Terman and the Gifted

Peter Van Valkenburgh
June 1928

Lewis M. Terman

Terman and the Gifted

MAY V. SEAGOE

Introduction by Ernest R. Hilgard

WILLIAM KAUFMANN, INC.   Los Altos, California

Library of Congress Cataloging in Publication Data

Seagoe, May Violet, 1906-
  Terman and the gifted.

  Bibliography: p.
  1. Terman, Lewis Madison, 1877-1956. 2. Psy-
chology--History. 3. Gifted children. I. Title.
[DNLM: 1. Psychology--History. WZ100 T319s]
BF109.T39S4   153.9'8'0924 [B]   75-19063
ISBN 0-913232-27-0

Copyright © 1975 by WILLIAM KAUFMANN, INC.

Printed in the United States of America

Contents

Introduction *by Ernest R. Hilgard*   *vii*

Preface   *xi*

CHAPTER I.   Father to the Man   *1*

CHAPTER II.   The Student Years   *16*

CHAPTER III.   The Making of a University Professor   *30*

CHAPTER IV.   The Binet and Mental Testing   *40*

CHAPTER V.   School Hygiene and Health Reform   *55*

CHAPTER VI.   Group Tests and the Testing Movement   *64*

CHAPTER VII.   The Gifted   *80*

CHAPTER VIII.   The Fruits of Eminence   *107*

CHAPTER IX.   Pioneering in Personality Research   *129*

CHAPTER X.   Public Affairs and the Social Conscience   *149*

CHAPTER XI.   Retirement   *167*

CHAPTER XII.   Perspective   *184*

APPENDIX A.   Publications of Lewis M. Terman   *187*

APPENDIX B.   Unpublished Manuscripts of Lewis M. Terman   *203*

APPENDIX C.   Ph.D. and M.A. Research Sponsored by Terman   *205*

APPENDIX D.   Related Publications   *211*

APPENDIX E.   Selected Unpublished Manuscripts   *216*

Index   *251*

Introduction

It was with some trepidation that I began to read Dr. Seagoe's biography of Lewis M. Terman, for I knew him so well, admired him so deeply, and owed him so much that I would be unusually critical of any attempt to capture in words his essence as a scientist, educator, and human being. Dr. Seagoe also expressed some self-doubts in undertaking the biography of a man who was himself an expert in biography. Once I began to read, however, my apprehension disappeared and I became absorbed and moved by this portrayal of Terman. Dr. Seagoe has been thorough, objective, and sensitive throughout; she gives the story of the man I knew. I believe this will be his definitive biography.

The account is more than the story of a man, for his professional life spanned the first half of the twentieth century, in which psychology grew from a handful of members in the American Psychological Association to upwards of 10,000. Although its membership has tripled since, the first large spurt came after World War I, when psychology established itself through psychological testing, in which Terman was a prime mover. Hence we have a reflection of the history of psychology in the history of one of its prominent figures.

It would be unfortunate if the contemporary uneasiness over psychological testing were to dim the appreciation of what Terman meant to psychology. In historical perspective, intelligence testing was psychology's success story, and it first gave psychologists access to the schools, to industry, and to government. Terman was not merely an IQ psychologist, however; if anyone is under that misapprehension, reading this book will provide the necessary corrective.

Terman's career demonstrates so well how the human influence of one person upon another transcends the professional, even when the occasion for the personal association is professional to begin with. As we read his story, we learn mostly about Terman's psychological colleagues and his students. As a shy person, he did not reach out to all manner of people on a purely social basis. That he could reach out is attested, of course, by his continuing relationships over the years with the "gifted children," who grew to adulthood while they participated in his long-range study.

The mutual admiration and respect shown among three of psychology's great men—Terman, Yerkes, and Boring—illustrates the triumph of personal affection over narrow scientific interest, even when the original basis for the friendship was professional. Yerkes, who was Terman's senior by a year, devoted his life as a psychologist to what he preferred to call psychobiology: the comparative study of animals and man in an evolutionary context. Boring's identification was with sensation and perception, deriving from the early days of experimental psychology. The primary interests of both Yerkes and Boring could not have been further from those of Terman, yet all three men remained intimates after their World War I experience together. Terman, the greater expert in tests, was little impressed by the point scale Yerkes and his collaborators had developed in 1915, the year before Terman's Stanford Binet appeared. Boring who was only nine years Terman's junior, became associated with him at an age when those few years made the difference between a young instructor at Cornell and the two established scientists with whom he worked. Yerkes was already president of the American Psychological Association at the time, and Terman was already widely known. So Boring always thought of Terman as a senior counselor to him, perhaps more a kindly uncle than a father figure.

Such personal attachments spread their influences to succeeding generations. Just as Lindley sent Terman from Indiana to Clark, and Terman's appointment at Stanford came through his Clark connections, I hope that I may be pardoned for telling how I shared in an extension of this process. It is as though each generation warms the hands of the next in a way that goes beyond letters of recommendation.

I first met Terman in 1931 while still an instructor at Yale. At that time, Stanford was well represented at Yale. Walter and Catherine Cox Miles, whose names appear in this biography, had come from Stanford first as visitors and then permanently, opening a position at Stanford during the Depression years when academic positions were scarce. Terman, recognizing the opportunities unfolding at the new Institute of Human Relations at Yale, had sent on a number of those who had earned degrees at Stanford, including Ray Carpenter, L. P. Herrington, Stanley Lindley (son of his former Indiana professor, who had since become president of the University of Kansas), Donald Marquis, Neal Miller, and Robert and Pauline Sears. The universal admiration they all expressed for

Terman enlivened my interest in meeting him when Yerkes proposed to introduce me.

Yerkes had been a supporter as a senior professor at Yale; he had invited me to spend the summer of 1931 at the then Yale Laboratories of Primate Biology at Orange Park, Florida, later to be renamed in his honor. Yerkes introduced me to Terman that fall, at the meetings of the American Psychological Association in Toronto. We sat on the grass for a long talk, and I was impressed both by Terman's warmth and by his willingness to talk to a 27-year-old instructor as though he were a colleague. I met Anna Terman at the meetings in Cornell the following year, when she came as his ambassador. The offer that brought me to Stanford in 1933 soon followed—to some extent a product of the Yerkes-Terman friendship.

The third member of the triumvirate, Boring, influenced my career somewhat differently. He was unusually kind and thoughtful toward me through many years. When I acknowledged that what he gave me seemed beyond anything I deserved from him, he told me how much Terman, as an older friend, had meant to him; he felt that doing all he could for me (and Stanford) was in some measure repaying Terman for what he had done for him.

A further testimony to the esteem in which colleagues held Terman came from Woodworth, a widely respected older psychologist who wrote the introduction to the *Festschrift* presented to Terman by his former students upon his retirement. Woodworth concluded his nine-page tribute with these words: "He is truly to be numbered among the pioneers, whose example is an inspiration to the younger generation and whose work and influence will long endure."

When Josephine and I arrived at Stanford, we were taken into the Terman household until we found a place to live. Unfamiliar with California houses, and having very little money, we took an unusually long time to make up our minds; but both Lewis and Anna were very patient as we spent one day after another with them. We enjoyed conversing with them about many mutual friends: the Stanford contingent at Yale; Arnold Gesell, under whom Josephine had just received her Ph.D., and his wife, to whom he had been introduced by Terman; and the Harlows and the Lindleys, whom we had visited on our motor trip across the country.

The next years under Terman's leadership were very happy ones indeed. When, after World War II, I succeeded to his position, he was an ideal ex-department head, busying himself with his own research and scholarly writing, available for consultation but never intruding upon his successor. I was around when the issues of our approaching participation in World War II were raised, and I am pleased that Dr. Seagoe has given such a full account. It is difficult to recapture the intensity and divisiveness of the feelings that then existed over the issue of America's joining the war against Hitler. Here we see the mild Terman committing himself in favor of fighting Fascism, taking leadership and standing firm as a rock, even though he was opposing some of his long-time friends and colleagues.

The temptation is very strong for a biographer to try to explain the subject of his biography—to account in Terman's case for the determination that led him to overcome the limitations of a country boy who suffered many illnesses and to emerge as an eminent, productive scientific scholar. Boring, in his brief biography of Terman, tentatively suggested that distractions can sometimes be motivating; he noted the Adlerian concept of overcompensating for handicaps. I am pleased that Dr. Seagoe refrained from excessive psychologizing and left Terman's career as either inexplicable, or as what can be expected when a well-endowed youth develops, for whatever reason, a desire for learning and the motivation to succeed.

The Terman story stands on its own merits, and it is told here clearly, honestly, and competently.

Stanford University

ERNEST R. HILGARD

Preface

Writing biography is precarious business at best. And writing the story of a biographer such as Lewis Madison Terman requires temerity bordering on madness.

For Terman published his own autobiography at the age of 55, taught a course in the psychology of biography, and voiced his own qualms about the biographer's task.

> As a more or less desultory student of biography, I have been much impressed by the daring that biographical writers have sometimes shown in their attempt to psychoanalyze the characters and careers of their subjects. ... One's memories are not only incomplete; they are also warped by systematic influences that distort the total picture. Memory of a given period of one's life is selective; what finally survives is determined partly by the nature of the events which follow ... (Terman, 1932f, p. 297).

He hoped to improve the art. He felt that most biographies are dull records of main events with little attempt to depict the personality, much less to explain how it got that way. He planned to give his last years of work to a semi-popular book on psychological aspects of biography, but time ran out.

According to Terman, biography should trace common threads through early life into later life, presenting case material descriptive of early behavior as it predicted later achievement. That, in his opinion, was the only way of defining individual entity.

He criticized the autobiographies of his friends, and urged biographers and historians to adopt his concept (Terman, 1941d). He condemned equally biographers who gave too little information on the critical years of childhood and autobiographers who bared their souls and enjoyed it. He felt that if personal dignity were to be preserved, no utterly frank autobiography should be written except for posthumous publication. The important thing was to find the right balance between openness and dignified reticence (Terman, 1953c).

When E. G. Boring urged him to round out the story of his life, Terman demurred. He needed his time for other work; and besides, the records were inadequate. He had always looked toward the future, and his memory of things past was fragmentary and unreliable. All he could add would be bits of personal philosophy, and that was not worth publishing. Such an attitude is characteristic in the man Terman was: a reserved though friendly person who never liked to talk about himself.

Yet Terman's life story should be written. His own impact on the field of psychology has been tremendous, and his fine human qualities extended his influence far beyond his own work. In addition, the problems that concerned Terman are as current today as they were fifty years ago, and his answers are too often overlooked. Most of all, Terman was a gifted man who shaped much of his career around the study of the gifted. His biography illuminates all attempts to understand the gifted, their educational needs, and their potential value for society as a whole.

Sources of information on Terman's life are limited. At no time in his life did he keep a diary; it was not the fashion when he was a boy, and later he was too busy. In school, he wrote few compositions and kept still fewer. All of his childhood family is gone, and his contact with them after he left home had been limited at best. Even the letters to his gifted "godchildren" were centered on them, warmly avuncular but giving little information about himself.

The search for material began with the six enormous boxes of professional notes and correspondence in the Stanford Archives, with particular attention to those written by Terman himself. They were colored by anecdotes, attitudes on events, news of a friend's illness, new research ideas. In addition, a number of unpublished manuscripts rounded out the whole, particularly with reference to his illnesses, religious beliefs, and social concerns.

Then fifty-five of Terman's colleagues, doctoral students, collaborators, and friends who were living in 1968 were contacted by letter for anecdotes and impressions. There were forty-one replies, leading in some cases to an interchange of letters clarifying information and impressions.

Interviews were arranged with Terman's children and with six close, long-term associates. The conversations were taped for later review. Those interviewed spanned Terman's whole life at Stanford, from 1911 to 1956.

Finally, Terman's own writings were explored with an eye to contemporary meanings and central interests. That meant becoming familiar with fifteen books, four monographs, ten pamphlets, thirty-two chapters, forty-eight articles, thirty-three reviews, twenty-seven forewords, and ten tests and manuals, as well as reviews by others of Terman's books. In addition, more than fifteen substantial unpublished manuscripts filled out and reinforced the whole.

All materials were then organized around major foci of interest on Terman's part. Those segments were placed in approximately chronological order, and the writing began. With such varied sources, all but the most pertinent references were omitted. The others may be found in Terman's file in the Stanford Archives, or in my own in the Archives of the History of American Psychology at the University of Akron. Admittedly, all impressions were filtered through my own memories of two luminous years of study with Terman as chairman of my own dissertation committee.

I am indebted for illuminating letters from Roger G. Barker, Nancy Bayley, Margaret E. Bennett, Robert G. Bernreuter, Bruce Bliven, Virginia Lee Block, Edwin G. Boring, Clarence Ray Carpenter, Harold D. Carter, Jessie Chase Fenton, John A. Gardner, Harry F. Harlow, Aden D. Henderson, Maud Merrill James, E. Lowell Kelly, John L. Kennedy, Samuel C. Kohs, Roger T. Lennon, Curtis Merriman, Neal E. Miller, Margaret Lima Norgaard, Jo Anne Pegg, Bronson Price, Albert Raubenheimer, Jesse B. Sears, Anne Roe Simpson, Keith Sward, Miles A. Tinker, Leona E. Tyler, Albert Walton, and Kimball Young.

I am grateful for interviews with Paul R. Fransworth, Ernest R. Hilgard, Helen Marshall, Melita Oden, Robert R. Sears, J. Harold Williams, and with Terman's children, Frederick Terman and Helen Terman Mosher.

Most of all, I am deeply appreciative of the generous helpfulness of the late Edwin G. Boring, before his death, in testing the validity of the interpretations; of Melita Oden in advising and assisting all along the way; of Malcolm S. MacLean for editorial reading; of Paul Farnsworth and Robert Sears for reviewing the entire manuscript; of Helen Terman Mosher for invaluable criticism; and particularly to Frederick E. Terman for incisive evaluation and practical assistance in completing the manuscript.

Los Angeles
October, 1975

MAY V. SEAGOE

CHAPTER I

Father to the Man

*Certainly it would be a mistake to ignore the indica-
tions of childhood experiences and preoccupations, even
though heredity and environments as causal agents can
never be clearly disentangled. ... My study of biography
and my work with gifted children incline me to believe
that the child is indeed often father to the man (Terman,
1932f, p. 297).*

SOUTH from Indianapolis, along the old roads, the past still
lingers. A land slashed by freeways and pocked by subdivisions still
holds scattered clumps of forest and occasional wooded hills. Gently
rolling grasslands surround secluded farms of soybeans and corn.
The villages of comfortable homes and closely clipped lawns are
thickly bolstered by churches—Baptist, Methodist, Nazarene,
Apostolic, Adventist, Lutheran. Franklin, the largest town in the
area, has a rich history: settlers first put down roots on an old
Indian trail; staunch abolitionists operated a station on the Under-
ground Railroad during the Civil War; and an early denomina-
tional college struggled and grew. Out from town on Hurricane Road
lies the old Hurricane Cemetery, its silence broken by bulldozers
building the new freeway.

In that placid country Lewis Terman spent his childhood. His
family had followed the westward surge from Virginia into the Ohio
Valley after the War of 1812. They were a mixed group, first arriving
in America around 1700, and subsequently intermarrying with other
immigrant stocks. Their occasional swarthy skin and characteristic
high cheekbones bore mute testimony to a native strain as well in
the heritage of the Termans, Tirmans, Tiermans, Turmans, Ture-
mans, and Tuermans.

Lewis's paternal grandfather was a farmer who followed the
frontier. He was born in 1790 of Scotch-Irish parents, served briefly
in the War of 1812, and then set out on horseback through Kentucky
for Ohio. In 1820 he settled fourteen miles south of Zanesville,
which for a brief time was capital of Ohio. Like his neighbors, he

1

cleared the land, built a log cabin, and brought to it his wife, a Welshwoman whose maiden name was Jones. After twenty-six years and the birth of ten children, he moved again to a farm in nearby Brown County, an area unpromising enough to attract only the sturdiest of pioneers. Both he and his wife lived into their sixties and seventies, a ripe old age.

Lewis's father, James Terman, was born in 1834. Like his brothers and sisters, he attended rural school for only a few months each winter for three or four years, and worked on the farm the rest of the time until his late teens. When he was twenty, he found a job with a prominent Pennsylvania Dutch farmer named Cutsinger and his French Huguenot wife, whose maiden name of Dupree (or Duepree) suggests why she never fully mastered English. After a year as a hired hand, James married Martha, one of Cutsinger's daughters, and moved to his own farm in the northeast township of Johnson County.

James Terman was known for his industry, honesty, and persistence. He became a prosperous farmer and even held a few local offices. But his family was large, and although there was enough for necessities, there was little for luxuries. Books, however, were among the necessities for him. His library included 120 to 200 books and a set of *Encyclopaedia Britannica*. In his spare time he read a great deal—newspapers, magazines, and the Bible, as well as the books in his library. He was a family-centered man, self-sacrificing, infinitely kind and patient, and fond of his children. To others he seemed quiet, seldom attending church or social gatherings. His health may have been less than robust, for most of his aunts and uncles had died of tuberculosis, and he himself had hemorrhages as a young man. Nevertheless, with care he lived to the age of seventy-two.

His wife, Martha Cutsinger Terman, provided a balance of temperaments. As a child helping with the farm chores, she had refused to let her father dominate her, though his positive personality overshadowed the other family members. When she married, her successful farmer-businessman father made an outright gift of land to her and her husband as evidence of his affection and trust. Martha was well educated, youthful, and volatile—a counterweight to her husband's composure. Yet after her marriage there was little time for the social life she loved. Cleaning and cooking, laundering and sewing, bearing fourteen children and bringing eleven of them to maturity kept her busy every moment, even when the children were old enough to help. She loved to cook and garden, managed the household well, and was devoted to the family; still, the children

2

felt closer to their quietly intellectual father than to their gay and energetic mother.

James and Martha Terman settled on a farm at Needham, in Johnson County, seventeen miles southeast of Indianapolis. When the Civil War came, James served in the Home Guards and cared for his wife and the three daughters born to them before the war began (Jane, Elizabeth, and Martha). Two more daughters and two sons were born during the Civil War (Alice, Flora, John, and Joseph). Soon after the war, two more daughters arrived (Sarah and Ida). By 1870, the family included nine living children; two sons had died in infancy.

Seven years later, after the couple had been married for twenty-two years, Lewis was born. It was on January 15, 1877, a year Lewis later placed as the halfway point between the presidency of John Adams and that of Dwight Eisenhower. Like his brothers and sisters, Lewis was large, weighing ten pounds at birth. As the first son in twelve years to survive infancy, his welcome was assured. His unique-ness, too, was apparent early, in the combination of his gold-red hair and his deep brown eyes.

It was a gay and lively family, with little or no quarreling and much mutual affection. Along with the warmth, there was a definite sense of discipline and order, and of work that must be done.

There was tragedy for his family in Lewis's early years as well. During his infancy, his oldest sister, then twenty-two, died of tuber-culosis. Since the home was crowded and medical knowledge limited, Lewis, along with the rest of the family, was undoubtedly exposed to the disease. Then, during his childhood, another elder sister died of scarlet fever. But two younger sisters, Bertha and Jessie, were born. These changes meant that of the fourteen children who had been born, two brothers and seven sisters made up the family in which Lewis spent his early years. Born the eleventh of fourteen, he became the eighth of the ten surviving Terman children. They were an able and lively group; much later, when Lewis was trying out a research instrument, he rated the intelligence of half of them as superior.

In the large families of the late nineteenth century, only the first two or three children claimed much attention from the mother. After that, the older ones took care of the younger ones, and the load was spread. So it was with Lewis. An older sister took over much of his mothering, caring for his needs, playing with him, and taking him with her wherever she went. The tie was warm and close—so close that when she started dating, three-year-old Lewis was very angry to be excluded. He always remembered that incident as an insufferable invasion of his infant territory.

In the same way, his fathering was shared by his oldest brother, John, fourteen years his senior. It was John's interests Lewis came to share, his books Lewis read, and his classroom in which Lewis was given independent study. Lewis even practiced on John's violin before a mirror, but he never learned to play it as John had taught himself to do.

It was a busy family. During the summer and the harvest, neighbors joined the family and the hired hands and threshing crews in ceaseless work in the fields. Martha Terman busily replenished a continuous smorgasbord for all comers. These days were among Lewis's most pleasant memories.

Every Sunday throughout the year he would go to the Hurricane Church to listen in desultory fashion to the sermon, often by a professor of Greek from nearby Franklin College. He learned the family attitude on political issues: Republican. No one read to him, but his immediate success in school suggests that he must have picked up reading on his own. It was a free and easy life for a small boy. Nobody paid much attention to him; when children were little they were just around, to be accepted as they were.

His health was good. He had the normal childhood illnesses, but there was no hint of anything more. His later associates speculated that Lewis must have been a delicate child, that the family tendency toward tuberculosis must have been apparent, that lack of vitality must have been the reason he showed no athletic prowess, and that life on the Indiana farm was rigorous and undermined his health. Nothing could be further from the truth. Lewis was well as a child. If he had no athletic prowess, it was simply that he was little interested in the things most children did.

Or perhaps he was interested, but simply did not have playmates of his own age. He was always too small, too young, or too far away from boys of his size. His red hair did not help; he was constantly teased about it, called every nickname, and considered an oddity.

But the thing that made him different ran deeper than age and red hair. The boys on the neighboring farms were not interested in intellectual things; most dropped out of school before completing the eighth grade. Even so, they were always superior in strength, agility, and skill, because they were three or four years older than Lewis. They could run faster, jump farther, dive deeper, throw a ball farther, wrestle more skillfully, and swear more nonchalantly.

Lewis came to feel that he did not count very much in their activities. He regarded them with an attitude ranging from respectful deference to admiration and awe. That he surpassed them in school-work as much as they surpassed him in play did not matter in a child's world. He was low in their pecking order; he could not fight them and win. So he settled for acceptance and trailed along with them as best he could.

When he was five and one-half, Lewis entered school. It was a red one-room schoolhouse, without a single library book. But the teacher was excellent. He was the prototype of all Lewis's teachers—men who had not attended school beyond the eighth grade, but who were intellectually able. In fact, two of Lewis's early teachers went on to become physicians; a third became a lawyer. And despite its disadvantages, the old-fashioned country school offered a range of opportunity seldom found in more modern elementary schools.

After six months in school, shortly after his sixth birthday, Lewis was promoted to the third grade. After finding him reading the books which children of nine and ten used, the teacher placed him in advanced history and grammar classes with even older children. Lewis loved school; he found no subject he disliked. At one time or another he thought his favorite was arithmetic—or history—or geography—or physiology—or grammar. Though his spatial memory was poor, he memorized verbal material easily; that made reciting easy. He habitually memorized his textbooks, including biographical footnotes and tables of population and area. The school day was long, from 8:15 to 4:00, and the time had to be put in somehow.

Lewis learned about people, too. All the Termans had a keen eye for the peculiarities of others; family events were enlivened by mimicry and by hilarious reminiscences about the eccentricities of people they knew. At school, Lewis saw others who were different. There was a feeble-minded boy, still in the first reader at the age of eighteen. There was a backward albino boy pathetically devoted to his small sister. There was a spoiled crippled boy given to fits of temper and to stealing. There was a "lightning calculator," and even an imaginative liar who was later accused of swindling and murder. All were different. Perhaps being different was just a part of being human; perhaps Lewis's own kind of difference was just an ordinary eccentricity.

When he was twelve, Lewis completed the eighth grade. He wanted to go on in school, but he was too young to leave home, and there was no high schol near enough for him to attend. So he stayed on in the same school for a year doing advanced work. Then, at thirteen, he began attending his brother John's elementary school to do independent study in high school subjects for two more winters. John had attended college for a time, and under his tutelage Lewis's insatiable curiosity was fed for two winters, until he could gain control over his own destiny.

During those two postgraduate years in John's school, Lewis met another gifted student, Arthur Banta, later a well-known biologist and geneticist. Banta was less bookish and less interested in people than Lewis, but he was much more concerned with plants, animals, and rocks. The two became fast friends. After both became "starred" scientists in Cattell's *American Men of Science*, Banta and Terman investigated the unlikely coincidence that two such prominent men should come from the same thirty-student, one-room rural school. They found three pairs of brothers who rose to prominence from such situations, but no other pairs of unrelated individuals. They concluded that John must have been an exceptionally capable and inspiring teacher, and that native ability will out despite meager opportunity.

At home, Lewis's life was that of an Indiana farm boy: he worked on the farm, played with the neighbor boys, went to church, read, and played as he wished. One experience when he was nine or ten stood out. A book peddler, selling books on phrenology, stopped at the Terman home for the night; that evening as the family sat around the fireplace, the peddler felt the bumps on each Terman head in turn. For Lewis he predicted great things, and the boy was much impressed. His brother bought a copy of the book; Lewis became familiar with it and held a firm belief in phrenology until he was fourteen or fifteen. More importantly, the prediction bolstered Lewis's self-confidence and encouraged him to seek more ambitious goals than he had thus far imagined for himself.

His education in sex, both factual and imaginary, was thorough. He watched the farm animals and learned obscenity from the rough boys of neighboring families. The hired hands expanded his vocabulary and information. That was the origin of the interest in sex which later led him to research in that area.

Church attendance bore fruit in baptism in the nearby river. Lewis continued to be interested in politics, with the family's strongly Republican viewpoint.

Until he was eleven, Lewis's vacations of five or six months each year were spent in unsupervised play, often alone. His sense of being different grew. His family played with him occasionally, especially

6

an older sister with whom he invented a word game. One of them would choose a word, the other would give an associated word, and so on until all evident connection with the original word was lost. The object was to get as far away from the starting point as quickly as possible, yet still to be able to justify each transition as natural and logical. The game sharpened Lewis's verbal awareness as well as giving him pleasure.

The household library helped to fill the hours. Lewis liked the *Encyclopaedia Britannica* best of all, then Hans Christian Andersen's stories, *Robinson Crusoe*, a book on Arctic and African travels called *The World's Wonders*, the novels of Cooper and Dickens, the Bible, pocket atlases, and *Peck's Bad Boy*. He did not care for *Pilgrim's Progress*; he later wished that his father's library had included Plutarch's *Lives*.

Much of the time he was on his own, wandering about the woods and farms. About a mile from his home lived a pair of flying squirrels; Lewis watched with fascination as they glided from tree to tree. He learned the names of the more common trees, plants, animals, and birds. His only collections, however, were of Indian relics, and he engaged in no systematic observations of nature beyond those required to satisfy the curiosity of a bright boy.

Instead, he often engaged in introspective play. He discovered for himself such phenomena as after-images, the flight of colors, and the association of ideas. When he was eleven or twelve, he found out that by monotonously repeating a formula, he could lose his sense of identity and his orientation in time and space. He would gaze fixedly at something and say, "Is this me?" or, "Am I living? Am I living? Am I living?" until all distinction between the subjective and objective worlds was lost in a kind of mystical haze.

He also investigated memory. He later recorded an experiment done at about the age of eleven.

I was pondering over the fact that, of the countless visual impressions which one experiences, the majority vanish quickly and none ever remains as indelibly fixed in memory as to be recallable in all its details. Can it be that there is no such thing as complete and permanent memory? I decided to find out. My method was to select a small object and gaze at it so long and intently that the exact 'picture' of it would *never*, so long as I lived, fade from my memory. After casting about for a suitable subject, I selected a small bit of material that lay on the north side of a potato hill from which I had just forked the potatoes. It resembled, as I now

7

recall it, a piece of semi-decayed straw or cornstalk; it was about a quarter of an inch long, had a brownish yellow color, and was shaped something like a tadpole with the tail downward. As I gazed at it, I kept repeating to myself "this time I will *never* forget—I *must* remember it—I *will* remember it if I live to be a hundred years old," and so on probably for several minutes. Even yet the image of this object seems fairly distinct and the details as I have described them fairly certain . . . (Terman, 1932f, p. 304).

Then, of course, there was farm work. Lewis loved the threshing, the harvesting, and the large family gatherings. He liked to help load the wagon with vegetables to peddle from house to house in Indianapolis. When he was eleven, he began to do a man's work with team, plow, and wagon. After that, each year until he was eighteen, he worked on the farm from April to September; his working day was usually ten hours, but sometimes from 5:00 in the morning to 8:00 at night. The long hours of repetitious work provided little intellectual stimulation, but at least his thoughts could be busy elsewhere. He did not dislike farm work or resent it, nor did he do it only from a sense of duty. He did it because it was there to be done, but he definitely did not want to spend his life as a farmer.

What he really wanted was more school. For the Indiana farm boy of 1890 the first step in getting an education was preparing to teach. Then, by teaching, he might earn money for college and prepare for a profession. Not to teach meant to continue forever ploughing the same fields, doing the same chores, and getting nowhere. Lewis decided to become a teacher.

His family encouraged him: if teaching was what he wanted, that was fine. His father could not give much financial help, because the panic of 1893 and several years of economic depression had given the family enterprise a close call. Nevertheless he offered Lewis a fine horse that he thought could be spared if Lewis could sell it to finance more schooling. Lewis had a pretty good idea what Nelly was worth, but when he took her around to all the potential purchasers, he found that the best offer was considerably below her true value. After wrestling with his conscience for several days, Lewis decided to keep Nelly and defer school. Ultimately, his brother John found the money to underwrite the expenses of a course at normal school, and Lewis was delighted.

At the age of fifteen, then, Lewis went away to the Central Normal College at Danville to prepare for teaching. At a time when public high schools were few and bad roads limited commuting to three or four miles, such private normal schools filled an important gap in education for those who could not afford to attend the established private colleges. The normal school was high school and college combined, with a vocational bent that was attractive to practical farm parents.

Most of the instruction at Central Normal College was supremely good, despite the fact that the teachers were poorly paid for a heavy load of twenty-five to thirty hours of teaching each week. Most of them were alert, witty, stimulating, and well informed. They were gifted in their fields, interested in research and in ideas, and well taught, though sometimes self-taught. Some were working toward advanced degrees in Boston or New York, or even at the newly established Clark University. Others were headed for influential posts in similar normal schools.

Good teaching had an electric effect on Lewis. Two of his favorite teachers held opposing views, one Hegelian and the other Herbatian. A running duel of wits ensued; classes were tense and exciting. Many thoughtful students took sides. Lewis became an enthusiastic Herbartian, perhaps because he could see nothing but words in Hegel. He read his texts avidly, then went on to independent reading: Hoffling's *Philosophy*, several volumes of Herbert Spencer, James's *Principles of Psychology*, (he read this surreptitiously because his advisor disapproved of James), Darwin's *Origin of Species* and *Descent of Man*, Huxley's *Lectures*, Haeckel's *The Riddle of the Universe*, Brinton's *Religions of Primitive Peoples*, Paine's *Age of Reason*, and the lectures of Robert Ingersoll. He browsed in the works of Aristotle, Plato, Hume, W. T. Harris, and Paul Carus. He read John Dewey for a time, but soon gave him up as dull and uninteresting.

That first school year (1892-93) Lewis attended Central Normal for thirty weeks. He spent the summer on the farm, and then returned for twenty weeks more. Intellectually, he came alive. His teachers recognized him as an obviously bright and enthusiastic student, and helped him to gain assurance as well as to explore new ideas. It was the good life.

It was a good chance to find friends as well. He stayed in a boarding house with other students; among his roommates were several men who later became eminent in their fields. One became a professor of American history and a recognized scholar; another became a nationally known geneticist; one came into prominence as an attorney; one went on to the United States Senate; and two others went on to become a school superintendent and a minister. With young men like these Lewis went spearfishing with pitchforks at Wabash Bayou; all his life he remembered the smell of the carcasses thrown on the banks and left to the elements. They went rabbit hunting, younger farm boys stirring up the animals for the young men to shoot. He rode his bicycle for miles to visit friends and share their good-natured banter. And through these experiences he formed lasting friendships.

He also started dating. He accepted it as inevitable that any boy between fifteen and twenty-four would be preoccupied with sex. When an early best girl was stolen by a friend, he recovered to be grateful to the thief. He found his life so exciting, in fact, that he failed to arrive home for Christmas the first year, and thus precipitated a family crisis. But his friends were staying over at the school, and he wanted to share the vacation excitement with them.

Then, at seventeen, Lewis was ready to teach. He was assigned to a one-room rural elementary school like the one he had attended as a child. The following winter he was employed in a similar school nearby. Later, he served for three years as teacher and principal in a township high school, handling the entire curriculum for about forty students. The students remembered him for his stimulation and for the sparkle of mischievous joy in his eyes.

During those early years of teaching, Terman's chief intellectual interest lay in the Teacher's Reading Circle. The cost of two or three books each year was deducted from each teacher's salary; the nine instructors in Terman's neighborhood met one Saturday each month at one of the schools for an all-day session. Most of the day was devoted to discussion of the books, according to definite assignments given to each participant in advance. In this way Terman became familiar with current professional books. He was particularly impressed with Bryan's *Plato the Teacher* and James's discussions of memory in his *Talks to Teachers*. He began to see teaching as a field interesting in itself, and not merely as a way to earn money.

At about this time Lewis lost all interest in organized religion; from then on, he seldom attended church except for marriages or funerals. This change paralleled his growing enthusiasm for Darwin and Huxley. As he became increasingly agnostic, and doubtless faced pressure from church and family, he was sometimes almost bitter against organized religion. But later, when one of his boyhood friends became involved in a controversy over teaching the theory of evolution, Terman mildly advised him to resign rather than to stand trial for heresy.

Terman wanted still more education. After his first year of teaching he returned to Danville for forty-eight weeks, this time to complete the scientific course and receive the degree of B.S. After another winter in the rural school, he again went to Danville for eighteen weeks to complete the pedagogy course for the degree of B.Pd. But two degrees were not enough for him. Instead of working the following year, Terman borrowed enough money to remain in Danville for still another forty-eight weeks to complete the classical course and receive the degree of A.B. By 1898, when he was twenty-one, he had completed 164 weeks, or about four and one-half school years. In addition to the courses designed specifically for teachers, his instruction was equivalent to the rest of high school and the first two years of college. Except for a few correspondence courses in German and in the history of education, this was the extent of his formal education before he entered the university.

Illness then added to the complexity of a life alternating between teaching and going to school.

> ... I was nineteen when I had my first serious illness, which
> proved to be typhoid fever. It was a severe case, and for a time
> I was not expected to live. I have always suspected that this illness
> may have made me less resistant to tuberculosis; at any rate, it was
> just three years later when I had my first hemorrhage of the lungs.
> Or was it from the lungs? After all, there were only two or three
> mouthfuls of blood, followed by a faint trickle that was over in a few
> minutes. If I had not known about the consumptive taint in my father's
> family I should probably not have given the matter a second thought,
> but the memory of that taint led me to consult a doctor. When the
> examination disclosed nothing wrong the doctor was inclined to think
> that the blood had not come from my lungs, but probably from
> injury to a tiny blood vessel in my throat. He told me to take my
> temperature twice a day, to eat heartily, get lots of sleep, and avoid
> strenuous physical activity; then if no symptoms had shown up by
> the end of the month I could forget that anything had happened.
> None appeared ... (Terman unpublished, 1953).

The specter of tuberculosis had materialized.

More happily, Terman's courtship of Anna Minton went well. Her parents had the same midwestern pioneer farmer background as his own. As a youth, Reuben B. Minton, Anna's father, had settled in Star City, Indiana, a small town on the Pennsylvania Railroad near Winamac. His schooling had gone no further than graduation from the eighth grade of a typical one-room rural school.

11

Subsequently, he had taught in such a school for several winters to help support his widowed mother and to develop a farm. In addition to his skills as a farmer, Minton had an unusual business sense. For many years he supplemented his farm income by acting as a commission merchant, buying cattle and hogs from his neighbors to build up carload lots, which were then shipped to Chicago or Pittsburgh. Later, Minton founded a country bank, which he ran with great success with no professional help but occasional advice from a banker friend at Winamac. Though limited in formal education, Minton was an intelligent man who became an important figure in his community; at the time of his death in 1927, at the age of seventy-nine, he was quite well off financially, relative to the community in which he lived.

Terman first met Anna Minton at Normal School when he was eighteen; she was already teaching in a neighboring county. When one of his friends mentioned that the prettiest girl who ever went to Danville was back in town, Lewis replied that he would take her home from the next social. He did. Anna teased him later that, had it not been so dark that she did not notice his red hair, she would never have consented. The friendship ripened into love during the next four years; in 1899, when Lewis was twenty-two, they were married.

The Termans settled in an old farmhouse near the country high school where Lewis had taught the previous year. Less than a year after the marriage, in June of 1900, their son was born. He was named Frederick Emmons Arthur Terman, in honor of three of Terman's closest friends. The name was later shortened to Frederick Emmons Terman for convenience. Fred enlivened his father's interest in child psychology in a very personal way. Yet only two months later, the tuberculosis was back.

> . . . I came down with a disabling attack of pleurisy that was diagnosed as tubercular. The country doctor I had then was ill-trained, but in the light of events that followed, I have little doubt that his diagnosis was correct. He kept me in bed for two or three weeks until my temperature was normal and the pains of pleurisy had subsided. When I was able to be up and around a little, he told me bluntly that if I did not want to die from tuberculosis in a year or two, I had better resign my job and move to a better climate. Badly scared as I was, I could not take his advice because I had nothing on which to support myself and family while getting well. I decided to stay where I was, but to ask for a month's leave of absence in the hope that I could then return to work. The leave was granted; I improved

12

steadily and went back to my job at the end of October, though I was still worried about the final outcome.

My regimen that year may be of interest. I usually rose early and took a brief walk in the near-by fields or woods before breakfast. As soon as school was dismissed at four in the afternoon, I strolled off again unless it was raining or snowing. On Saturdays and Sundays the walks were somewhat longer, though still carefully rationed. I took my temperature every day and counted my pulse at the end of my walks. As a measure of safety to my family, I slept in a separate room which was large and had cross ventilation. All through the winter I slept with doors and windows wide open, often waking to find snow drifted half way across the room. I came to enjoy "outdoor" sleeping, and during most of my life since then, I have usually slept in open or half-open rooms (Terman unpublished, 1953).

Gradually the regimen paid off. Life returned to normal and planning for the future was resumed.

This, then, was Lewis Terman at maturity. His origins, like those of many eminent scientists, were humble and mixed. He was a blend of Scotch-Irish, Welsh, Pennsylvania Dutch, and French Huguenot, in about equal parts. He came from pioneer farm people, who worked hard for a living but were successful in their difficult task. Although he had two aunts and an uncle who had been teachers, farming was the predominant occupation in the family. For Terman, too, the future would normally have suggested high school graduation as the limit of education and farming or small business as a career. It was not an ancestry of distinction in the professions, and did not indicate an intellectual career.

As a young man, Terman was troubled by his ordinary ancestry. He could not account for himself. Others could trace their ancestries far back through illustrious men; he could not. When he later found Termans, Turmans, and Tearmans scattered from coast to coast, most of them farmers and artisans, he wondered how it could be that their children seemed quite bright. When a Terman turned up in his gifted group in 1921, he was amazed. And when he found that his own children and grandchildren were bright, he insisted that it must come from his wife's side of the family. Unable to see anything in the life of a poor farm boy that would lead to eminence, he looked to heredity for an answer. Perhaps he was a biological sport. Heredity, being inscrutable, could not disappoint him; but he still had a sense of not quite measuring up.

Perhaps Terman undervalued the pioneer way of life as a challenge to thinking and innovation; he may have forgotten that

13

taming a wilderness was not conducive to writing letters, keeping diaries, and composing biographies such as those he read from families that were economically secure. More likely, his own low self-esteem, fostered in a lonely childhood, was reflected in a low valuation of that from which he came.

At any rate, Terman's own case does not make a good argument either for heredity or for environment. He must simply be accepted as a fact.

His early environment did hold distinct assets. His family was relatively prosperous for its time and place. It had some intellectual interests: Lewis had a brother who taught and a sister who played word games with him. The whole family provided a warm acceptance around him, and its hospitality drew in neighbors and acquaintances. Work was important and achievement valued. Most of all, there was freedom, independence, and encouragement to find his own way.

Yet his isolation from others his own age led Lewis to a sense of distance from people. He was a low sibling in a hierarchy of fourteen; he was always smaller than his playmates. Although he was an intellectual maverick, he was never talkative, and even became skilled in shutting off conversation when it led nowhere or led too close. He became an onlooker, friendly but seldom intimate; he disliked crowds but liked persons. He particularly admired those who had little education but developed strong intellectual interests without it.

His natural reticence was compounded by his constant fear that disease would strike again before his children were grown, and that his wife would be left with no capital with which to raise them. With his intense striving for an education while the door of opportunity stood so precariously ajar, with the threat of his frail health, and with the uncertainties of the future, it is small wonder that Terman had little time for the trivial in living.

Along with his feeling of not quite measuring up, Lewis developed an awareness of status very early. He had to keep up in his own way in order to hold his own with larger, stronger, more aggressive boys. He found excitement and success in ideas. He came alive when he went to normal school and to college, and felt the need to justify himself through intellectual achievement.

On the other hand, his sense of being different led him to be concerned with the differences of others. He was primarily concerned with those who had his kind of difference—giftedness—yet he gave much time to a wide variety of exceptionalities and to the need for understanding the individual. He even wrote of his strong impression that illness, frustration, and personality maladjustment are all related in a vital sense to professional motivation.

Like the men of eminence he later studied, Terman showed an early precocity in school subjects. He learned to read by the age of five and was advanced rapidly in school. He read widely and memorized much of what he read. But beyond the elementary school, he was blocked. He had no access to the classics or to foreign languages, and little to the arts, philosophy, and natural science. He found his way into teaching early, but even that was a steppingstone to more demanding intellectual work.

Terman's boyhood shows parallels to the early history of renowned scientists studied by Anne Roe (1952). He was placed on his own resources early in a busy household. He was concerned from the beginning with human differences. He was curious, particularly about psychological phenomena. He was forced into an early autonomy in mastering his environment, by the life to which he was born and by not fitting his age group. He had the persistence essential in the large farm family. And he was capable of great concentration in mastering ideas.

In common with other social scientists, he was concerned with people as people; made a relatively late vocational decision; felt ostracized from his family and schoolmates; valued social status; experienced physical problems during early adulthood which drove him further into reading and isolation; was fascinated by books; gained his first knowledge of science through agriculture; had early work experience; and became independent for himself and uncritical toward others. He did not share the social scientists' common explicit rebelliousness or their early isolation, except in relation to his playmates. Otherwise, his early history is typical of eminent social scientists.

CHAPTER II

The Student Years

As for myself, everything I have done since 1905 was foreshadowed by my interest—at that time—in psychology of genius, the measurement of intelligence, the phenomena of individual differences, in general, and the problems of hygiene (Terman, 1932f, p. 321).

By the spring of 1901, Terman's health seemed to have returned to normal. He began to think of earning a bachelor's and perhaps a master's degree at a university, so he could teach psychology or pedagogy in a normal school or college. Failing that, he thought, he could always fall back on a high school principalship or a superintendency of schools. His three normal school degrees would permit him to enter Indiana University as a junior; he could complete the work for both the B.A. and the M.A. in two years plus summer school. The Ph.D. was a remote, shimmering mirage.

Indiana University had been recommended by some of his normal school teachers and classmates as stimulating, but not too far away and not too expensive. His father and brother could manage a loan of $1200 to keep him and his family for the two years. Anna was willing to take in roomers to help out. So the Termans rented a big house in Bloomington and filled it with students. For Terman, the days and nights of hard work, stimulating talk, and games of cards formed the life he loved.

He set about his studies with his usual eagerness. During his two years at Indiana University, he took all the psychology courses offered, a year of neurology, as much philosophy and education as he could, a year of sociology, a year of economics, and French and German. He completed three and one-half years of work, including the requirements for both the A.B. and A.M., in the two years he had allowed.

From his teachers at Indiana he gained personal associations and the excitement of working with ideas—something far more important than the two degrees. His eagerness, earnestness, and

16

thoroughness impressed fellow students and teachers alike. For example, his French teacher, Anton Boisen, remembered Terman years later as the student who began the language in the spring of 1902, read ahead so he could be admitted to the third term's work during the summer, completed a double course during the six-week summer session, and took private tutoring between the close of the summer session and the beginning of the fall term. Thus Terman entered third-year French that same autumn, covering two years of French in less than eight months. Small wonder that Boisen considered Terman one of the ablest students he had ever taught; and from a man who later entered the ministry and wrote *Religion in Crisis and Customs*, that was high praise. Boisen also strengthened Terman's belief that psychology gained value only as it was of service to man—an attitude basic to Terman's championship of work in applied fields.

There were courses with Bryan as well, though at the end of Terman's first year he became President of the University of Indiana and largely withdrew from teaching. There were instructive sessions with Bergstrom, a modest man who lacked the personal force of Terman's favorites, but who was a wizard with apparatus and an able experimentalist in the Wundt tradition. But not even Bergstrom, could overcome Terman's mechanical ineptitude. Setups were difficult for him, and machinery was an obstruction between him and the thing he was trying to get at. Brass-instrument psychology was not for him.

It was the brilliant, inspiring Lindley who contributed most to kindling Terman's ambition to become a professor of psychology. He became Terman's instructor, personal guide, and friend. Recently returned from a postdoctoral year of study in Germany, he introduced Terman to the works of Wundt, Ebbinghaus, Kraepelin, Kulpe, Ribot, Tarde, Binet, Charcot, Morgan, Galton, Ladd, Hall, Sanford, Burnham, Cattell, Titchener, and Baldwin. Terman read widely, in German and French as well as in English. He found Immanuel Kant unnecessarily obscure, and began to lose interest in philosophy as he gained dedication to psychology as a field of empirical study.

During Terman's second year at Indiana, Lindley scheduled a weekly conference of an hour with him, which often stretched to two. Under Lindley's guidance, Terman formulated seminar reports on such topics as "Degeneracy" and "The Great-Man Theory." He read all he could find in his three languages on mental deficiency, criminality, and genius. He settled on leadership as the topic for his master's thesis on the basis of his reading, his interest in Binet's recently published book on suggestibility, and Hall's articles on child study. Because of his aversion to apparatus, Terman wanted to do a gadget-free experimental study with children, and because of his interest in genius he wanted to work in the field of the development of leadership.

His master's thesis became Terman's first publication (Terman, 1904). He defined leadership as the tendency to rise to a position of influence in a group. He covered the literature on animals and primitive peoples as well as on children, and then designed his own study patterned after Binet's investigations of suggestibility. He constructed tests consisting of ten pictures of objects mounted on cards, which he showed to groups of four students each of the same age and sex, all drawn from a pool of 100 children in the second, fourth, sixth, and eighth grades in the Bloomington schools. Students responded to twenty-three questions about the pictures, eleven of which required inference. Terman identified as leaders those who gave the first response in each group; he then asked teachers to rate those leaders in relation to their classmates on a list of characteristics including size, dress, quality of work, appearance, and selfishness. His conclusion was that leadership is related to a feeling of superiority and competence which results in a quickness in speaking up before others.

The experimental study was followed by a questionnaire about the characteristics of student leaders, which yielded more than 400 returns from teachers in the eastern states. From the results, he concluded that boys were more dominant and gregarious than girls, and that the leadership that emerges in preadolescence and adolescence is based on dominance, spontaneous attraction, skill in games, and social position. A discussion of the "outcast" as the opposite of the leader and of the "bluffer" as a special case, together with a review of studies of children's values in relation to leadership, rounded out the whole.

Terman was always quick to point out that as a scientific contribution, his master's thesis had little worth. Yet as a biographical document, it reflects his own early concern with social acceptance and foreshadows his later work with the gifted. It even anticipated later studies of patterning, pecking order, self-concept, and value systems in children. Most of all, it was a vehicle for personal and professional development for Terman himself.

In 1903, near the end of the family's second year at Indiana, Helen Terman was born. Fred was then nearly three; he carried the announcement that he had a baby sister as his earliest memory. She was warmly welcomed. Yet Terman's health and his heavy schedule, as well as the midwestern custom of turning daughters over largely to their mothers, meant that her care became predominantly Anna's responsibility. To a considerable extent, Anna managed Helen's life from early childhood, something she did not attempt with Fred. As a result of her mother's tendency to make important decisions for her, Helen early developed less self-confidence and independence than her brother.

Now Terman had his M.A. degree, relatively good health, a family of three, an empty purse, and a substantial debt to repay. He needed to find remunerative work, yet hated to leave his studies. He was offered a position teaching psychology and pedagogy at the Central Normal School, but the salary was too low to enable him to pay his debt and save for more college, so he declined.

He consented to having Lindley nominate him for a fellowship at Clark University without any expectation that it would be forthcoming. But it was, and Terman was torn between his obligation to his father, brother, wife, and children, and his desire to complete work on the Ph.D. degree in educational psychology. Lindley, Bryan and Bergstrom urged him to accept, to go on with his studies without delay. Again, he went to his brother and father, who agreed to back him for another $1200. Anna courageously approved, and he accepted the fellowship. Then, when their belongings were packed for shipment to Clark University, Terman was offered one of the best high school principalships in Indiana. Had the offer come two weeks earlier, he would certainly have accepted, and a quite different career could have resulted.

The young family set off for Worcester, with a brief stop at Niagara Falls. Anna handled the arrangements, with the help of three-year-old Fred, who was already developing his lifelong protectiveness for his little sister. When the baby was left with the landlady while he and his parents viewed the Falls, Fred protested forcefully that someone might steal her. When they reached Worcester, he objected to her being used as an experimental subject by other students at Clark. Even when Anna let her play outdoors, knowing she would not wander far, Fred complained, "Would you please keep her in? I have to keep running after her and bringing her back." Such warm concern within the family, coupled with Anna's identification with her husband's ambition and her efficient management of daily routine, freed Terman to make the most of his opportunities, despite the threat of his frail health and the uncertainties of the future.

19

The Clark University of 1903-05 was very different from the Clark of today, just as it was from its contemporaries in America. Chartered in 1887 and opened in 1889, it was the second institution in the country (after Johns Hopkins) dedicated exclusively to graduate study and research. When Terman attended, Clark offered work only in biology, chemistry, mathematics, physics, and psychology. It was the American mecca for aspiring young psychologists. Later, in the 1920's, alumni from the early years nostalgically regretted the inclusion of undergraduate work, which they saw as detracting from the university's early creativity and daring.

Terman described the early Clark University as:

> ... in spirit much akin to the German university yet differing from it because of the small student body. It enrolled in all its departments only about fifty full-time students. .... Possibly thirty of the fifty were there primarily for psychology, philosophy, and education. The informality and freedom from administrative red tape were unequalled. The student registered by merely giving his name and address to President Hall's secretary. He was not required to select formally a major or minor subject. There was no appraisal of credentials for the purpose of deciding what courses he should take. *Lernfreiheit* was utterly unrestricted. There were professors who proposed to lecture and there were students who proposed to study; what more was necessary? The student could go to three or four lectures a day, or to none. No professor, so far as I could see, kept a class list. Attendance records were, of course, unheard of. No marks or grades of any kind were awarded at the end of the year or semester. One could attend a course of lectures all year without being required or necessarily expected to do the least reading in connection with it. There were no formalities about candidacy for a degree. The student was allowed to take his doctor's examination when the professor in charge of his thesis thought he was ready for it. No examination except the four-hour doctor's oral was ever given. ....
> The manner of conducting the library was in harmony with the general spirit of the university. The only formality was that books had to be signed for when they were taken from the building. ... Stacks and reading room were combined. Each student could have an entire alcove of perhaps ten by sixteen feet, and a large table to himself. .... No student ever wanted a book that the librarian would not gladly get, whatever the cost and in whatever language it was printed. (Terman, 1932f, 313-314).

Most of all, Clark University meant G. Stanley Hall, its founding president. Hall was one of the giants of the new American psychology; he was a contemporary of James, almost twenty years older than Cattell and Baldwin. Terman's ambition soared at the thought of a Ph.D. with Hall; their interests were similar, and neither was an apparatus man.

Hall's eminence was well deserved. No one in the history of child psychology had so great an opportunity to influence the course of development of a discipline as judged by seniority, volume of publications, public speaking ability, and personal control of publication media. Hall had studied under Fechner, Helmholtz, and Wundt in Germany, and under Bowditch and James in America. He had been Harvard's—and America's—first Ph.D. in psychology. He founded and edited four psychological journals, and the American Psychological Association itself was founded in his study. He became the first president of that Association, and was the only person other than William James to be elected its president a second time. He was the dominant figure in the child study movement of the 1890s, and his publications ultimately numbered more than 400. His students included such later luminaries as James McKeen Cattell, Joseph Jastrow, E. C. Sanford, H. H. Goddard, Arnold Gesell, and John Dewey, in addition to Terman (McCullers, 1969).

Hall was essentially a synthesizer, not a proponent of radically new ideas. Nothing in his theory of research strategy was specifically original with him. Even the questionnaire method frequently attributed to him was suggested by others, and his recapitulation theory of mental development was a blend of contemporary thought in several disciplines. But he had a passion for fresh ideas, and often used them for their shock value.

He was an ardent evolutionist, in touch with the contemporary literature in biology, embryology, psychology, sociology, and philosophy. He extended the doctrine of evolution to social development. His two basic theories, recapitulation and the inheritance of acquired characteristics, were widely acclaimed. He advocated a return to nature and to the simple, rural way of life, extolled the benefits of free play, and praised the programs developed in the Boy Scout movement.

A man of Hall's eminence inevitably drew detractors, particularly following his death in 1924. His basic theories lost their scientific respectability because they were essentially untestable as hypotheses; and he lost his following because his writing style was ponderous and full of complicated sentences. Terman agreed in those judgments, but pointed out that such things were outweighed by the tremendous inspiration Hall gave to students, even those who were distinctly not his disciples. His mind was the richest they had known. They were profoundly impressed by the amount of reading he did and by his offhand memory for nearly everything he read.

In 1904, Hall was preparing a course to bring together the whole field of psychology. Students saw books, monographs, and magazines taken to his study by the wheelbarrow load. In one lecture, he told of reviewing eighty monographs and articles on an aspect of perception, and students believed him because he worked until after one o'clock every night. They knew, for they had an understanding among them that whenever they came home in the early morning, they were to report whether the light in Hall's study was still burning.

The rest of Hall's schedule was equally busy. From eight to nine each morning he transacted all the business of a university president. From nine to eleven he prepared for his eleven o'clock lecture. From half past one to six he worked in his study, where students might consult him, preferably by appointment. After dinner he returned to his study to work until after midnight. Scholarship was his life, and Clark University profited from his efforts during his life and from an endowed professorship and his personal library at his death.

For most of the students, Hall's influence was felt most through his seminar.

When Clark students of the old days get together, their conversation invariably reverts to Hall's seminar. All agree that it was unique in character and about the most impotant single educational influence that ever entered their lives. . . . It met every Monday at 7:15 and was attended by all the students in psychology, philosophy, and education: in my day about thirty in number. Each evening two students reported on work which had occupied the major part of their time for several months. . . . The longer or more important report came first. It was always under way before 7:30 and might last an hour or longer. Ordinarily, though not always, it was read from manuscript. It might be either a summary and review of the literature in some field or an account of the student's own investigation. When the report was finished Dr. Hall usually started the discussion off with a few deceivingly generous comments on the importance of the material presented, then hesitantly expressed just a shade of doubt about some of the conclusions drawn, and finally called for "reactions." . . .

Soon, however, a student bolder than the others would dare to
disagree on some fundamental proposition; others would then follow
suit, and the fat was in the fire. When the discussion had raged from
thirty minutes to an hour, and was beginning to slacken, Hall would
sum things up with an erudition and fertility of imagination that
always amazed us. . . . Then we were herded into the dining room,
where light refreshments were served, and by 9:00 or so we were in
our chairs listening to another report. I always went home dazed and
intoxicated, took a hot bath to quiet my nerves, then lay awake for
hours rehearsing the drama and formulating the clever things I should
have said and did not.

   If there is any pedagogical device better adapted to put a man on
his mettle than a seminar thus conducted, I do not know what it is
(Terman, 1932f, 315-316).

   A student might cut all lectures for a week and reduce sleep to
half in preparation for a seminar report. If his presentation was
disapproved, a nervous collapse might send him to bed; in one case,
a breakdown resulted, necessitating several months of vacation.
There had been interesting seminars at Indiana under Lindley and
Bergstrom, but Hall's was beyond all comparison. Terman gained
more from it than from anything else at Clark University.
   At their first conference Hall let Terman know that, because
of his splendid training and the fine report of his Indiana teachers,
great things were expected from him. This favorite pedagogical
device left Terman with a burdening sense of responsibility during
the following months. Hall also advised Terman to sample all
courses in which he thought he might be interested and to drop
those he cared for least. Students in psychology usually began by
taking most of the courses given by Hall, Sanford, Burnham, and
Chamberlain, perhaps together with one by Hodge in neurology or
physiology. Nearly all classes, therefore, started out with an attendance of twenty to thirty, often reduced to ten or fewer by mid-
semester. One class even dwindled to two, and that would have been
cut in half had Terman not stayed too long to drop out without
embarrassment. Each professor lectured three or four times a week
on whatever he pleased. No effort was made to make courses
dovetail.
   E. C. Sanford became a major influence for Terman at Clark.
It was not that Sanford's experimentalism made Terman apparatus-
apt, or that his matter-of-fact lectures inspired; instead, his rare
personal charm and fineness of soul appealed to Terman, and his

scientific objectivity and keen critical judgment appealed to Terman's free-ranging curiosity.

Then there was W. H. Burnham, whose brilliant lectures helped Terman to see the beauty of the good English style that Hall did not have. Burnham always read from a manuscript ready for publication—but publication was always postponed. In his classes he gave a splendid systematic orientation in educational psychology, and his course in school hygiene particularly influenced Terman's reading and teaching for many years.

Hall lectured from notes, with sweeping statements and a wealth of allusion. Students judged the freshness of his preparation by the amount of fumbling with notes and by the verve of his delivery. Chamberlain and Hodge were unorganized and sometimes rambling, Chamberlain wandering off into his extensive browsing in anthropology, and Hodge into personal associations. For the other professors, lectures were not particularly important; they were there primarily to carry on research and to guide students in doing likewise. There was no systematic instruction in statistical methods, an omission that Terman regretted.

Reading ran a close second to Hall's seminar as a way of learning. From every quarter, Terman felt the influence of European psychology as it went on in Germany in the new laboratories, in France with Binet and his studies of children, and in England with Galton and his studies of genius. Thorndike's tests of school achievement caught his imagination. He became interested in the work of Freud and, until 1935, read a good many articles and books on psychoanalysis. He read everything he could find on the method of tests, including the publications of Bourdon, Ebbinghaus, Kraepelin, Aschaffenburg, Stern, Cattell, Wissler, Thorndike, Gilbert, Jastrow, Bolton, Thompson, and Spearman. He noticed the similarity between the earlier and later work of leading psychologists in topic, method of work, psychological views, and literary expression. Even such men as Hall, Kraepelin, Binet, Titchener, Spearman, and Thorndike set a pattern early and elaborated it throughout their careers.

Then there were the free hours for walks, and the evenings with other students. Hall attracted able students; among psychologists listed in *American Men of Science* were fifteen who named Hall as their chief intellectual stimulus, either directly or through his students (M. Boring, 1948). Terman's own classmates included a number who later became eminent: W. F. Book, A. A. Cleveland,

Edward Conradi, Arnold Gesell, E. B. Huey, J. R. Jewell, F. Kuhlman, W. Libby, G. E. Myers, Josiah Morse, J. P. Porter, J. W. Slaughter, and Charles Waddell.

Arnold Gesell shared Terman's interest in childhood and his enthusiasm for Hall; he enjoyed Terman's friendly companionship and Hoosier humor as well. The two joined forces in observing children. They used the forbidding immensity of the steep wooden staircase to the main academic building at Clark to study the motor coordination of bright and backward boys. Terman would marshal the boys while Gesell would serve as timekeeper to record speed of climbing and descent. They explored puzzle books, games, and children's books, looking for materials that would tease out the critical factors in mental growth, while Binet's work was still on the horizon.

Huey had just returned from Europe, and he spent evenings telling the other students about the work of Binet and Janet. Three others from Indiana—Book, Conradi and Porter—were close friends. Book was at work on his typing experiments; Conradi, who lived across the street from the Termans, was deep in his study of imitation in birds, an enthusiasm shared by Porter. Cleveland was involved in the psychology of playing chess. Even five-year-old Fred listened to discussions of his father's work and was tested on Binet-like scales. These formed a close community within the larger group of students.

They looked on with interest at the others. There was a semi-psychotic Swede who had ridden the trucks of freight trains 3000 miles to study with Hall, only to find himself the imagined victim of persecution by Hall and others. There was a tradesman who had been struggling for years to win the doctorate; and there was a foreign "university tramp" working toward his fourth Ph.D. There were assorted older spinsters with an enthusiasm for child study but little feminine charm.

The experience at Clark was even richer than Terman had expected. He suffered some disillusionment about Hall as a scientist, and reacted against some of the courses. However, he had never worked well under much direction or restraint, and at Clark he was placed on his own responsibility. He gave his best with enthusiasm. He learned the need for intense concentration and developed a taste for research monographs rather than textbooks. But most of all, he found at Clark freedom to work as he pleased, unlimited library facilities, and Hall's Monday evening seminars. That freedom was crucial in his development.

At Hall's suggestion, and after some protest, Terman circulated a questionnaire on leadership among children; that experience convinced Terman that the questionnaire method was not for him. Similarly, he did a study of the literature on "precocity" in which he carefully separated natural development in advance of an assumed norm—"precocity"—from forced development through outside interference, or "prematuration" (Terman, 1905). He argued the importance of infancy and pointed out that the social need is to lengthen rather than shorten the period of childhood. Excessive pressure might induce chronic fatigue, neurasthenia, delinquency, and more serious emotional disorders. Such a point of view is directly opposed to the educational trend of the 1970s. In his study, Terman met Hall's negative attitude toward the gifted neatly by excluding them from the discussion, and by defining prematuration as forced rather than natural development.

So far as Terman's health was concerned, the first ten months at Clark were uneventful. The new environment was stimulating, and he worked harder than ever before, averaging about eighty hours a week. Then came his third pulmonary hemorrhage.

> . . . around the middle of the vacation period, just after I had finished a game of tennis, a hemorrhage broke loose in such quantity as to leave no doubt as to its origin. Four years had passed since the attack of pleurisy and I had pretty well recovered from the fright it had given me. The shock I experienced from the new threat was profound, particularly after the nature of it was confirmed by a TB specialist. When I informed the doctor of my desperate situation—a wife and two children, debts of more than $1500, and the necessity of getting my degree the following year—I fully expected to be told to forget my plans and spend a year regaining my health. Instead, he suggested that I go to bed for two or three weeks to see how things developed. If there were no further symptoms, he thought it might then be safe to work a few hours daily provided I rested in bed the remainder of the day. I have always believed that if I had been sentenced to a year in a sanatorium I should probably have died of worry about the future of my family and my career. As it turned out, I was feeling so well within a month or two that I was working six or seven hours a day.
>
> Although no symptoms reappeared during the following school year, I developed something like an anxiety neurosis which remained fairly quiescent during the day but often woke me in the middle of the night and left me sleepless for hours, worrying about my health, my debts, and my chances of getting the degree. Before that year I had

never experienced insomnia but for the next five years I was rarely free from it (Terman unpublished, 1953).

As the months passed and his health again improved, Terman's anxiety abated a little and his working efficiency increased. Anna nursed him and walled him off from casual visitors; when they stayed too long, she indicated that he was tiring and must get some rest. Terman welcomed the protection for his work as much as for his health. He did not particularly enjoy casual visits, just as he seldom went out in crowds to lectures or concerts; his life was in his study. The friendships he really valued were those he initiated for himself. Anna regarded him as a man of genius who must be allowed to go his own way, freed from interruption. He must, if at all possible, complete his studies at Clark. She even arranged for financial help from her father to ease the difficult financial situation, making it unnecessary for her husband to feel he must undertake supplementary activities to generate income. Anna wanted for her husband what he wanted for himself.

In the spring of 1904, Terman had decided to base his dissertation on an experimental study of mental tests in relation to brightness and dullness. It cost him a heavy soul struggle to desert Hall in favor of E. C. Sanford as mentor, but Hall's emphatic disapproval of both mental testing and giftedness as fields of study made it essential. In addition, Hall distrusted what he termed the "quasi-exactness" of quantitative methods as misleading, while Terman was a firm empiricist. When Hall finally gave his blessing to Terman's project, Sanford took over the chairmanship and followed the work with friendly interest, though he rarely ventured a suggestion.

The time for such a study was ripe. Gilbert, Cattell and Farrand, Sharp, Wissler, Thompson, and Thorndike had all published research recently on mental and physical development. Kuhlman had a study of the feebleminded in press. Spearman was working on his theory; though Terman admired the originality of his ideas, he found them over-dogmatic, self-contradictory, excessively dependent on mathematical formulas.

At first, Terman's interest in mental tests was more qualitative than quantitative. He wanted to find out what processes were involved in "intelligence." He had enough experience as a teacher to know that great differences exist in the capacity to learn; and his own boyhood was evidence that high talent may well be lost without recognition and encouragement. There was something provocative in the idea of measuring complex mental processes.

The dissertation was wholly his own, from concept to finished document. He selected the topic, devised the tests and procedures, and wrote up the results unaided. He tested subjects six hours a day for five months, accumulating more than forty hours of testing per subject. Yet he thoroughly enjoyed the whole process. In June 1905, the dissertation was complete.

Genius and Stupidity: A Study of Some of the Intellectual Processes of Seven "Bright" and Seven "Stupid" Boys was the title (Terman, 1906). Terman first argued that psychology had too long been preoccupied with structure rather than process, and that only intensive, qualitative analysis of a limited number of cases would disclose the deep differences in mentality between individuals.

Principals of three schools in Worcester, with the help of their teachers, selected twelve "bright" boys and twelve "stupid" boys from a population of five hundred—roughly the extreme two percent at either end of the hypothetical distribution of intellectual ability. Of the twelve in each category, seven were able to devote the necessary time to Terman's exhaustive testing program at the University. All were ten to eleven years of age, and home conditions and educational opportunity were matched for the two groups.

Terman devised tests in eight categories: inventiveness and creative imagination; logical processes; mathematical ability; mastery of language; insight, as shown in the interpretation of fables; ease of learning to play chess; memory; and motor ability. Many of the tests are familiar to contemporary psychometrists; the water-measuring problem, ball-in-field, tracing figures, making change, developing a rule, repeating a story, giving words, completing a sentence, following directions, interpreting fables, and reproducing geometrical forms were all among the forty tests. The statistical treatment of the data from the boys was crude—a simple judgment of rank for each individual on each task, with simple comparisons between the "bright" and the "stupid" groups.

The "bright" boys were superior on all mental tests, though inferior on the motor items. They uniformly preferred to read, while the others liked to play games. Inventiveness was least linked to brightness; emotional reaction was highly individual; and there was little difference between the two categories in persistence. The rankings of the subjects were strikingly uniform from test to test. The whole project strengthened Terman's impression of the importance of endowment over training as a determinant of the individual's intellectual rank among his fellows.

Most of all, through the dissertation Terman learned an exciting method of investigating complex mental processes. Though this study was hardly a definitive statement about the nature of brightness, it supplied a method for the future.

Terman's final oral examination lasted four hours, including a fifteen-minute intermission at the end of the first two. In addition to the usual questioning about psychology and about the dissertation, Hall—who had been a minister and had lectured on the psychology of religion—inserted a question about St. Thomas. Terman, the agnostic, replied that he knew nothing about St. Thomas. Nothing was said for about five minutes, Hall staring into space and Terman fearing that his orals were being terminated. Finally Hall broke the silence, changed the subject, and the examination went on. Terman was his own man with his own point of view.

CHAPTER III

The Making of
a University Professor

*At last I found the opportunity I had so long wanted,
in a perfect climate and with the university I would have
chosen in preference to any other (Terman unpublished,
1953).*

His degree completed, Terman faced the problem of what to
do next. He had dreamed of college teaching and research, but his
precarious health imposed limits. Fortune dictated a circuitous
start toward his goal, but his direction never wavered—his drive
and his love of learning held him steadfast.

Terman's physician at Clark warned him that he should find a
congenial climate. That ruled out the East, where he would have
liked to stay. Of course he wanted a university position, but the
only such offer he received carried a salary much too low to support
his family, to say nothing of paying off his debt of $2500. That sum
was the equivalent of more than $10,000 in the early 1950s, and
still more today.

Late in the spring of 1905, after months of anxious waiting, he
received three offers in as many days. The first was the presidency
of a struggling normal school in St. Petersburg, Florida, which he
accepted. Then, forty-eight hours later, he was simultaneously
offered a one-year temporary position at the University of Texas at
half salary, and the principalship of the high school in San Bernardino, California. After two sleepless nights, anxiety over his health
won out over professional ambition, and he secured a release from
the Florida presidency to go to San Bernardino. Other Clark men
took the other offers: Conradi that in Florida, and Morse that in
Texas.

The attraction of the San Bernardino principalship lay almost
wholly in the semiarid Southern California climate that he thought
safest for him. He did not like administrative work particularly, but

30

he had done it well and could do it well again. And he knew he still suffered from active tuberculosis, though he was sensitive about his condition and rarely mentioned his precarious health. He could live above such limits.

... Although I have had numerous bouts with tuberculosis, I have lost an estimated total of not more than eight months from work, have been bedridden with the disease less than half of that time, and recovered quickly from every attack. Nevertheless I have had my full share of anxieties: the possibility of a premature death was a nightmarish specter that haunted me for years. ...

It was September of 1905 when we arrived at San Bernardino after an unforgettable ride through the Mohave Desert. As our train coasted down through the Cajon Pass, and the San Bernardino Valley opened up before us almost encircled by mountains of 4,000 to 11,000 feet, the valley seemed to be truly the paradise that the Chamber-of-Commerce literature had depicted it. Here, if anywhere, I should be able to rid myself of the threat that had been hanging over me. The people we met were so proud of their climate that I was constantly being told of this or that person who had come to San Bernardino twenty or thirty years ago as a 'one-lunger' and was soon restored to health. My new friends who told me these stories could not know what an eager listener I was!

The high school work proved to be interesting; the teachers were competent and cooperative, and the townspeople were as friendly and kind as the climate itself. Life was so pleasant and so filled with hope that I was ill-prepared for the shock that came eight weeks later when I awoke about five o'clock on a Thursday morning with my mouth full of blood. The hemorrhage lasted several minutes and was more copious than any other I was ever to experience.

Imagine my predicament. No one in San Bernardino knew that I had ever had TB, and to admit the fact now might have serious consequences. Instead of calling a doctor, I reported to the school that I was not feeling well and would remain at home the rest of the week. During the following week I was on duty half of each day to attend to administrative matters, while other faculty members taught my classes. Just eleven days after the hemorrhage I went back to work on a full-time basis. The desperate gamble I had taken paid off, for there was no serious trouble the rest of the school year. I carried my duties as lightly as possible, avoiding over-exertion, and went to bed early. As soon as school ended in June we packed off to the mountains where we camped out in tents for nearly three months. By the time we had to leave I felt so well that I could look forward to the next year's work with confidence (Terman unpublished, 1953).

31

Terman's handling of his own illness in such cavalier fashion had justification in more than his anxiety. He knew that he often registered negative on tuberculosis tests after a hemorrhage, and the diagnosis was seldom unmistakably clear. He had pulled through on his own regimen before, and financial necessity was a strong master.

There were friendly people all around with whom Terman and his family corresponded for years after. He was comfortable and reasonably happy in his work.

Terman was reappointed for a second year as principal at an increased salary, but his plans changed unexpectedly. A telegram from a teachers' agency told him that the Los Angeles Normal School needed a man in educational psychology, though Terman had not applied for the position. It was much nearer to the kind of thing he wanted to do; perhaps after a few years he could find a university position. He took the next train to Los Angeles for conferences; in a few days he asked release from San Bernardino and accepted the position as Professor of Child Study and Pedagogy at the Los Angeles Normal School.

This was a critical turning point in Terman's career. The new position was his first involvement in higher education and in the training of teachers. It brought him in touch with new professional colleagues, where as principal of a high school he had much less chance for such intellectual associations. And it showed much more promise of leading ultimately in the direction he had chosen.

The Termans moved to Hollywood, then a quiet suburb with a population of four thousand. Later in the year, they bought an acre in an orange grove at the foot of the Vedugo Hills in the San Fernando Valley (now in Glendale) and drafted plans for a house. After another summer of camping in the mountains, they moved to their new home. The location was ideal, for in those presmog years the climate of the San Fernando Valley rivaled that of Redlands and San Bernardino. Terman commuted to Los Angeles by interurban trolley, and his schedule was light enough that he had time for an hour or so in his garden each afternoon before dinner. Anna's cheerfulness and her frequent singing while about her work added to the family contentment. Terman read moderately during the evenings and on weekends, spent as much time as he could outdoors, and tried to forget that he had ever been interested in research.

Arnold Gesell was appointed Professor of Psychology at the Los Angeles Normal School in 1907, and the Gesell-Terman partnership was renewed. They became neighbors in their respective citrus groves opposite each other on picturesque Valley View Road.

When Gesell and his brother undertook building their own bunga-
low, the Termans were helpful in emergencies and always
hospitable.

Fred, then seven, was appointed chief assistant builder; Gesell
later insisted that the eager boy showed signs of engineering talent
even then. Gesell was a reasonably eligible bachelor, so Terman
introduced him to a colleague who was gaining a reputation as a
creative teacher of young children, and who soon became Mrs.
Gesell. Terman and Gesell were not only fellow students and neighbors; they also shared professional interests, a common illness when
Gesell once fell ill from tuberculosis, and even a common invitation
to teach at Stanford later (Terman, 1925g; 1946c).

In 1907, Terman's old friend from Clark, E. B. Huey, spent the
greater part of the summer with the Termans in the San Bernardino
mountains. He brought more talk of clinical psychology and mental
examination methods. Again in 1910, Huey visited for two weeks
during the summer, bringing Terman up to date on the work of
Binet and Goddard; he urged Terman to start some work at once
with the 1908 Binet scale.

Terman's teaching schedule during his four years at the Los
Angeles Normal School was not too heavy, requiring only moderate
preparation. His only outside work was an occasional lecture before
a teachers' institute; he prepared these lectures with considerable
care. Just what courses he taught, and what his own impact was on
the nature of those courses, can only be inferred. The *Los Angeles
Normal School Catalog* for those years contains only descriptions
of courses and programs. Professors' names are given only in the
general faculty lists, and no schedules of classes are available. Yet,
in the light of Terman's interests and point of view, the trace of his
influence can be seen. The first semester for students included a
required course in psychology which covered the "fundamental facts
of consciousness," effects of environment on mental development,
and the limits and meaning of education from a biological and
genetic point of view. In the second semester, there was an elective
course in experimental pedagogy, skills in special subjects, and
economy in learning. In the senior year, concurrent with two semes-
ters of student teaching, were two courses in educational psychology. "Child Study" included mental and physical growth,
individual differences, and the cultivation of an "intellectual sympathy" with children. "Pedagogy" focused on the application of
educational psychology and child study to teaching itself. In addition, there was an elective course in school hygiene, which included

33

mental hygiene (fatigue, work and rest, home study, sleep, "nervous-ness"); the hygiene of learning, with special reference to skill sub-jects; health inspection, with special attention to defects of the eye, ear, and throat; the health of the teacher; and the care of school buildings.

The library facilities at the Normal School were unusually good, and Terman used them to write eight rather general articles on teach-ing (Terman, 1907, 1908a, 1908b, 1908c, 1909a, 1909b, 1909c, 1909d). He criticized William James's thesis that man had a reserve of physical and mental power he seldom used, saying that such a reserve was only a safety factor for emergencies, and that man need not use all of his energy all the time. He proposed a book on the mental characteristics of occupational groups such as teachers, whom he cited for their false mannerisms, devotion to petty devices, didactic style in human relationships, air of omniscience, pedantry, and rigid conventionality. He traced the history of child beating to produce learning from ancient Egypt to the twentieth century, concluding that this practice was a far more serious deter-rent to learning than the written record shows. Claiming that con-temporary pedagogical methods neglected the child's bodily well-being, he stressed the need for health supervision as an essential part of teaching. He advocated more vocational education so students could see a direct relationship between their studies and their vocational aspirations. So it went. The articles reflected Terman's own experience as a teacher in the light of his later training and point of view. The issues were timeless, the writing was clear and forceful, yet the articles were not the research documents he had learned to love.

The four years in Los Angeles brought renewed health, and Terman became restless in his somewhat sterile intellectual environ-ment. Gesell left for Yale, but Terman had to wait for an opportunity in the right climatic location. Five years beyond the doctorate, at age thirty-three, he could not wait many more years before the chances for a good university position would begin to dwindle.

Then his friend Bergstrom, who had gone in 1909 to a newly created professorship of educational psychology in the Department of Education at Stanford University, died suddenly within his first year there. The position was offered to Huey, who declined in favor of continuing his work at Johns Hopkins. Huey recommended Terman to take his place, a suggestion that substantially influenced the faculty at Stanford.

Then there intervened one of the strange chance factors that influence careers. Wilfred E. Talbert, an Orange County teacher and an early motorcycle enthusiast who had persuaded the county superintendent of schools to ride on the back seat in his excursions, was asked to suggest a speaker to share the platform at a teachers' institute with Elwood Cubberley of Stanford. Talbert replied that Terman was the most popular teacher at Los Angeles Normal, at least with the ladies; Terman had always been attractive to women and liked them in return as long as their interests matched his. The matter was arranged. After the meeting, Talbert and a friend invited Terman and Cubberley to lunch in a crowded cafe where the food was barely edible. The two men were so much interested in each other that neither noticed the limited menu or the crowding, but talked constantly the whole time.

The result of this chain of events was that in March 1910, upon Cubberley's recommendation, supported by Huey's evaluation, President David Starr Jordan of Stanford University offered Terman an assistant professorship in the School of Education at Stanford. Terman had found the opportunity he had dreamed of—a perfect climate and the university in which he would most like to teach. But for the tuberculosis which brought him to California, he might well have missed such an ideal position. All the anxiety the disease had caused him was worth such an outcome. Terman eagerly accepted the offer.

The move to Stanford represented another major turn in the road, because it placed Terman in an environment that gave him an opportunity to express the latent talents that had shown only as a brief flash of promise in his work at Indiana and at Clark.

In the summer of 1910, the Terman family moved to a charming country cottage a mile and one-half from Stanford, just near enough for Terman to commute by bicycle. The house had a living room, a bath, a large kitchen, a study, two bedrooms, and a screened sleeping porch more than forty feet long, where the entire family could sleep in the open air.

Jesse Sears, a member of the faculty of the School of Education, and his family were early friends of the Termans. The two Sears boys were somewhat younger than the Terman children, but the two fathers found much to talk about, and the families were soon exchanging visits and dinners. Sears found Terman friendly, though not impressive in stature, with a pleasant smile and a way of speaking that revealed real charm. Always informal and personally comfortable, Terman conversed freely and knowledgeably without ever dominating or directing the conversation. In faculty meetings he was much the same, giving his ideas readily and freely but never growing formal or vociferous. He listened attentively, spoke gently, and seemed always the gentleman in manner and speech. He liked to hear a good story, though storytelling was not among his own accomplishments. He seldom opposed views expressed by others, though he was quick to defend his own proposals. He never tried to draw attention to himself. His most outstanding characteristic was a generous friendliness which marked all his personal and academic relationships and brightened the distinction of his career.

Though Terman liked people, ideas were his first love. He was happy alone, wrestling with facts. He delighted in discovery and creation. Even in conversation, he often seemed to be looking inward for possible weaknesses in his own argument; such self-criticism served his burning desire to find truth. The ideas he proposed were frequently ingenious, but his suggestions were usually empirical rather than theoretical—common-sense standards by which theory could be stated. He was intolerant of the diversified and sometimes superficial theories then current. He disliked students who expected to be spoon-fed, people who were pompous, and people who preferred snap judgments to factual data. His idealism, along with the pace of his scholarly work and his friendliness, made him attractive to students from the beginning.

Students at Stanford saw in Terman a man slightly below average in height (five feet seven inches) and weight, fond of gray- and sand-colored suits, with light auburn hair and deep brown eyes looking out from behind his glasses. Just when Terman started wearing the glasses is uncertain, but from the early Stanford days on he wore them constantly. His carriage gave no hint of his recent illness, though he was slightly round-shouldered and seemed far from robust. He never called off a class, but the eyeshade he often wore and his habit of raising a hand to protect his eyes hinted of frequent headaches. Some of his associates wondered why Terman read so much about tuberculosis; he talked little of his close acquaintance with that disease, though he made no secret of it either.

Terman liked children, as both Fred and Helen would agree. At home, a wind-up phonograph with a huge horn played a whole stack of "red seal" records of the best music, including selections from grand opera and recordings of great violinists. Later the family had a player piano as well. Yet Terman seldom spoke of his children to his friends, just as he seldom spoke of himself. He was there when they needed help, but the initiative lay with them. Further, his dedication to his own work and his philosophy that children should be self-directing kept him from spending much time with them. He never questioned them about what they were doing in school or about their grades, but assumed, like Rousseau, that they would educate themselves.

One result of Terman's philosophy was that Fred did not learn to read until he was eight years of age. As a child, Fred had many interests and was less dependent that the average boy on the companionship of other children. As a result, his parents did not bother to start him in school at the usual age of six. Shortly after his eighth birthday, however, they decided that Fred should learn to read; so his mother, who had been a teacher, spent half an hour or so each day during the following winter giving him lessons in reading and arithmetic. The following fall—1909—Fred started school in the third grade, one year behind his age group. He had no difficulty in adjusting. Four years later, at thirteen, he graduated from the eighth grade; in seven more years, he graduated from Stanford Phi Beta Kappa. In addition to his schooling, Fred developed a vivid interest which eventually focused on electronics, first by setting up his own electric shop in the garage, later by becoming a ham radio operator. Terman was sympathetic and proud of his son's scientific bent, though he shared little of such interest himself.

With Helen it was a different story. She was lonely without other children, so she started school in the first grade at the normal time. Around 1912, her schooling was interrupted for almost a year when she was ill with a form of rheumatic fever. But despite the loss of time from school, she entered high school at the age of thirteen and went on with her work at Stanford, where she graduated in 1924 "with distinction," that is, in the top fifteen percent of her graduating class academically. From Stanford, she went to a small, rather rural elementary school north of Santa Barbara for a successful year as a teacher before her marriage. For Helen, caught between a positive father and a dynamic mother, school meant a life of her own, which she thoroughly enjoyed.

Anna, too, developed independent activities. An even-tempered woman with abundant physical energy, she joined her husband on family occasions and for essential social events, and went her own way at other times. She and her husband called at faculty homes, dined at the tables of their best friends, and joined in general activities. Faculty children saw much of Anna but seldom met Lewis, not only because of his great involvement with work, but also because their parents were afraid Lewis's former illness might still be contagious. Most of all, the Termans were a congenial family, combining mutual respect with an emphasis on individuality.

In 1912, Terman was promoted to the associate professorship, evidence that he had successfully established himself in the Stanford environment. By that time he had demonstrated his promise as a productive scholar in the field of school hygiene as well as in his work with mental tests. He had graduate students working with him as partners in research; that is, he was beginning to train disciples. He had become a full-fledged, productive faculty member of a university, training university teachers and conducting scholarly research of the highest calibre.

In the summer of 1912, Terman built a house on the Stanford campus that served as a family home for the rest of his life. The house was important in several ways. First, it was a sign that he felt his position at Stanford to be secure. In addition, living on the campus meant closer contact with his academic colleagues than continuing to live isolated in the country or moving to Palo Alto, where only a few of his neighbors would have been associated with the university. For a man who was friendly but never gregarious, living on the campus in the midst of colleagues with similar interests resulted in his being much more a part of the university than would have otherwise been the case. This fact in a subtle way enriched Terman's life and made him a more important and influential personal force on the Stanford faculty.

This home on the campus was a fairly substantial place, built on a superbly located lot of approximately one and one-third acres. The house was a full two stories, with three ample bedrooms, a large study, and two sleeping porches on the second floor; the arrangements on the first floor were correspondingly spacious. With only minor additions, this home served Lewis and Anna very well for the rest of their lives. The home was made possible through a gift of roughly $1500 from Anna's father to each of his three daughters, which provided a down payment supplemented by a loan from Stanford.

Terman arranged his study upstairs, adjacent to his bedroom and next to those of the rest of the family, remote from the living quarters and their distractions. There he could rest two hours during each day, reading professional material or biography. And he went up to his study immediately after dinner and worked there until late at night. He loved to collect and compile information, and he read all significant publications in French and German as well as English.

38

He kept carefully indexed files on his reading all around his study, on half sheets of paper grouped by topic in envelopes; each entry carried a complete bibliographical reference and annotation. When preparing to lecture or to write, Terman simply pulled out the right envelope from his file. He needed elaborate notes because his memory for the fine structure of factual details was inadequate to satisfy his passion for precision. He could easily recall people and their ideas, but titles and dates of articles and books often escaped him.

The files fit in with Terman's way of working. His many books and articles were written longhand because, as he said, the current of his thought refused to go through a typewriter. He had seen illustrations of monks of the Middle Ages writing at lecterns; from his reading he knew that the posture at a lectern placed the arm in an optimal position for writing. He therefore devised a lectern for himself and used it for some years for his writing.

Terman's teaching load was light for the times—eight hours a week, excluding seminars and the supervision of independent studies. An examination of the Stanford Register for the years 1910-13 and 1915-16 shows the development of the seven or eight courses per year to which Terman was assigned and which he undoubtedly shaped. The first cluster centers on child and adolescent psychology, together with related courses in "Social and Moral Education" and "The Literature of Child Psychology;" these gradually merged into two basic offerings, adolescent psychology and child psychology. The second cluster is more constant, focusing on school health and school hygiene. The third shows the development of Terman's work in individual differences, with clinical child psychology and his research interest spinning off a specialized course in intelligence tests. The fourth represents an attempt to handle the broad field of educational psychology, through courses in experimental pedagogy and educational psychology, or alternatively through a problems approach in independent research or a discussion of educational problems. The fifth nucleus is the teaching process and teacher education, with courses in the supervision of instruction and the training of teachers; these interests faded into the background with Terman's deepening interest in school hygiene and in individual differences.

For a man who had at one time been the principal and the only teacher in a four-year high school, and who from the age of twelve to fifteen had worked from dawn to dusk on a farm, any such load would seem light and stimulating, since it reflected his own driving interests.

39

CHAPTER IV

The Binet and Mental Testing

*In collaboration with one of my graduate students,
H. G. Childs, I began at once an experimental study of
the Binet tests and continued with this problem until the
publication of* The Measurement of Intelligence *in
1916. . . .*

*. . . I knew that my revision of Binet's tests was
superior to others then available, but I did not foresee
the vogue it was to have and imagined that it would
probably be displaced by something much better within
a few years.*

*Apart from the possible fate of my own work, I did
not expect mental tests to gain acceptance nearly so
quickly as they did. . . . Between 1910 and 1916 I made
no trips East and did not even apply for membership in
the American Psychological Association. I had the feeling
that I hardly counted as a psychologist unless possibly
among a few kindred souls like Gesell, Goddard, Kuhlman, Thorndike, Whipple, Yerkes, and a few others who
had become 'tarred by the same brush' (Terman, 1932f,
p. 324).*

ALTHOUGH Terman divided his research and writing time more
or less equally between mental tests and health studies during his
early years at Stanford, his work on tests had more continuity
with his earlier research and a stronger relationship to his later work.
In that sense it came first. By 1912 his health was so good that he
was able to get life insurance at normal rates. His record in teaching
and research was brilliant. Promotion from associate to full professorship came in 1916, as soon as the Stanford Binet test was published. As an ambitious person, Terman was sensitive to the implications associated with the promotion, and was intensely gratified

40

when he received it. Cubberley, for his part, quickly appreciated the importance of Terman's work and acted accordingly. As a result, Terman always felt that Stanford in general, and Cubberley in particular, had treated him well, and he was loyal to both. His mind was at ease.

Psychology as a science was moving, too, away from "brass instrument" problems and toward Terman's concern with behavior and personality. Mental testing had been proposed by Cattell, but the studies of Wissler and Sharp triggered a violent reaction against it on the part of those preoccupied with studies of "consciousness." Then came Binet, trained in the clinical method as a physician, and an astute observer of children. A new point of view breathed new life into an old dilemma.

Binet was an insightful, inventive psychologist, as well as a scrupulously careful researcher. His stress on measurement through performance was in tune with the emerging behaviorism in American psychology. His belief in letting facts lead rather than in limiting them by stating a theory at the outset undoubtedly influenced Terman. Defeated in his early espousal of hypnotism and suggestibility (Wolf, 1964), Binet turned to child psychology and mental testing. He proposed tests to measure eleven different mental "faculties," but ten years later he was flexible enough to abandon faculty psychology completely. He had found that any "faculties" involved in intelligent behavior were so interwoven that it was only possible to measure combined functional capacity.

In 1904, when Terman was embarking on his dissertation at Clark, the Paris School authority asked Binet and a physician named T. Simon to devise a screening device, in order to remove from public schools children who were hopelessly unable to learn there and who needed special schools. Binet did not try to define what he wished to measure, since whatever it was had never been fully isolated. He knew that teachers could not make valid judgments of mental ability, unbiased by family background and child personality and behavior. Instead, he adopted the medical practice of choosing tests to distinguish between clinical groups—the normal and the feebleminded.

Binet brought a rich background to the task, for he had been working on differences between bright and dull children since 1893. He had tried recall of digits, suggestibility, size of cranium, moral judgment, tactile discrimination, mental addition, graphology, palmistry, and many other devices. He quickly found that physical measures and tests of such simple functions as sensory judgment were of little significance in relation to mental ability. He turned to tests of more complex functions, such as the tendency to take and maintain a definite direction, to make adaptations, and to criticize one's own effort. Finally, he put together the best items he had been able to devise in the *1905 Binet-Simon Scale*, consisting of thirty tests of increasing difficulty (Binet and Simon, 1905).

The *1905 Binet-Simon Scale* met a mixed reception. It was impartial and independent of the preconceptions of the tester, and it was highly useful in identifying and studying subnormal children. Nevertheless, it was crude in many ways. Binet had used only ten cases each at ages three, five, seven, nine, and eleven years, selected by teachers as average, as the normal group, together with an unstated number of feebleminded individuals. The scale was scored simply by the number of tests passed, with arbitrary cutoff points at six for idiots and fifteen for imbeciles. But the scale was a turning point in mental testing because it combined mental abilities into a single measure, approached intelligence through performance in everyday tasks, and used clinical criterion groups for its validation.

Binet knew that mental ability increases with age, and he quickly turned to constructing an age scale (Binet and Simon, 1908). This time his subjects were 203 children within two months of a birthday, from ages three to twelve. He revised his original test items, added others, and grouped all according to age level. He chose items on which success was markedly related to age and to success on other items on the scale. The assignment of an item to an age level was based on sixty percent of children of that age passing the item. The age scale was another tremendous stride in testing. It was enthusiastically received, despite criticisms that the number of tests at each age varied from three to eight, and that mental age had meaning in prediction only when related to chronological age.

The *1911 Binet-Simon Scale* (Binet, 1911) was less revolutionary. It relocated many items in different age groups, built the number of tests to five at each age level, and extended the scale to fifteen-year-olds and adults. It was a refinement of the 1908 scale rather than an essentially new approach.

A chorus of criticism arose against the whole idea of intelligence testing, particularly against the Binet scales. Psychiatrists and teachers were incredulous. Psychologists claimed that the tests were improperly located—those at the lower levels were too easy and those at the upper levels too hard. Besides, any quantitative approach to measuring intelligence neglected important qualitative differences. The scale lacked a zero point, and no ordinal ranking such as the Binet provided could be a true measure. Neither could it measure native endowment, because the tests were contaminated by experience (Tuddenham, 1962).

Binet agreed that tests might need to be relocated, but he claimed that quantification was possible without establishing a zero point. He explained that the knowledge called for in testing was within the common experience of children. He even urged teaching children how to learn, to give attention, to memorize, and to exercise judgment. Binet believed that "intelligence" could be improved through appropriate instruction, contrary to Terman's later view.

There was a surge of interest in the tests from other psychologists. Goddard, who had been critical of the 1905 scale, adopted the 1908 revision and translated it into English for use at Vineland. He became an eloquent advocate of the test, applauding its concept of the functional and unitary nature of intelligence. Both Whipple and Huey issued adaptations of the Binet in 1910. Kuhlman and Wallin each added to the list of translations and revisions in 1911. Meanwhile, Cyril Burt in England was paralleling much of what Terman was beginning to do. There was no communication between the two men, but they shared both a common approach to the task and a distrust of Spearman's factor analysis, his dogmatism and his wholly quantitative approach. But it remained for Terman to set the next major landmark.

Terman had, of course, been interested in mental testing from the beginning. His childhood feelings of frustration at being unable to match the athletic performances of his older, stronger schoolmates may have been the origin. In his master's thesis on leadership, he was groping for some kind of process for selecting the able. He then focused strongly on mental tests in his doctoral dissertation, despite the disapproval of Hall. All this activity predated the publication of the first Binet scale. Terman had read Binet's early articles with interest and admiration: they were unusually clear and perceptive; Binet's procedure in test construction was excellent; and his inductive-empirical approach held great promise. Terman even admired Binet's lucid style and consciously tried to model his own on it.

Except through his reading of Binet's publications, it is doubtful that Terman had any direct personal contact, despite statements by Tuddenham (1962) and assertions by Simon to Theta Wolf. Binet's first publication on his mental test appeared in 1905, concurrently with Terman's own work, done quite independently.

There is nothing in the Terman archives to suggest any correspondence. Terman was never in Europe. None of his associates at that time heard Terman mention any personal interchange, though he often praised Binet and his work. Besides, Terman was so preoccupied with health and finances from 1905 to 1910—when Binet was revising the test most energetically—that he was trying to forget research until Huey urged him in 1910 to revise the Binet. Binet's work did, however, give the subject of intelligence a new meaning and provide a framework for moving ahead with tests of intelligence, at just the right time to fire Terman with new interest. The whole approach was just what he had been looking for.

Typically, Terman searched through the related background laid by other psychologists in connection with his work with Binet's concepts. He studied particularly the work of Janet, Meumann, Spearman, Stern, Ebbinghaus, Thorndike, Whipple, and the Freudian writers (Terman, 1932f). He was most stimulated by Thorndike's writing, perhaps because of his search for a method of quantification, and perhaps because he found himself in perpetual disagreement with Thorndike's theories. Next in order of usefulness were the writings of Meumann, Stern, and Whipple. He reread all of Binet's contributions on mental testing, prepared lectures on Stern, published an extensive summary and criticism of Meumann's *Experimentelle Pädagogik* with its applied emphasis and elaborate test series (Terman, 1914i; 1915i). He read regularly almost everything in *L' Année Psychologique*, the *British Journal of Psychology*, *Zeitschrift für angewandte Psychologie*, Kraepelin's *Psychologische Arbeiten*, *Zeitschrift für pädagogische Psychologie*, and all the American journals. He also made careful notes on the important monographs on mental development; reread Ellis, Krafft-Ebing, and others on sex differences; and even followed what he considered the "singularly sterile" writings of Titchener.

Terman's publications showed his deepening interest in the Binet scales. He gave Binet credit for being the first to attempt to test higher mental functions, to measure general intelligence rather than separate mental faculties, and to use age norms (Terman, 1913b). He pointed out that the Binet tests measured intelligence only, not the "entire mentality," and that caution should therefore be used in applying them to vocational guidance and school instruction. He criticized the chance factors present in Binet's standardization, defects of procedure and scoring, the absence of any instruction on gaining and maintaining rapport, and the use of arbitrary cutoff points for feeblemindedness. From the beginning he recognized the influence of educational and social opportunity on test results: "... in our efforts to measure intelligence, therefore, we always measure intelligence plus a certain kind and amount of training" (Terman, 1913b, p. 98). Terman was Binet's enthusiastic supporter, but also a rigorous critic.

In 1913, Terman attended the Fourth International Congress on School Hygiene at Buffalo; it was one of his first trips east after going to Stanford, and perhaps his first public appearance at an important meeting of more than local character. At the Congress he presented a paper which suggested revisions, extensions, and supplements for the Binet scales (Terman 1913c). He discussed sample bias, placement of test items, and criteria for choice of tests. In a similar paper in more extended form (Terman, 1913h), he pointed out that a retardate with a mental age of five is quite different as a person from a child of five. He asserted that the age level of a test should be determined not by a particular percentage of success at a particular age level, but rather at the point where the number of children testing more than one year above is equal to the number testing more than one year below. He argued that tests must be practical in terms of time and equipment; that there should be six per age level for ease in computing mental age; that there should be alternate forms of such tests, and well as a shortened form and group tests for accuracy and convenience; and that achievement tests should be developed to aid teachers in interpreting the child's learning. This was essentially a chart of his future life work in mental testing, planned in bold strokes on a large scale.

Terman asked forbearance for the emerging science of mental testing from its theoretically-oriented critics (Terman, 1914a). He welcomed the work of Goddard in interpreting the Binet scales (Terman, 1914n), though he was critical of Goddard's translation; he corresponded with Goddard regularly while preparing the Stanford revision. He differed strongly with Haines's criticisms of Goddard's work, contending the age scale was superior to the point scale Haines proposed (Terman, 1916n). Terman was moving into the broad field of psychology in the nation as a whole and solidifying his position as an authority in the construction of mental tests.

Terman began his own experimentation with the Binet scales in 1910, immediately after his arrival at Stanford. He continued his revision until it culminated in the first Stanford revision in 1916, became his own severest critic in the years leading to the 1937 revision, and directed the 1960 revision in its early stages until his death. Though his major interest turned to other matters after World War I, Terman assiduously perfected the measure as best he could.

Terman began by defining intelligence as the ability to do abstract thinking. It included the ability to formulate concepts, to apply them to practical tasks which were new, and to evaluate the results. It was functional; it involved adaptation, as did the Binet tests; but it was characterized generally by the level of the thought process involved.

As for items, Terman had tried out a host of tests for his dissertation, and had continually added to them from his reading and the ingenuity of his students. He wanted to use many different tests, because intelligence itself has many aspects, and because the accidental influence of training and environment must be minimized.

With a graduate student, H. G. Childs, Terman tested 400 unselected children on an improvised extension of the Binet-Simon scale in 1910-11 (Terman, 1911a; 1912h). A few years later, he followed up eighteen of these cases and found that intelligence was relatively stable (Terman, 1915k).

A picture of Terman at work during that period is given by Robert Sears, whose childhood recollections of Terman bring those days to life. As the son of Terman's colleague Jesse Sears, Robert was a family friend. One day, when Robert was about six years old, Terman invited the boy to his office on the Stanford quad to take the 1914 version of the Binet revision. Robert remembered the musty smell of the office next door to that of his father. He remembered Terman's manner, soft and gentle, keeping him working, pushing for his best effort. He remembered hashing up the ball-and-field test and knowing intuitively that he had not done the right thing, though Terman let it go without comment. He noticed that when he began to have trouble with the tests, the session came to an end. He liked the tests and thought the tester a very nice man. From the vantage point of later distinction in child psychology, Sears judged Terman a superb mental tester.

The final revision of the Binet included six tests at each age level; each test carried a prorated number of months of mental age equivalent. The mental age equivalents were added to a basal age—the age level at which the child passed all tests—for a total "mental age." Perhaps the most useful innovation in scoring was Terman's adoption of Stern's proposed "intelligence quotient," or index of brightness, computed by dividing the total mental age by the chronological age (Stern, 1912; 1914). The IQ, as it came to be known, resolved the dilemma of finding a relatively stable index of mental ability in a developing child to permit prediction of later growth. The IQ also became the symbol for attack on the whole concept of mental testing, first by educators, and more recently by environmentally oriented psychologists.

In the process of developing and placing tests and standardizing the scale, Terman's unfamiliarity with statistics became critical. He realized that his past approaches had been crude and tried to understand statistical procedures in order to test the reliability and validity of his method and his conclusions. Statistics became his armor and defense against the violent attacks on his early tests. But he disliked the drudgery of computation, as he had disliked using brass instruments. He therefore enlisted the aid of Arthur Otis, and later of Truman Kelley and Quinn McNemar, in handling the data. For himself he reserved the meat behind the statistics and the invention of new ways of working with the results.

Another of Terman's graduate students, Irene Cuneo, worked intensively with the Binet at the kindergarten level. To her research contributions she added, at her death, a substantial bequest to Stanford, one-third of her estate, as an endowment to support fellowships in connection with "studies in the field of mental testing." By 1973, the university had received $217,000 for this purpose.

Terman labored with his material exhaustively. Dissatisfied with his first attempt at revision, he reworked each test and its placement. If a test did not fit at one age, he modified it and tried it out at another. It was a long, trying process.

Finally, in 1916, he was ready to publish the results. The book (Terman, 1916g) was dedicated "to the memory of Alfred Binet, patient researcher, creative thinker, unpretentious scholar, inspiring and fruitful devotee of inductive and dynamic psychology." It was high praise for Binet, and it was also a statement of Terman's own ego-ideal.

The Measurement of Intelligence (Terman, 1916g) was based on the testing of approximately one thousand subjects. It began with a discussion of mental testing as a method and its uses in working with children. The discussion touched on misconceptions about the nature of brightness and dullness, variability during adolescence, sex differences resulting from environmental pressures, and social class differences. Terman had found that high social status children were seven points above the norm in IQ, whereas low status children averaged seven points below. His own interpretation was that such differences are ". . . probably due, for the most part, to a superiority in original endowment" (Terman, 1916g, p. 72). The discussion also presented the rationale for initially choosing sixteen as the age at which mental development could be assumed to be complete.

General instructions for administering the test followed. Terman emphasized the importance of establishing rapport before beginning testing and using tact thereafter; adhering to the given formula in response to questions; entering the entire response in the test booklet for later evaluation; adhering to the sequence prescribed, except as essential to maintain rapport; and receiving special training to assure comparability in scoring.

Then each test was presented, from age five to adult. In each case Terman gave the rationale and related research behind the item, weaving in his own research and experience with practical questions. He also gave interpretations for retarded and accelerated children, as well as normal children. The scoring instructions were equally detailed. Terman even warned that the chronological age should be checked with school records; that chronological age should be reduced to months before it was divided into mental age; and that all computations should be checked twice.

The test's claim to validity lay within the standardization of the items themselves, their relationship to increments in chronological age, the internal consistency and cohesiveness of the test as a whole, and comparisons between bright and dull students (Terman, 1917d). Later extensive testing verified that the Binet is positively, though far from infallibly, related to teacher judgment and to school success.

Even after its publication, Terman continued to evaluate the test. The coefficient of reliability (on a scale from 0.00 to 1.00, on which coefficients above .75 are remarkable and those above .90 quite rare for such data) on repeated testing of kindergarten children turned out to be .94 for a half-year interval between tests, and .85 for a two-year interlude (Terman, 1918g). There was little practical effect in repeating the test after forty-eight hours. There were few sex differences, and no indication that radical change in age placement of items was needed. Fully one-third of errors in scoring were errors in arithmetic—more than half of them harmless, since they changed the IQ only five points as a maximum (Terman, 1918b).

Terman continued to study certain items in detail. A test which simply required naming words as they come to mind yielded a mental age within a year of the total test in fifty percent of the cases (Terman, 1919c). This test was little affected by reducing the testing time from three minutes to one, and showed little foreign language influence in bilingual children after they had attended school for three or four years. It met the usual criterion of regular increase on successive mental age levels, and it also showed that dull students slowed down in successive minutes markedly more than bright students.

He urged special care in scoring any verbal material, and worked exhaustively with the vocabulary test (Terman, 1918k). Vocabulary correlated to a high degree with total mental age, showed no sex difference, increased with age with remarkable regularity, and was closely related to other vocabulary samples.

So it went. In 1915 and 1916 he set his seminar to assembling and modifying promising items further. The group came up with twenty-three serial tests of five to fifty items each, including picture naming, oral reading, origin of familiar things, orientation in time, orientation in direction, mastery of space concepts, memory for sentences, memory for digits reversed, mental arithmetic, similarities, differences, opposites, absurd pictures, absurd and incongruous statements, picture interpretation, resourcefulness, finding reasons, building sentences, disarranged sentences, ball and field, and finding the shortest road. That survey of possible items for intelligence testing was planned for ultimate inclusion in the Binet, but impending events led to incorporation of many of the items in the emerging group tests.

In all his research Terman was well aware of his debt to graduate students and assistants. It was not really modesty that caused him to name his revision the *Stanford Revision of the Binet* rather than the Terman Binet. It was a mere matter of justice to the half-dozen or more students who had helped gather the data on which the 1916 revision was based. It was Terman's life-long experience that the senior author of any research based on collaboration with students gets far more credit than he deserves. So he always leaned over backward to avoid the appearance of taking credit for what others had done.

Many of his graduate students had helped with the development of the Binet. H. J. Childs had aided in the first revision attempt. Neva Galbreath and Grace Lyman and done master's theses on related aspects of the subject. Arthur Otis brought his knowledge of mathematics to bear on the statistical aspects of the Binet, and later developed a dissertation on the point-scale concept. Virgil Dickson related mental testing to school problems. Each in his own way helped the new field to expand at a rapid rate.

Terman's chief reliance, however, came in time to be Maud Merrill, later Maud Merrill James. She had assisted his fellow student at Clark, Kuhlman, at the Minnesota State Bureau of Research. She had also worked in institutions for the mentally retarded, as well as writing popular material on the feebleminded. She came to Stanford as a graduate student in 1919, later became a member of the faculty in psychology, and became Terman's chief collaborator in the two later revisions of the Binet done under his supervision.

The first Stanford revision of the Binet was an immediate success (Cronbach, 1949). For more than twenty years it was the leading test for individual mental measurement (Traxler, 1937). It was translated into approximately twenty languages within fifteen years, and was used in schools and other institutions at the rate of fifteen to twenty million cases annually. In retrospect, its success seems to have been largely a consequence of skillful work in selecting the individual items and in their placement with respect to age, though its success in testing complex mental activities and the ease with which the intelligence quotient could be understood added to its usefulness. It has stood the test of time; the early Binet tests gave IQ values nearly as reliably as tests constructed twenty or forty years later. Since the amount of test data involved in compiling the original test was very limited in comparison with that available in formulating revisions, Terman's subjective judgment in such matters must have been remarkably good. In addition, the practical results of testing corroborated his early point of view. Most inventions stem from a good idea started by one person and improved by others, but the Stanford Binet, as the first test of its kind, has stood out as a leader during all the nearly sixty years that have elapsed since it was first put together.

Terman expressed the hope that ten or fifteen such scales would soon be devised, each more perfect than his Stanford revision of the Binet, exploring every line of ability, whether intellectual, "volitional," motor, personal, pedagogical, social, or linguistic. He wondered why his fellow psychologists were so lacking in initiative as to accept his work with little criticism. But the advantage of a common standard, and the colossal job of revising a scale which did not permit piecemeal change, meant that the first revision of the Binet remained the dominant instrument in its field for twenty years. When the "something better" did come along, it was the 1937 revision from Terman's own hand.

During the period 1914-18, Terman was active in pointing out the implications of mental testing in a variety of fields. He suggested studies of the effect of physical problems on mental functioning and mental illness, as well as of the use of the Binet in vocational guidance (Terman, 1914l). He pointed out that the Binet tended to overestimate intelligence at younger levels, and that overageness or underageness in school grade tended to blur the accuracy of the teacher's judgment of a child's potential (Terman, 1915j). He criticized schools for their heavy rate of nonpromotion, often for normal and gifted students (Terman, 1915e). He advocated use of the Binet by teachers with special training (Terman, 1916n). He was critical of Pearson's claim that there is little difference between the feebleminded and the normal (Terman, 1916l), and praised Goddard's work in reporting the use of the Binet with criminals (Terman, 1916j). He pointed out the distinction between the psychological use of the term "feebleminded," using mental tests as a criterion, and the social use of the term based on ability to care for oneself (Terman, 1916d). He defended the use of the Binet in the courts (Terman, 1916c), and even served as expert witness for the defense of a clearly feebleminded murderer (Terman, 1918d).

Long after the first revision appeared, Terman's students continued working with the Binet and its applications. Samuel Kohs developed his *Block Design Test*, Florence Goodenough her *Draw-A-Man Test*. Helen Davidson, Phillip Rulon, and others worked on the analysis of the Binet itself. Curtis Merriman, Giles Ruch, Beatrice Lantz, and Barbara Burks were among those concerned with more theoretical problems related to the nature and origins of intelligence. There were studies of sex differences and of minority groups, including the dissertation of Kimball Young. Other studies related mental testing to school practice and explored the vocational implications of mental testing. Studies of delinquency continued with such students as Herbert Knollin, Norman Fenton, A. S. Raubenheimer, and Vernon Cady. Maud Merrill James and R. C. Challman added studies in mental retardation.

Other psychologists devised tests for special purposes and special groups following the Binet pattern: the *Merrill-Palmer Scale* for infants and young children, the *Herring-Binet* for brief testing, the *Hayes-Binet* for the blind. Such tests based their claims to validity chiefly on correlation with the *Stanford Revision of the Binet*. During the 1920s and 30s, the Binet came very close to constituting a meter-bar standard in the domain of mental measurement.

By the late 1920s, Terman set about the painstaking and systematic revision of the *Stanford Binet* ultimately published in 1937 (Terman, 1932e; 1942b; 1953b). First there was a preliminary tryout on about one thousand school pupils who had previously been given the 1916 *Stanford Binet*. Items were again studied, and the final selection was made chiefly on the basis of the steepness of the age curve for the item. That is, Terman used the demonstrated fact that the ability to perform any task follows an S-shaped curve, rising slowly at first, then accelerating, then slowing and leveling off. He used the age of rapid rise as the criterion for placing a particular test at a particular age level. Two provisional forms—L and M—were devised and administered to more than three thousand subjects by seven trained examiners who received two months of intensive instruction.

This time great care was taken to avoid bias in selecting the standardization population. The subjects came from seventeen communities in eleven different states. In each community, schools of average social status were selected on the basis of four objective estimates of socioeconomic status. In those schools, all children between six and fourteen who were within one month of a birthday were examined. This selection process resulted in a population of roughly one hundred boys and one hundred girls at each age level. For ages fifteen to eighteen, dropouts and part-time students were included as well as regular students. For ages two to five, siblings of the school children tested were asked to cooperate. All were native-born whites, and for that reason Terman later questioned the applicability of the Binet norms he derived to members of other ethnic groups.

All tests were then returned to Stanford, where Maud Merrill and two assistants rescored the more than six thousand blanks. The less satisfactory tests were eliminated, age placement of each item was reevaluated, and equivalence of the two forms item for item was assured.

The result was a still more reliable and valid test (Terman, 1937a; 1937b). It showed a high degree of internal consistency. In addition, the test differed from the 1916 revision in several significant ways. Two equivalent forms were available in case retesting was needed. There were more nonverbal tests, particularly at the lower age levels. There were six tests for each half-year at ages two to four; the gaps in age at eleven and thirteen were filled in; and the scale was extended to include three levels of superior adults. Binet's fifty-four items, which had been built to ninety in the 1916 Stanford revision, were expanded to one hundred twenty-nine in the 1937 Stanford Binet. A correction for chronological age was introduced at fourteen to sixteen, so the new research which showed an average adult mental age of fifteen rather than sixteen was incorporated, and so the rate of growth showed a gradual leveling off just before maturity, rather than an abrupt break. The sampling for the norms was more than three times as large as that for the 1916 revision, and the whole structuring process was a model of its kind. Full test kits were made commercially available rather than having the examiner assemble his own, and the form and content of the manual was improved. Terman pointed out, too, that the standard deviation on the 1937 revision was seventeen rather than twelve as it had been in the 1916 revision, which increased the spread between the mentally retarded and the gifted. At the extremes, the IQs from the two revisions were not fully comparable. For example, a mentally retarded child with an IQ of 70 on the 1916 Stanford Binet would have an IQ of 60 on the 1937 revision, and a gifted child with an IQ of 130 on the 1916 test would measure 140 on the 1937 version.

Terman again emphasized the importance of good examining procedure. He recognized the limits of the test, affected as it was by age, level of intelligence, language facility, physical handicap, and emotional factors. He claimed that for children of two or three the results were more often right than wrong, but subject to much error. For children of four to six the test was quite accurate and useful. Beyond the age of six it was quite stable: Marked changes of as much as twenty points in IQ occurred in only one case in a hundred. Terman reminded psychologists again that such a test must always be used in connection with other data, preferably in the context of a complete case study, if action was to be based upon the results.

Reviewers commended the precision of the new instrument (Traxler, 1937) and predicted for it a "long and productive career comparable to that of the first edition" (Freeman, 1938, p. 388).

The process of revision still goes on, updating items and matching new research findings. In 1960, after Terman's death, the third revision appeared. It combined the best tests of the two 1937 forms into a single measure, adopted tables to replace computation based on mental age, and extended the basis for IQ calculation to the age of eighteen to accommodate new research showing that mental age continues to increase beyond the chronological age of sixteen.

Terman's willingness to measure intelligence as a whole, rather than specific abilities, and to leave in abeyance the question of the ultimate nature of intelligence, represented a triumph of pragmatism. It led to the development of other kinds of tests, and to the use of mental testing in education, industry, and the military services (Postman, 1962).

CHAPTER V

School Hygiene and Health Reform

Professor Elwood Cubberley, who brought me to Stanford and was my 'chief' from 1910 to 1922, gave me every opportunity and encouragement. . . . I was given free range in the selection of courses anywhere in the field of educational psychology and mental development. In the meantime, through my courses in school hygiene and by writing The Hygiene of the School Child, *I was giving vent to another of my deep-seated interests. This had its origin with Lindley and Bergstrom at Indiana, gained new life from Burnham's lectures at Clark, and was given imperative need for expression by my personal health problem. There is an old saying that if you scratch a health reformer you will find an invalid (Terman, 1932f, pp. 323-324).*

TERMAN was initially employed as Cubberley's specialist on the physical aspects of child development in relation to schooling. Most of his teaching and his service to schools and governmental agencies were concentrated on that field. He taught courses, participated in surveys, conducted research, and wrote articles and books. He gained national and international recognition for his work in school health.

The quality of his relationship to his growing group of graduate students was clearly demonstrated in those years. J. Harold Williams, subsequently (1914-15) recipient of the newly created Buckel Fellowship for the study of the mentally retarded and Terman's first graduate assistant, found Terman clearly interested in individual students. Terman at once noticed that Williams illustrated his notes and reports with graphs and charts; he suggested that Williams prepare a book on using graphs, and aided in placing it for publication (Williams, 1924). Williams went on to join the staff of the University of California at Los Angeles, and still later served as Provost for the University of California's Santa Barbara campus.

The story of Samuel Kohs is an even better illustration of Terman's concern for his students. Kohs came to Stanford after working with Goddard at Vineland and with Hall at Clark, as well as working in the House of Corrections in Chicago. He wanted to develop a performance test of intelligence, a project about which Terman was initially skeptical, though tolerant of a student's whim. That project was Kohs's Block Design Test, subsequently regarded as an important contribution to the mental testing field in diagnosing brain damage and in assessing the intellectual ability of the blind. When Kohs arrived at Stanford with his wife and infant son to look for a home, he landed instead in a hospital with typhoid fever. During his entire hospitalization, the Termans took the Kohs family into their own home. Then it was Anna who found a place for the family to go for the long convalescence.

Once Kohs was able to work again, he pursued his work and defended his position to the point that it made sense to Terman; he thereafter received encouragement and rescue whenever he needed it. Terman did not demand that his students become disciples with evangelical drive in his own pattern, but freed his students to follow their own bent. Much later, when Kohs found anti-Semitic sentiment interfering with his college teaching, Terman urged him to accept the directorship of the Jewish Welfare Federation in Oakland. Terman's concern for his students was unlimited: they were his friends.

Others of his students, too, later became prominent. Virgil Dickson became an administrator who wrote influential books. Marvin L. Darsie studied the intelligence of American-born Japanese children and became the first Dean of the School of Education at the University of California at Los Angeles. Appendix C lists students who wrote theses or dissertations under Terman's guidance.

The relatively light teaching load left more than half of Terman's long days for research and writing. His interests lay in the field of educational psychology, broadly defined to include instinctive tendencies and the controversies about them, individual differences and their causes, psychometric methods, mental development, and the psychology of learning (Terman, 1931e). To these interests he added education as a whole, and particularly health work in the schools. It was a wide area for his curiosity to roam.

In the context of these concerns, Terman argued repeatedly for vocational education (Terman, 1911d; 1911e), not only because of its practical value, but also because in his opinion it cultivated sustained attention and possibly even "quickened the intelligence." He strongly advocated anything that would help to bridge the chasm between school and life, for he saw education as an apprenticeship for a busy, practical adulthood. He was an early enthusiast for the kind of education contemporary students call "relevant."

Yet he was aware of his obligation in the field of child health, and his early publications reflect that focus. He reviewed the literature and did original research on the sleep of children (Terman, 1913e; 1913f; 1914c; 1914m), placing the results of a study conducted in California, Oregon, and Arizona against the backdrop of existing knowledge. He also compared this study with detailed research on the sleep of the feebleminded done at Vineland Training School. He found that the quantity of sleep a child had was far less important than the quality of that sleep, and he recommended that each child have his own separate bed in a room kept near sixty degrees, to which he should retire at a fixed time.

He urged research on the effects of sedentary study on sleep, eyestrain, and general health. He believed that the five-hour school day was too long for young children, especially when followed by homework or private lessons in music or art (Terman, 1912b). He claimed that more intensive work for shorter periods would result in equal academic gains, according to the data on half-day sessions, and that such shorter sessions might well improve child health. In fact, he had found evidence that compulsory education for long hours may slow growth, promote malnutrition, create poor posture, lead to emotional stress, and result in loss of weight, headache, insomnia, and nervous symptoms (Terman, 1914c).

He led an influential crusade for attention to children's dental health (Terman, 1912f; 1914m; 1915f). Diseased teeth, he claimed, were often responsible for indigestion, anemia, general debility, retarded growth, and nervous disorders, because of the decreased power of mastication as well as the toxic effect. He advocated attention to mastication and to cleaning of the teeth as well as to early childhood nutrition. Most importantly, Terman suggested dental clinics similar to those in England and Germany, where early diagnosis and treatment would be available to all free of charge (Terman, 1913g; 1919b). He argued that the child's right to good health supersedes the parent's right to control the child (Terman, 1912f). According to his friend Bronson Price, Terman's crusade stimulated the United States Children's Bureau to publish a monograph on the subject; this publication laid the groundwork for trying out such school dental clinics some years later in Australia, with phenomenal results (Fulton, 1951).

Other problems received less comprehensive attention. Earache was an important cause of child problems (Terman, 1915b). Eugenics had much to offer in correcting social problems relating to feeblemindedness (Terman, 1916i). George Crile's *Man, an Adaptive Mechanism* provided important evidence that mental and physical disorders often come from a disregard for fundamental biological processes (Terman, 1916k). In fact, Terman explored the whole host of ailments from which children suffer, the anatomical and physiological background of such problems, and particularly their environmental and school causes.

Terman's earlier concern with the health of the teacher resulted in a monograph and a book (Terman, 1913i; 1913j). It was his first book, and he was justly proud of it. A school medical director had found that eighty-four percent of the teachers in a Massachusetts city suffered poor health after five to ten years of teaching; they developed such ailments as tuberculosis, asthma, deafness, defective vision, malnutrition, anemia, heart disease, or neurasthenia. Terman pointed out the effect of such teachers on children. His book was favorably reviewed, and the theme recurred in his works in later years. In 1928, Terman suggested that teachers become involved in something analogous to his early Indiana Teachers Reading Circle to "humanize" them—he suggested that they read and discuss a number of professional books each month and pass a test on three books at the end of the year, that they also read general books such as biography for perspective, and that they participate widely in community affairs (Terman, 1928c). As late as 1931 he wrote a message to teachers in Philadelphia in which he advised openness and freedom in teaching, saying that the worst crime a teacher can commit is to stifle curiosity and instill a habit of taking things on faith, fencing off certain fields as sacred against the intrusion of independent thinking.

Terman's concern included all types of health work in the schools. He traced the history of school health through legislation in California, pointing out the difficulties and dangers in passing laws that anticipate public opinion (Terman, 1911b). He recommended the development of preventive school hygiene, including routine examinations for physical defects; supervision of physical training; study of the heating, lighting, ventilation of classrooms; and child psychology as a whole. He envisioned what has become specialized training in school public health work, for he found the average physician unable to handle such a task (Terman, 1912d). He criticized educators for placing too much emphasis on buildings and too little on children (Terman, 1913d), and praised Gesell for countering that trend (Terman, 1912c). He suggested open-air rooms, improved nutrition, and systematic instruction in oral hygiene (Terman, 1913g). He devised a scheme for grading the adequacy of school buildings, studied the problems of rural children and of teacher candidates, and deplored the gap between medical knowledge and what he saw in schools and homes (Terman, 1915c).

Like all reformers, Terman found no adequate textbook in his field (Terman, 1913a; 1913d; 1913g; 1914k; 1915c; 1916a; 1916c). He liked writing and wrote well, and though he did not enjoy writing texts, he published two of his own. *Health Work in the Schools* (Terman, 1914d) was written in collaboration with E. B. Hoag, a physician. Collaboration seldom goes smoothly, and ultimately Terman did more than his share of the job. The book presented the school's responsibility for the prevention of physical defects, as distinguished from the curative task of the medical profession. Sixty percent of school children, Terman claimed, had physical defects which were remediable but uncorrected, including both communicable diseases and faulty physical conditions. He advocated health grading by teachers, school clinics, open-air schools, careful school housekeeping, alertness for communicable disease, teaching children about health, safeguarding the teacher's health, and knowing about school health organizations. The book was met with reviews ranging from "splendid" to "no better book for superintendents, principals and teachers," and "clear, balanced, concise and attractive."

Terman's second book, *The Hygiene of the School Child* (Terman, 1914e), was a pioneer textbook for teacher candidates in normal schools and for teachers' reading circles; in its revised form (Terman, 1929b), it was recommended for parents as well. Terman argued that man is much like the animals in his physical needs and his heredity, and that a biological perspective is essential to the understanding of how man can be educated. Thinking is important only insofar as it leads to adaptation on the part of the learner; the school must therefore consider the body in which the mind resides. Important factors influencing growth include physiological maturity (not chronological age), posture, malnutrition, tuberculosis, ventilation, dental hygiene, disorders of the nose and throat, problems of the ear and hearing, visual disorders, and preventive mental hygiene. The book was liberally sprinkled with statistics and charts, as well as with practical suggestions for teachers. It urged vigorous reform in school practice. Reviewers agreed that Terman succeeded in putting the case exceptionally well, though they questioned whether teachers were really capable of making routine physical tests.

The book and its later editions was a standard text in teacher education for nearly twenty years. It shifted the focus of concern with school hygiene from Europe to America and kindled interest in problems of school health. When nearly one-third of the men drafted in World War I were later found physically unfit for war service, national health became an issue, and research was stimulated. The combined sales for *Health Work in the Schools* and *The Hygiene of the School Child*, including a revision of the latter done with J. C. Almack, totaled about 200,000 copies.

Such active promotion of more attention to health conditions in the schools inevitably drew fire from established groups, though Terman limited his advocacy to professional circles. For years he received annual protests from the Church of Jesus Christ, Scientist requesting that certain passages be eliminated. Medical fringe groups such as the League of Medical Freedom objected to the whole idea of preventive health work in the schools. The medical profession, as a whole, at first opposed the appointment of special school physicians, then let the issue die. Teachers and superintendents sometimes disagreed with Terman's views, but because of his intimate personal knowledge of teaching, he could adapt to their point of view and explain his own. The whole crusade for school health work presented Terman, the activist, at his vigorous best.

Terman even tried popular writing during these years, largely motivated by a need to generate supplementary income. His articles had a rather high rate of acceptance and publishers paid fairly generously for those they liked. His articles were published in *Popular Science Monthly* (Terman, 1911d; 1912d; 1914c), *Harper's Weekly* (Terman, 1909b; 1912a; 1912b), *The Youth's Companion* (Terman, 1914b; 1915b), *The New England Magazine* (Terman, 1909c; 1911c), *Forum* (Terman, 1914g; 1914m), and a number of others (Terman, 1908c; 1911e; 1911f; 1913a; 1913g; 1914g; 1914n; 1915f). His files also contain brief unpublished articles on such topics as worry and the efficient use of time (Terman unpublished, 1929b; 1929c), designed for monthly house organs and syndicated production. After 1916, when royalties from the Stanford Binet and his texts became significant, he discontinued popular writing.

Terman was drawn into the public service activities of the university as well. In his role as health specialist, he participated with Cubberley in school surveys in Portland, Salt Lake City,

Denver, and elsewhere. Often he suggested that school medical supervision be taken over as a function of the Board of Education rather than the Board of Health, and that the schools assume a more active part in preventive health work (Terman, 1923e). He deplored the use of basement rooms for instruction (Terman, 1915a). Wherever he found children with handicaps, he advocated special educational programs for them (Terman, 1914f). He was the reformer in his field work, as in his publications.

When Hiram Johnson became governor of California in 1911, the state prisons and other institutions were under attack for their therapeutic programs as well as for their cost. There was no diagnostic service for inmates other than a routine medical examination. The Governor consulted Terman, who welcomed the opportunity to apply both his knowledge of institutional health and his emerging new mental tests. His survey of the Whittier State School for Boys became the prototype for a number of studies of delinquency, including San Quentin Prison and the Preston School of Industry (Terman, 1914q; 1915g; 1918f). One finding was especially significant in demolishing the myth that delinquency was for all practical purposes synonymous with feeblemindedness: Terman found that only about one-fourth of the delinquent boys were mentally defective. This result underlined the need for institutional reform. Then Terman went on from prisons and training schools to institutions for the feebleminded and orphanages (Terman, 1912g; 1918a; 1918e). Though his work in public custodial institutions spanned only a few years, his concern remained. As late as 1928, he was named a member of a commission for the study of problem children by the California Executive Department.

His publications also reflected his active concern with individual differences. He had been inspired by James McKeen Cattell's awareness of the importance of studying differences, and as a child he had been keenly aware of his differences from others.

> . . . as far back as I can remember I seem to have had a little more interest than the average child in the personalities of others and to have been impressed by those who differed in some respect from the common run. . . . I am inclined to think that the associations I had with such schoolmates were among the most valuable of my childhood experiences (Terman, 1932f, pp. 300-301).

He saw ability and personality as infinitely variable and contradictory (Terman, 1911c; 1911f), and for a time much of his own and his students' research fell into this field (see Appendix C). True, Terman's was a ground-breaking approach, lacking the later refinements of intercorrelation and factor analysis (Anastasi, 1970), yet it sampled the rich ore awaiting later investigators of human diversity. He actively encouraged and endorsed the work of others, including Grace Fernald's kinesthetic method with nonreaders (Terman, 1943b). He was a critical reader of the work of others in the field well into his retirement (Terman, 1947e).

He was concerned with the mentally retarded, and administered the Buckel Fellowship (Terman, 1915a) which was dedicated to the study of backward and feebleminded children. He pointed out that not all children who are slow in school are mentally retarded; some had physical handicaps or failed to respond to the kind of instruction usually offered in schools. He insisted that mentally retarded children require small, ungraded special classes in which the academic curriculum could be modified and work individualized. He was convinced that as long as mentally retarded children remained in classes for normal children, no learning could occur. Even after his retirement, his continuing concern made Terman lend his name to the exposure of a fellow psychologist in the field whose work bordered on charlatanism (Terman, 1949a). In the study of the education of the mentally retarded, Terman foreshadowed much of the thinking of the next fifty years.

He was equally concerned with the mental health of children. He knew that stuttering was related to mental health and advised special speech correction teachers in public schools (Terman, 1912a). He compared suicide rates in other countries with that in the United States (Terman, 1914a) and asked empathy for children in periods of crisis, since about one-third of the child suicides were traceable to school-related problems (Terman, 1913k). He strongly endorsed Dorothy Canfield Fisher's *Self Reliance* as a model for developing independence and self-direction from infancy, which would lead to individual happiness and social progress (Terman, 1916a).

Terman also published in the field of juvenile delinquency. He urged research and gave liberal support to the new *Journal of Delinquency* through editorials and reviews. During the 1920s he found time to assess the use of personality tests in the identification of potential delinquents (Terman, 1925f) and to advocate specialized programs for such individuals (Terman 1928f). He eulogized the work of Fred Nelles, the forward-looking superintendent of the Whittier State School for Boys (Terman, 1927a), and wrote to the then Governor Young urging selection of a successor to Nelles who could work with human case problems rather than simply administer an institution. He said that such a superintendency was at least as important as a college presidency. When Normal Fenton, a former student of his, was appointed, Terman publicly applauded (Terman, 1928a). He even analyzed the contribution of psychology to the practice of law in the fields of evidence, testimony, deception tests, expert testimony, jury reaction, and legislation (Terman, 1931f; 1947e).

In the field of working with exceptional individuals, Terman achieved enough visibility to be approached in 1921 to head a proposed new research department at the Clark School for the Deaf. The department was to be dedicated to broad investigations of personality and ability differences among the deaf, and to a study of the "deaf style." But Terman's heart was in his work at Stanford, so he discouraged the approach.

Even in those early years, Terman's writing was remarkably lucid and pleasant. He had an ear for words; he studied the styles of those he admired, such as Binet. He abhorred over-generalization, failure to use words with great precision, dramatizing facts, and the scattered use of case material without unifying principles. The full rigor of his style was developing rapidly.

Terman's contribution to the study of school health was significant. He added to knowledge in a neglected field and forcefully promoted a movement that bore fruit for many years after he turned to other things. To the pre-World War I psychologist, Terman was still an educator concerned with the problems of psychology; he was just beyond the periphery of what was then the American movement in psychology. He was not even a member of the American Psychological Association until 1917. Between 1910 and 1916, Terman moved away from education toward psychology as a focus, from what Boring called a psychotropic educationalist on the model of G. Stanley Hall to a sociotropic psychologist (E. G. Boring, 1945). By the time World War I broke out, Terman's work on the Stanford revision of the Binet had firmly established him as a psychologist.

CHAPTER VI

Group Tests and
The Testing Movement

*... Then came the War, with service on the committee
that devised the army mental tests: on Yerkes' staff, first
as Director of Research on the army tests and later as collaborator with Yerkes, Boring and others on the historical
account of psychological work in the army: and as a
member of Scott's Committee on Classification of Personnel. It would take us too far afield to enter into the new
world of experiences which the war work opened up to
me. Their most important aspect, so far as my personal
development is concerned, was in the opportunity they
gave me to become acquainted with nearly all the leading
psychologists of America. ...*

*One result of the war experiences was to confirm and
strengthen my earlier beliefs regarding the importance of
mental tests as an integral part of scientific psychology.
Whereas I had thought that only a handful of psychologists were of this opinion, I now learned that many were.
I could return to my work with more confidence than ever
that, in the long run, contributions to the field of mental
tests would receive the recognition they deserved
(Terman, 1932f, pp. 325-326).*

TERMAN'S meteoric rise to eminence with the Stanford Binet,
amplified by his war work in the development of group tests, meant
more than fame. His life became infinitely more complex. He worked
with his graduate students and maintained a heavy writing and editorial schedule. He launched his monumental longitudinal study of
the gifted. He was asked to rebuild the Department of Psychology
at Stanford as its chairman. At almost the same time he was elected
president of the American Psychological Association, with all the

front-man responsibilities such a position entailed. And in the midst of it all, Fred became seriously ill. But one thing at a time.

Terman accepted invitations to teach summer sessions in New York during the summers of 1916 and 1917, which were memorable for their record heat. He continued his exploration of mental testing in the schools and even in civil service examinations (Terman, 1917e). He supervised the work of a number of graduate students on testing, and the future looked bright.

Then, on April 6, 1917, the United States entered World War I. The army expanded at an explosive rate, and psychologists were called upon to provide group tests to select candidates for officer training, to reject the unfit, and to classify the remainder so that balanced companies could be created.

Robert Yerkes, then president of the American Psychological Association and known for a 1915 test of intelligence using the point-scale later adopted by Wechsler, was made chairman of the committee. The membership of the group read like a *Who's Who* of American psychologists in the first quarter of the twentieth century. Many had originally been hard-bitten experimentalists, and some were former associates of Terman. The original committee consisted of Yerkes, Boring, Bingham, Otis, and Terman. Other luminaries who later worked with army testing from time to time included Thorndike, Whipple, Woodworth, Truman Kelly, Goddard, Scott, and Dodge, along with less well known psychologists such as Yoakum, Mabel Fernald, Bridges, and Wells.

The presence of Arthur Otis in such a group deserves comment. Otis was a unique individual, extremely bright and highly innovative, but with very little social understanding. As a graduate student at Stanford assisting Terman with statistical problems, he had done an exploratory study of adaptation of the Stanford Binet approach to a group technique, following the precedent established by earlier standardized group tests in arithmetic, handwriting, and spelling. His experience was invaluable. Otis went on to get his doctorate with Terman in 1920, and later pursued a successful career as consultant on tests for the World Book Company and its successors. When he died, he left a significant part of his substantial estate to Stanford University.

The committee met first at Vineland during the summer of 1917 for a total of two weeks; some weeks intervened between the first and second sessions. Terman shared a room with Bingham and got to know him well. From those meetings came the *Army Alpha Test* for literates and the *Army Beta Test* for illiterates and non-English-speaking men. Both were group tests, simpler than the existing individual tests, capable of being applied to large numbers of men simultaneously, and adapted for routine scoring. These tests introduced the multiple choice item, and objective scoring came of age. Tests included following directions, simple reasoning, arithmetic, and general information. The administration procedures were carefully standardized; answers were recorded by marks rather than by writing words; scoring was done by stencils; and five equivalent forms made coaching relatively unproductive in influencing the score. A preliminary trial on four thousand men during 1917 demonstrated the usefulness of the tests.

From September 1917 to January 1919, more than 1,750,000 men were tested with the *Army Alpha* alone. In placing men for greatest military usefulness and reducing time for organizing training units, the *Army Alpha* clearly demonstrated its value (Terman, 1918h; 1918j; 1921g). Inductees were grouped in eight classifications, based largely on the test scores. The members of the lowest classification—probably below a mental age of ten—were designated unfit for service and dismissed. The second and third lowest groups, approximately fifteen percent of those accepted, were assigned to simple work under careful supervision. The middle groups were assigned to homogeneous or heterogeneous batallions, depending upon the kind of work required. At the other end of the distribution, the top two groups, or about ten percent, were recommended for officer training. And men in the third group from the top, about fifteen percent, were trained as noncommissioned officers, responsible for routine work in their companies. The rationale of the psychologists was that a high score meant not only ability to learn specialized skills, but resourcefulness and adaptability as well. Again Terman urged that the tests be used as only one element in classification, that fuller analysis should be made in each case. The test was validated through comparing its results with the judgment of commanding officers, through studying the performance of men selected for officer training, and through analyzing the performance of those who rated low on the measure. The Army testing was a major achievement in practical psychology, and for years the data was a prime source for information on occupational, ethnic, racial, and geographic groups.

In 1917, Terman joined the newly created general psychological staff at the Surgeon General's office in Washington. The staff was to conduct inquiries concerning the value of psychological examination, improve methods of work, and take charge of writing the 200,000-word historical account of the development of psychological examination methods in the Army (Terman, 1921g). Terman was a civilian in 1917 and early 1918; he went into uniform as a major in October 1918, just before the armistice. When his students of 1917-18 sought his counsel about war service, he almost invariably advised them to remain in graduate school working toward degrees, rather than diverting to the military services. When he became a major they were amused by the incongruity between his rank and the gentle, unassuming man they knew. Late in the summer of 1918, Anna and Helen moved to Washington with Terman where he found time to take Helen to see all the Charlie Chaplin and Fatty Arbuckle movies and to hear Harry Lauder sing. Fred remained at Stanford as a student.

Yerkes, in whose home Terman and E. G. Boring stayed for long periods during these days, became a lifelong friend. Yerkes had urged Boring to join the testing division in the Army, and had called him to Washington to work on the same mammoth report after the armistice in 1918. Though Boring had heard of Terman a year or two earlier, he came to know him only as they worked together. Terman, who had become a member of the American Psychological Association in 1917, quickly catapulted into prominence. As early as 1918, he suggested Boring as secretary of the Association and supported him so effectively that Boring was elected to a term of office from 1919 to 1922—an office which did much to advance Boring's career. The relationship led to a lasting friendship, never social because neither man valued purely social events, but consisting of endless talk of professional matters, at work and during the evenings and weekends.

In 1921, Boring taught at Stanford during a summer session, and had a wonderful time giving graduate students there much of the kind of material he published eight years later in his *History of Experimental Psychology*. Later still, he visited Stanford during World War II. After Terman's death, Boring wrote a biography of Terman for the National Academy of Sciences (E. G. Boring, 1959). In addition, he warmly supported the writing of the present biography, supplying anecdotes, checking on characterization and structure, and providing leads in a characteristically voluminous correspondence shortly before his death.

After World War I, a civilian revision of the Army tests was extensively applied, and comparable tests were developed by various psychologists. The *Army General Classification Test* which replaced the *Army Alpha* in World War II made no basic break with the earlier test, though it reflected increased sophistication and was a far more refined instrument. Terman characteristically welcomed the refinements but rejected the factorial approach to intelligence implicit in the new measure. His interest in federally sponsored testing continued until his death. In the 1950s, he urged the Surgeon General to revise the manual of mental examinations for aliens, praising the use of nonverbal tests as equally fair or unfair to all groups, but cautioning against confusing ignorance with stupidity. He again suggested a cooperative approach through appointing a revising committee to improve the selection of the tests to be used.

Most of all, the Army testing in World War I convinced the public that to some degree, mass testing could effectively predict success. Schools and industry were quick to demand similar measures for their own use. The need was widely recognized, and the way was paved for an expansion of testing into many different endeavors. And Terman, because of his role in planning intelligence tests for the Army, rapidly gained acceptance and attention as a psychologist.

Terman's work on group mental testing for the Army was seized upon as a model not only because of its intrinsic merit, but also because it met a pressing social need. Schools were burgeoning under new compulsory education laws. Teachers were eager to get away from lockstep methods and adapt to individual differences. Because of this demand, Terman spent most of his time for two years after World War I developing tests for schools.

At the same time, immediately after World War I, the World Book Company sought to arrange the publication of intelligence and other tests for schools. At first, such a development was opposed by the prestigious American Educational Research Association, but the opposition was withdrawn a year later.

The *National Intelligence Tests*, designed chiefly for elementary schools, were published in 1920 (Terman, 1920a). They and the *Otis Test of Mental Ability* which appeared in 1918 were the direct outcome of Army experience, though Terman was already looking toward improvement of the instrument. Terman urged the National Research Council, which shared the profits from the National Intelligence Tests, to use the funds to construct additional forms and to look toward revision within ten years. He published a list of tests which might correlate with other intelligence measures (Terman, 1918i). He extended the norms for the *National Intelligence Tests* and proposed applications to work in schools (Terman, 1921a). These early tests were largely group efforts, though Terman's leadership emerged clearly as time went on.

In 1920, the *Terman Group Test of Mental Ability* appeared (Terman, 1920d). It extended and refined tests similar to those used in the Army testing, for students in high school. Widely used over an extended period, this test was later revised and extensively analyzed by Quinn McNemar and Terman (Terman, 1941e) for still more years of service.

In 1921, Terman started developing an all-around achievement test covering all school subjects in grades three through eight. Terman planned the grand strategy; he was greatly aided in its implementation by Truman Kelley and G. M. Ruch. The *Stanford Achievement Test* appeared in 1923 (Terman, 1923f). The original battery consisted of four intercorrelated forms standardized on 345,735 children from 363 school systems in thirty-eight states—a tremendous undertaking. Yet no detail was too small for Terman's attention. A class record sheet was included in each package though Terman maintained that a class list could never replace the essential individual analysis of each test to identify the relative strengths and weaknesses of the individual. Scoring was completely objective; even arithmetic problems had to be carried out accurately to two decimal places, so that there could be only one correct answer. Terman opposed separate publication of the subtests in particular subjects, because he feared that such tests would give the impression of too great reliability for the shortened measures. However, he was overruled by his collaborators and the publisher. He defended the designation *Stanford Achievement Test* because of his characteristic insistence on recognition of all who worked with him. The test was later revised in 1929, 1940, and 1964, and a revision was in progress in 1975 to keep the test current with developments in education (Terman, 1929c). The *Stanford Achievement Test* led all other achievement measures in reliability and became the most widely used test battery in the United States for many years.

Giles M. Ruch, who was a full coauthor of the original *Stanford Achievement Test* with Truman Kelly and Terman, was a graduate student of Terman's while he was aiding in the development of the test. He went on to college teaching in educational psychology at the University of California at Berkeley after completing his doctorate in 1922, and was extensively involved in at least one revision of the test before his death.

During these same years, Terman enjoyed talking with Albert Raubenheimer, a graduate student whose South African Boer background made him distinctive. Raubenheimer went to the University of Southern California, where he became Vice President for Academic Affairs for twelve years prior to his retirement.

Much later, Terman published an additional mental test designed to judge the ability to deal with abstract ideas at a high level, the *Concept Mastery Test* (Terman, 1956a). This was the natural fruition of his early work with mental tests, applied to his extended work with gifted students. The *Concept Mastery Test* measured power rather than speed, drawing on concepts from a wide range of subjects, including mathematics, physical and biological sciences, history, and literature. Norms were provided for college seniors, graduate students, and selected adult groups. The test correlated positively with childhood Stanford Binet scores and with level of education attained. The measure has proved to be a useful research and predictive device for advanced students and for the gifted.

Other psychologists joined the growing test movement, contributing specialized measures for use in clinical, educational, and industrial settings. In more recent years, special aptitude tests have proliferated. The use of multiple scoring keys for a single personality test was developed by Bernreuter under Terman's supervision; the practice has been widely adapted in other personality measures. Such special ability and personality tests were usually used as supplemental devices to general mental tests, initially derived from the work of Binet and of Terman.

While developing tests of intelligence and achievement, Terman was busily explaining how to use the new instruments. His first major publication after World War I, continuous with his earlier work on individual differences, was *The Intelligence of School Children* (Terman, 1919a). Its subtitle is significant: *How Children Differ in Ability, the Use of Mental Tests in School Grading, and the Proper Education of Exceptional Children.* Terman demonstrated that large individual differences in mental ability exist, and applied that concept to such widely varied school problems as grade classification, vocational guidance, promotion, teacher grading, courses of study, skipping and repeating grades, delinquency, and special classes. He argued that, since a spread of six years or more in mental age is found in each grade above the first, and since a deviation in mental age of two years below the grade norm makes learning the standard grade content impossible, it is no wonder that many children drop out of school at the earliest opportunity. While they are in school, their failures often lead to severe frustration, lack of encouragement at home, and poor attitudes toward the teacher. Though the cultural status of the home does affect school work, the chief problem lies in such children themselves, as studies of siblings who are superior and inferior students from the same home show. Whatever the cause, the effect of poor environment either at school or at home is a downward slump in achievement which affects superior students along with their less able classmates.

Though group tests are valuable, Terman argued that every child should be given an individual mental test upon first entering school, administered by a teacher with specialized training and interpreted with help from a competent psychologist. Such a test, though it is less exact than measures used in the physical sciences and should be used only in the context of fuller knowledge about the child, greatly increases the teacher's ability to plan suitable work for the individual. Without tests, teachers too often overate children who are vivacious, responsive, self-confident, good-looking, and conscientious; conversely, they tend to underrate those who are placid, plain, diffident, timid, and annoying in behavior. Yet the result of an intelligence test is remarkably stable.

> The fact is that, apart from minor fluctuations due to temporary factors . . . the feebleminded remain feebleminded, the dull remain dull, the average remain average, and the superior remain superior. There is nothing in one's equipment, with the exception of character, which rivals the IQ in importance (Terman, 1919a, p. 10).

Tests are also a valuable aid in vocational guidance, Terman claimed, for the individual's native ability should be matched approximately to the median of a vocation if he is to succeed. Such assistance is particularly needed by girls because of their limited vocational opportunities, a situation that still exists fifty years later. Today Terman might well add socioeconomic disadvantage and ethnic difference to sex in his advocacy of intensive vocational guidance.

Terman emphasized the importance of preprimary instruction for children too immature for school (Terman, 1920e). He suggested that such children either should be sent home or assigned to special classes to help prepare them for school work. Similarly, the gifted should be identified early and suitable instruction provided for them. When children reach the third grade, group tests should be administered, and all who deviate markedly from the norm should be given individual tests. At this point, ratings should be secured on character traits, educational tests should determine achievement level, and further teaching should be adapted to the individual child.

71

Terman's second book on the implications of testing for schools, *Intelligence Tests and School Reorganization*, appeared in 1922 (Terman, 1922c; 1922f), after being foreshadowed by several general articles (Terman, 1921c; 1921e). It was concerned with classification according to mental ability, methods of individualizing instruction in regular and special classes, and the conservation of talent in the gifted. In addition to reinforcing the arguments he had used previously for testing, Terman warned against over-enthusiasm and false hope for the mental testing movement and urged a wholesome respect for the probable error in any test used. After all, he said, the intelligence test can only be a point of departure for further study, and "... the child is more than intelligence, and education is more than the cultivation of intellectual faculties" (Terman, 1922c, p. 3).

Terman pointed out that the purpose of mental testing in schools is to make a difference in the educational treatment of children, not simply to gratify curiosity. In fact, unless the results of tests were so used, it would be better not to give them at all. Grade assignment should reflect test results along with other factors. Teachers are seldom aware of the full significance of mental age: in a given class, older children who are less able tend to be overrated, and younger children who are often highly capable tend to be underrated.

The solution to instructional problems in school, said Terman, lies in individualization of instruction and homogeneous grouping. Learning is essentially an individual matter, whether instruction occurs alone or in a group. Social values will not be lost through individualization if suitable playground experience and frequent group discussions on topics of general interest are provided. As for homogeneous grouping, it is practical if it is geared to systematic teaching and long-term planning, both of which require skill and resourcefulness in the teacher but lead to greater academic gains. Terman suggested that five homogeneous groups in mental ability be used as an aid in adapting instruction—two and one-half percent at each extreme, fifteen percent in a group at either end of the distribution next to the extreme, and a middle sixty-five percent in the average classroom.

More general articles (Terman, 1922d; 1924f) and reports of conference participation (Terman, 1932c) followed in later years. One of the most thoughtful was an editorial which was never published (Terman unpublished, 1928). Terman believed that educational historians would characterize the era of the 1920s as the one which saw the birth of the testing movement—a thrust which left its mark on school organization, instructional method, curriculum, and even educational ideals. He predicted that the next two or three decades would turn chiefly to an assessment of educational ideals in the light of what has been learned from the testing movement. Tests show, he claimed, that the emphasis in schools may well have been misplaced. There has been too much talk of achievement as a result of teacher quality, school expenditure, days of school attended, class size, correction of physical disability, and even method of instruction. All those factors count for something, but they are less important individually than the mental level of the child. It follows, therefore, that we might well reconsider the aims of the school. Attention should be redirected more toward ethical-social ends, attitudes, and interests, and the analysis of general and special abilities for educational adaptation and vocational guidance. Terman's argument is diametrically opposed to the trend of the 1970's, when schools are asked to correct for so many social ills with the help of federal dollars.

Though Terman stressed education in elementary schools, he was also concerned with secondary schools, as his work in vocational guidance and his development of the *Terman Group Test of Mental Ability* demonstrated. He heartily approved a proposed nationwide survey of intelligence in high schools as a way of leading toward important reforms in secondary education. He read and responded to current publications on secondary school reform (Terman, 1922h). He even discussed the possibility of establishing a new teachers' journal in psychology with a potential publisher.

Terman felt also that intelligence tests had an important place in colleges and universities. He advocated their use in student admissions and in research (Terman, 1921d). He presented a detailed case study of a Stanford student who managed to be admitted with a mental age of twelve or thirteen, and who failed spectacularly during his first term (Terman, 1922a). In publishing this case, he opened himself to a charge of intellectual snobbishness in characterizing the man as a satisfactory clerk but never a manager, a mediocre citizen who would never be elected to an important office, and a loyal party adherent and devout repeater of catchwords. At any rate, Terman found the conventional course-credit system in colleges indefensible, and advocated individual tailoring of college instruction (Terman, 1939f).

Terman was available to educators and laymen for advice as well. He advised a superintendent of schools not to report numerical intelligence quotients to teachers, saying that it was less easy to misinterpret a category such as "very superior" or "somewhat below average" than a specific number. He counseled another that the apparent drop in average mental test scores in his eighth grade might well result from an increasing tendency on the part of teachers to promote on chronological age rather than from a decrease in ability. To a Boy Scout official who asked about using intelligence tests in that movement, he suggested that character tests might be more meaningful than mental tests, though such tests were still too much in the experimental stage to justify their practical use.

Most of all, Terman was critically responsive to requests for help from others working in the mental test field itself. He answered Ruml's criticism of mental test methods by pointing out that a wholly theoretical attack on a problem is often sterile, while a more concentrated focus on an immediate, practical problem often leads to a major theoretical advance (Terman, 1921b). The important thing is not to lose sight of the nature of the historical development in a science, and to discriminate between what science is ready to explain and what it is not. He praised Goodenough's work with the *Draw-A-Man* test as being far better than more conventional tests for first and second grades. He pointed out that Thurstone's factor analysis approach to mental testing led to instruments which did not predict scholastic success any better than the *Terman-McNemar Test of Mental Ability*. He warned Guilford against correlating ratios such as the IQ, since using derived scores magnifies errors. He advised Cyril Burt that American tests would need considerable revision to make them suitable for English children, since many items were heavily dependent on the social environment. He explained to the Office of Education that decreasing selectivity in high school attendance brought no drop in mental test scores because students were becoming more "testwise" and scoring higher; he gave to the same reply Sir Godfrey Thompson in connection with the testing of Scottish children. He advocated the use of data processing in its earliest years (Terman, 1935a), for he was always the innovator, receptive to new ways of getting rid of routine.

Some years later, Terman turned to tests of personality (Terman, 1929a) as a supplement to clinical judgment (Terman, 1934a; 1934c), and went on to devise and appraise his own instruments for measuring factors with which he was most concerned (Terman, 1936a; 1936b; 1938a). Yet from the early 1920s, his interest in test construction *per se* waned, and he turned to other fields of research.

Meanwhile Terman had discovered, to his initial surprise, that constructing tests can be lucrative. The poor farm boy who worked his way and borrowed what seemed like huge sums to go to school, who worried constantly lest his family not be cared for when his health was poor, was quickly relieved of financial anxiety. But he still led the life of a somewhat frail academician, never ostentatious, never extravagant. He lived to see America become test-conscious; that he profited from the sale of tests was incidental. He remained tireless in his work, his achievement drive in no way diminished. His sense of work—that it was waiting to be done—may have arisen in childhood frustration, but it became habitual for his entire life.

Another vindication came in 1923 in a letter from his old mentor, G. Stanley Hall, who had discouraged him from working with mental tests. Hall expressed keen appreciation for the marvelous work his former student was doing, and predicted that the whole business of calibrating human abilities had a far vaster future ahead. It was morning, but by no means high noon, in the testing movement.

In addition to his own publications and his new administrative posts, Terman was called upon to serve as associate or cooperating editor on an increasing number of professional and other journals. Before World War I, he had helped to establish the *Journal of Delinquency*, later renamed the *Journal of Juvenile Research* (1916-18). He became an editor for the *Journal of Applied Psychology* (1917-42), the *Journal of Educational Research* (1920-42), the *Journal of Educational Psychology* (1921-33), and the *Journal of Personnel Research* (1922-27). He served briefly in a similar capacity for the *Education Film Magazine* (1921), the *Journal of Social Hygiene* (1922), and the *Ungraded Magazine* (1923).

He established the *Genetic Studies of Genius* series as editor and author (1925-56). He added editorial responsibilities to the *Journal of Genetic Psychology*, formerly the *Pedagogical Seminary* (1925-56), *Genetic Psychology Monographs* (1926-56), *Vocational Guidance Magazine* (1929-33), *British Journal of Educational Psychology* (1931-56), *Journal of Personality*, formerly *Character and Personality* (1932-38), and *Applied Psychology Monographs* (1943-48), as well as serving briefly as a consultant for *The Nation's Schools* (1927) and *The Junior Home* (1931). His editorial load was stupendous.

Around 1920, Terman's association with the World Book Company (later Harcourt, Brace and World, and still later Harcourt Brace Jovanovich) began in a small way in connection with the publication of some school survey reports. He went on to publish with them the *Terman Group Test of Mental Ability* in 1920 and the *Stanford Achievement Test* in 1923. During those early years,

Terman increasingly gained respect and confidence from his test publishers as well as psychologists and educators.

The World Book Company had quickly recognized the need for specialized, professional editorial help in the development of tests, and sought specialists in measurement to handle the task. Terman served as test editor for a time, then suggested Arthur Otis as a successor to ensure the quality of the tests produced. Terman was not only the outstanding figure in test development at the time, but also enjoyed the reputation of being an "easy" author to work with— cooperative, considerate, and dependable.

The World Book Company soon found that the greatest difficulty in promoting the use of the new standardized tests was the gap between the psychologists and research workers producing the tests and the consumers, typically school administrators or teachers. To help bridge that gap, the World Book Company launched the Measurement and Adjustment Series of professional books on measurement and its applications. Terman was already active in writing books to meet that need (Terman, 1922c; 1923e); he was an author the publisher wanted. In 1921, he was named editor of a new textbook series to accomplish this purpose.

Terman proposed a textbook series on measurement which might take the name "Testing and Training Series," or "Intelligence and Adjustment Series," or "Measurement and Adjustment Series." He canvassed thirty to forty of the older, established educational psychologists for suitable manuscripts. Then he proposed sixteen possible books; the probable sales for the entire group totaled 100,000 copies or more. When the publisher expressed interest in the series, Terman had serious second thoughts about taking the time for such an extensive editorial job, saying that he was sure others could do it equally well, while he doubted that the others would be likely to do the research he was anticipating. But the publisher insisted, and Terman again reversed himself and became the editor of the *Measurement and Adjustment Series*.

Nearly half the titles originally proposed for the series are clearly parallel to volumes ultimately published. Dickson's *Mental Tests and the Classroom Teacher* (Terman, 1923a) grew out of "How to Use Tests," for which Dickson and Norton had been suggested. Wood's *Measurement in Higher Education* (Terman, 1923b) came from "Measuring the College Student," for which Wood or Thorndike had been proposed. Stedman's *Education of Gifted Children* (Terman, 21924c) replaced "Testing and Training the Gifted," which Terman had suggested for himself, with the cautious marginal note "not promised." Otis's *Statistical Method in Educational Measurement* (Terman, 1925c) was the final form of "Statistics of Tests and Measurements: Introductory Course," proposed for Otis, Franzen, or Dearborn, to give teachers a simple, non-mathematical introduction to statistics as an aid in using test results. Kelly's *Interpretation of Educational Measurement* (Terman, 1927b) apparently replaced two suggestions proposed for Kelly, "Statistical Methods: Advanced Course" and "Educational Tests" or "Measuring Achievement," designed to point out the limits of educational measurement, particularly of group testing. Wells's *Mental Tests in Clinical Practice* (Terman, 1927d) developed from "Testing the Psychopath," proposed for Wells, Mateer, or Goddard, which stressed the need for clinical judgment to supplement psychological examination.

What happened to the other titles is not clear. They included a two-volume "Manual of Mental Measurement," suggested for Whipple; "Testing and Training the Dullard," proposed for Merrill or Gesell; "Testing and Training the Delinquent," suggested for Williams; "Vocational Testing and Guidance," with no author proposed; "Trade Testing in the Selection of Employees," again with no author; "Training the Maladjusted" or "Testing and Training for Special Defects," suggested for Fernald or Sutherland; "Teacher Self-Measurement," with no author proposed; and "The Intelligence of the Nation," which Terman thought he might write himself, but again carefully hedged by the note "not promised." Some of the proposals may have been too highly specialized for the publisher to risk; others were doubtless converted to a slightly different slant; and still others may have failed to find a productive author.

The series included a number of additional publications, some of them educational classics. Peterson's *Early Conception and Tests of Intelligence* (Terman, 1925d) presented the psychological assumption on which the mental testing movement rested and the historical development from which it grew; its audience was teachers who were trained to give individual tests. Fenton's *Self-Direction and Adjustment* (Terman, 1926d) placed the prevention of behavior disorders previously scheduled for a book on delinquency into a broader setting. Goodenough's *Measurement of Intelligence by Drawings* (Terman, 1926c) was a landmark in nonverbal testing for young children. Hull's *Aptitude Testing* was equally innovative in its analysis of the range of talent in the individual and in the population as a whole; it gave a thorough review of test construction and interpretation. Hildreth's *Psychological Services for School*

Problems (Terman, 1930a) mirrored Terman's concern with something more than testing and classification alone as the proper contribution of the psychologist to the school. Madsen's *Educational Measurement in the Elementary Grades* (Terman, 1930b) and Stutsman's *Mental Measurement of Pre-School Children* (Terman, 1931b) reviewed testing for particular age levels. Dunlap and Kurtz's *Handbook of Statistical Monographs, Tables, and Formulas* (Terman, 1932a) replaced earlier proposals in the field of advanced statistics. Washburn's well-known *Adjusting the School to the Child* (Terman, 1932b), which presented the Winnetka plan of individualized instruction in basic skills with balancing socializing activities, reflected Terman's concern with individual differences. Hollingworth's *Children Above 180 IQ* (Terman, 1942a) was a major contribution, pointing out the acute need for highly specialized education for the highly gifted. Finally, Cattell's *Description and Measurement of Personality* (Terman, 1946a), based on a meticulous assessment of research and factor analysis, became another classic in individual differences, this time in the emerging field of personality. Of all the authors who contributed to the series, approximately one-third were former graduate students of Terman's, which gave a remarkably personal touch to the whole enterprise.

Nor was that the sum of Terman's editorial responsibility. He was called upon for forewords or introductions to other books he encouraged: Cady's *Estimation of Juvenile Incorrigibility* (Terman, 1923c); Fryer's *Measurement of Interest in Relation to Human Adjustment* (Terman, 1931e); Bennett's *College and Life* (Terman, 1933b); Fenton's *Delinquent Boy and the Correctional School* (Terman, 1935b); Howard's *The Road Ahead* (Terman, 1941a); and Lantz's *Easel Age Scale* (Terman, 1955b). Of this entire group, half the authors were former graduate students of Terman.

In such an extensive editorial load—particularly in the *Measurement and Adjustment Series*—all did not run smoothly. The initial arrangement, dividing the editorial responsibility between Otis and Terman, proved unworkable, and Terman soon made full authority the condition of his continuing as editor. He gave geographic distance and difficulty of communication as the reason, though Otis's old limitations in social and intellectual awareness are suggested by Terman's added comment that Otis knew statistics and test techniques, but that his judgment on books was inflexible and undependable.

In 1924, Terman proposed a monograph series to supplement the textbook enterprise. It was to include perhaps the best one-third of his students' doctoral dissertations. Of course, it would not make much money, but neither would the publishers lose, and it would be a service to the profession. The publishers differed, and declined to publish the monographs.

The *Measurement and Adjustment Series* was highly successful; many of the books went into several editions and translations. In its later years the series essentially combined the monograph idea with the original text format for such books as those of Hollingworth and Cattell. The influence of the *Measurement and Adjustment Series* on the education of teachers in the period between the two world wars was tremendous.

This, then, was Terman as he developed from 1916 to 1922, with many lines of activity reaching into later decades. He had focused on mental testing and developed the significant *Stanford Revision of the Binet*, which gained him national prominence. He filled a major role in the Army testing program during World War I, refining his techniques, adapting them to group testing and research, and moving to a position of national leadership in the testing movement. When he returned to Stanford, he buried himself in a flurry of projects on testing intelligence and achievement in the schools and using the results.

Terman's growing recognition as a psychologist brought him a new personal position. He was no longer primarily an educator, but a full-fledged psychologist. He had joined the American Psychological Association in 1917, a sign that he had begun to consider himself a psychologist rather than a pedagogue. He became active in Association affairs, leading to his election to the presidency of the American Psychological Association in 1923. And still later, in 1928, his growing eminence led to his election to the National Academy of Sciences, a major distinction awarded to one or occasionally two psychologists each year, based on broad support from the psychologist members of the Academy. It is no wonder that the election to the Academy meant a great deal to Terman. It meant that he no longer was an unknown educator, but a nationally and internationally recognized psychologist. He had "wanted to get to the top and did, the top of the particular mountain on which he was" (E. G. Boring, 1959, p. 439).

CHAPTER VII

The Gifted

It is a curious fact that special classes for bright children are strenuously opposed by a few of the country's leading educational authorities. Their opposition seems to derive from an extreme democratic bias which minimizes native inequalities of endowment and scents the danger of class favoritism in every departure from the plan of a single curriculum for the entire school population. The opposition as voiced displays more emotion than logic. True democracy demands that every child, whether superior, average, or inferior in ability, be given the fullest opportunity ·to develop to the limit of his mental capacity. It is the gifted child, more than any other, who has hitherto lacked this opportunity (Terman unpublished, 1929).

TERMAN pioneered in still another field during his early years at Stanford. He had always been interested in individual differences, particularly in the kind of differences he himself personified. In his opinion, gifted children are not the queer, "early ripe and early rot" individuals of popular opinion. Instead, they are a major national resource.

Terman's thesis for the master's degree at Indiana University had covered the early literature on genius and its role in social change. He had been impressed by Galton's finding that high intellectual achievement occurs in families, an indirect application of Darwin's theory to human intelligence. At Clark University he had become familiar with then current ways of measuring physical characteristics, sensory acuity, and mental imagery. He had followed the work of J. McKeen Cattell, who brought together a mixture of procedures from Wundt and Galton in order to identify mentally superior individuals through measures of sensory acuity, strength of grip, sensitivity to pain, and memory for dictated consonants.

Terman tried out Cattell's tests, along with many others, on bright and dull boys in his dissertation. Throughout, he was driven by a conviction that the common belief that brightness was undesirable was utterly false. Bright children were not sickly or weak, neurotic or maladjusted. They were mentally and physically strong, and they were the hope of society.

By 1910, Terman had devised an adaptation of the 1908 Binet and applied it to four hundred unselected children. He described the characteristics and abilities of those children with IQs above 125, following them to see what happened (Terman, 1911a). It was a prototype of his later longitudinal study. During his years of work with school health, he took time to point out that despite public opinion, mental superiority accompanies physical superiority—a fact significant for education (Terman, 1914e). He was interested in measuring intelligence as a whole and in devising an instrument to identify children of various levels of ability ranging from gifted to feebleminded. The Stanford revision of the Binet provided an instrument that was carefully standardized and that reached higher levels of ability in late childhood; this led naturally into his studies of the gifted (Terman, 1916g).

In those early years Terman also made a number of case studies of gifted individuals. He refuted Pearson's contention that Galton's ability was mediocre by pointing out that Galton's biography reported childhood incidents which could be explained only by an IQ of near 200 (Terman, 1917a). Galton recognized letters before he could speak; wrote simple communications to his family at the age of four; knew Latin well enough to read the *Iliad* and the *Odyssey* at six; classified insects and minerals at about the same time; devised drawings of a flying machine at thirteen; and was admitted to college as a medical student at fifteen. Contrary to popular stereotype, Galton was open-minded, modest, and affectionate—not at all the temperamental tyrant. Terman concluded that the case of Galton illustrates the common failure to judge performance in terms of the mental age to which it corresponds. He asked for cooperation in finding case descriptions of children whose IQs were between 150 and 200. The Galton study also foreshadowed a future effort, Terman's large-scale study of historical genius.

Terman received reports of a number of gifted children. There was Martha, who knew the alphabet at the age of nineteen months; recognized sentences at twenty months; and was reading primers independently by the age of two, with a reading vocabulary of more than 200 words (Terman, 1918c). And there was a gifted young author in the 1911 study who knew the alphabet at nineteen months; read *Heidi* at four and one-half years; and went on to Shakespeare and Dickens, while writing a hundred poems and seventy-five stories by the age of eight (Terman, 1921f).

A later case study is Terman's most unusual account. Henry Cowell was a gifted boy who became a musician with almost no formal schooling. J. Harold Williams, Terman's first graduate assistant, worked half time at a little one-room school near the Stanford campus; Henry, at the age of twelve, was janitor for the school. He was the world's worst janitor, for he would skip the cleaning and sit down to play at the piano instead. Williams mentioned the boy to Terman, who got in touch with him and studied him in detail (Terman, 1926a).

Henry's socioeconomic background was anything but privileged. His father was a ne'er-do-well of good family who was caught up in the activities of Jack London and his crowd in San Francisco. Henry's mother was a writer for major journals. His parents were able to give Henry violin lessons in early childhood, and according to neighbors he was a virtuoso; but soon Henry's father left home and the violin had to be sold. By the time Terman knew him, Henry was the chief support for himself and his mother, with his fifteen dollars a month for janitor work supplemented from time to time by weeding lawns or selling wildflowers to neighbors.

Henry had made one attempt at school, but dropped out at the age of seven because he did not like it and could not get along with the other children. In those days there was no way of enforcing compulsory education, so Henry's mother taught him writing and English informally. The boy spent his time hanging around the great estates in neighboring Menlo Park and Atherton, listening to pianos and trying them out for himself. He also taught himself botany, through wildflower excursions and independent reading of textbooks; in fact, he was for a time uncertain whether to become a plant breeder or a composer. Finally, Mrs. Thorsten Veblen arranged access to a piano for Henry, and members of the Stanford faculty made financial contributions to relieve him of the necessity of keeping the janitor's job. They even persuaded musicians in San Francisco to give Henry free lessons, and subsidized more than a year of formal training at the University of California at Berkeley. But the formal training did not take; Henry's unconventional style was already established. Somehow, too, he managed to get hold of a piano of his own.

Perhaps Paul Farnsworth, whose psychological specialty was aesthetics, knew Henry's musical talent better than anyone else. He followed the whole of Henry's career, from his childhood until his death at the age of sixty-eight. Henry's innovations were particularly in cross-rhythms and the timbre of the tone, not in melodic structure. He took the piano and used it in his own way, massaging and pluck-ing the strings by putting his hands inside the piano and playing directly on them. He used tone clusters to get different effects, playing with the flat of his hand, or with his arm or elbow. He produced rocking effects, and became highly proficient in playing such cross-rhythms as three-four time against four-four, four-four against five-four, and so forth.

Because of his own interest in cross-rhythms, Farnsworth had made player-piano rolls and phonograph discs which yielded cross-rhythms. Wildly enthusiastic, Henry got an engineer to make three boxlike devices called "rhythmicons" which also produced cross-rhythm effects. He later played one of these instruments with the Paris Symphony Orchestra. Henry's melodies were at first rather simple, but his contacts with Chinese groups in San Francisco stirred an interest in Cantonese music, which colored some of his later works. Henry went on to help organize the New Music Society and the American Musicological Society and to become the pet of an *avant garde* musical group in San Francisco and Carmel, which kept him going with commissions to write compositions for parties. Eventually he was awarded a Guggenheim fellowship for study and went on concert tours abroad. Henry's music was the first by a contemporary Westerner to be published in the Soviet Union. On his sixty-fifth birthday, he was honored by President Kennedy at the White House.

Henry himself described his way of composing music (Cowell, 1926). He thought in terms of sound rather than instruments, for until he was fourteen he had no musical instrument of his own. As a youth he could not attend concerts often, though he wanted desper-ately to hear them. When he did hear music, he mentally rehearsed the compositions he liked until he could play them over in his mind whenever he chose. At first, he could get only melody and some har-mony and had to listen for sound-quality, but gradually the full composition emerged.

Then his own compositions came into being. Leaps of glorious tone-quality would come spontaneously, with original melodies and

83

harmonies. They would develop until Henry could reproduce what he heard without interrupting the music. Then he practiced directing what he heard into channels for a few instruments at a time, rehearsing mentally until he could produce the flow of sound at will, centering on a germinal theme and enlarging it. Only then did he sit down to write. The composition usually took its final form on his first attempt to put it down. To him, musical creation was a distinctly emotional process; the only function of intellect was to steer and govern the meteors of sound that flashed through his mind.

When he attended a concert and disliked the performance, Henry would stop listening and turn his attention to his own vivid and persistent eidetic auditory imagery. By recalling in minute detail the performance of some more talented artist, he could enjoy his evening while the other listeners suffered.

Yet Henry's life was troubled. He was once arrested as a homosexual. Work was sporadic. His *avant garde* group eventually lost interest in him. Though he did much for music on the theoretical and organizational side, his melodies were humdrum and, musically speaking, he never got to the top. By the time he achieved a reputation as an artist, his mother had died and his father had remarried. His new stepmother bought a piano, fixed up an apartment for Henry, and began to foster his career in no uncertain terms. Later, Henry married a wealthy girl and thus solved his financial problems, but he had already reached his peak in musical productivity.

Terman, who was admittedly not musical, nevertheless tried to learn in order to understand Henry. He believed talent in the arts to be highly specialized, but thought that the artist could not go far without a high degree of general intelligence as well. Henry had the intelligence, with an IQ above 140 in childhood despite his unusual background. Terman was fascinated by Henry's combination of high general ability, unusual musical talent, scientific promise, and absence of formal education. He was attracted by what he called the most original mind among all his gifted proteges.

There were other objects of Terman's interest. There was a young man who had been dismissed from the Stanford Law School for cheating on an examination. He had quoted long judicial opinions almost word for word. The student protested the dismissal, saying that he could not help giving that kind of answer; he sought out Terman. Terman found that the young man had an extraordinary visual memory—eidetic imagery again, but in the visual-verbal area. The young man was reinstated.

And Terman found another young man who had taught himself to read Roman numerals at the age of five. He did most of the quarter's work in physics the first day and never needed to take another course. He became a renowned scientist and later a college president.

From time to time, as Terman gained recognition, he was asked about famous persons. In 1927 he replied to a request to name the twelve greatest living individuals in certain categories. He could give no names in sculpture, painting, finance, or philosophy. But he named Mussolini (and later dropped him) and Hoover in statecraft; J. J. Thompson, Neils Bohr, and Einstein in science; Paderewski in music; Knute Hamsum and G. B. Shaw in literature; Henry Ford and J. D. Rockefeller in industry; Edison in invention; and Foch in military science.

Challenged in 1941 to name gifted persons who promoted democracy, Terman gave a list of individuals with high childhood IQs who had contributed basic concepts. The list included Hugo Guershayst, the French jurist who helped to develop international law; John Stuart Mill and John Milton, who wrote tracts on democracy; Benjamin Franklin and Thomas Jefferson, who aided in establishing early American democracy; Harriet Martineau; Charles Hughes; and Adolph Berle.

Terman also continued his more general exploration of contemporary research in the study of the gifted. He supplemented his earlier review of the literature on the gifted, emphasizing the years from 1914 to 1920 and covering a list of ninety-five references Terman, 1920b).

Then in 1921 came the opportunity for which Terman had hoped. He was already actively seeking research funds from endowment foundations and federal and state agencies. In fact, in 1921 he was already supervising two grants of $10,000 each, one in character development and the other in teaching hygiene to children. Then came a grant from the Commonwealth Fund to gather research data on an extensive sample of the gifted (Terman, 1921k). Between 1921 and 1956, grants for this purpose totaled nearly $200,000. In addition to these funds, Terman assigned all royalties from the gifted studies to a special university fund to continue the research, and added some $35,000 of his own personal funds as well. At that time, it was a fantastic sum for such studies.

Terman planned a two-pronged approach to the study of the gifted, whom he defined as the top one percent of the population in the ability to acquire and manipulate concepts. The first approach was to study historical men of genius who had achieved greatness by tracing their development during childhood and youth. The second was to identify a sample of living gifted children, measure their abilities, and follow them through the years in order to evaluate their achievements as adults.

The study of historical genius grew out of Terman's case studies, his analysis of the childhood of Galton, and another review of the literature (Terman, 1922e). For Terman, reading biography was a continuing hobby. He believed that biographers and historians should know something of general psychology, the nature of human abilities, social behavior, motivation, and abnormal as well as normal behavior (Terman, 1941d). For a number of years he gave a course in the psychological study of biography. He even severely criticized the autobiographies of psychologist friends for giving only professional information and neglecting the intimate and personal incidents and events, maladjustments, and childhood hobbies that were significant· in shaping adult life and motivating scientific achievement (Terman, 1953c).

Terman's interest in historical genius sparked a doctoral dissertation done by Catherine Cox (Miles) and reported in Volume II of the *Genetic Studies of Genius* (Terman, 1926f). Miss Cox selected the top 500 names from Cattell's list of the 1000 most eminent individuals of history as judged by the amount of space devoted to them in biographical dictionaries. She eliminated those born before 1450, those who belonged to an hereditary aristocracy, and a few others whose eminence had little basis in intellectual achievement. For the 300 individuals remaining, she combed biographies for evidence of interests, education, school standing and progress, friends and associates, reading, and achievement. She used an outline covering ancestry and family, parents and siblings, wife and children, a chronology of events, a characterization, a statement of influence, and bibliography. Documentary evidence such as letters, compositions, poems, and mothers' diaries received special attention. The case material thus assembled ran to some six thousand typed pages.

Then the evidence for each of the 300 cases was examined independently by three psychologists intimately acquainted with age norms for mental growth; Terman, Merrill, and Cox. Each of the three estimated the minimum IQ that would account for the subject's reported childhood performance at age seven, and again for his performance at ages seventeen to twenty-six. Each psychologist also specified the level of confidence in the evidence for each opinion.

The three estimates were then averaged for each age and for reliability.

For the entire group, the IQs ranged from 100 to 200 with an average of 155, more than four standard deviations above the norm on the 1916 Stanford Binet. Estimates between 100 and 120 usually meant that there was little biographical information about the early years, and that the estimate was unreliable. Philosophers ranked highest, with an average IQ of 170; poets, novelists, dramatists, along with revolutionary statesmen, were next at 160, followed by scientists at 155, musicians at 145, artists at 140, and military men at 125. The main conclusion was that the individual who achieves eminence is one whom intelligence tests would identify as gifted in childhood. In addition to high intellectual ability, the eminent showed persistence and self-confidence, well-directed interests, energy, character, and in many cases a superior early environment (Terman unpublished, 1941a; Fenton, 1932).

The study gave many illustrations of the nonintellectual factors which influence achievement. Newton, Victor Cousin, and Faraday became eminent largely because of chance factors which operated at critical periods. Goldsmith, Scott, Liebig, Hunter, and von Humboldt were supposedly backward in childhood—a finding which Terman had challenged and which the Cox study disproved. The direction of later achievement was foreshadowed in childhood in at least one-fourth of the cases, including Macaulay, Goethe, Franklin, Pascal, and Leibnitz. Versatility was the rule, particularly for writers of non-fiction, followed in order by statesmen and philosophers, scholars, religious leaders, scientists, poets, mathematicians, novelists and dramatists, musicians, artists, and the military (Terman, 1947d).

The second prong of the research, and the more ambitious, was the longitudinal study of the living gifted. Terman wanted first to find out what traits characterize children of high IQ, and then to follow them as long as possible to find out what kind of adults they became. Though he used the term "genius" for many years, and as early as 1921 titled the series of books reporting the results of his studies *Genetic Studies of Genius* (Terman, 1921f; 1921j), he began to refer to the children in his longitudinal study as "gifted" rather than "genius." The word "genius" seemed to set such individuals apart as a separate, peculiar species rather than showing their relationship to the rest of humanity; "gifted," on the other hand, carried the meaning that such individuals were simply an extreme on a scale of intellectual ability, continuous with everybody else. For his study, Terman defined the term to mean an IQ above 140 on the Stanford

Binet; that represented the highest one-half of one percent of the population in ability to acquire and manipulate concepts.

The initial identification of the gifted group was described later by Helen Marshall, who was recruited at Ohio State University in 1921. She worked on the project not only from 1921 to 1923, but also in all the field follow-up studies (1927-28, 1939-40, and 1950-51) and in the mail follow-up of 1960. Each time, she took a leave of absence from her teaching post to help Terman, to whom she was deeply devoted.

In the summer of 1921, a training program was conducted at Stanford for the four assistants who were to work on the initial identification of the gifted. Besides Helen Marshall, there were Dorothy Yates, who had done her doctoral work at the University of California on a small group of gifted children; Florence Goodenough, who had completed most of her work toward a doctorate at Columbia; and Florence Fuller. The four went to class regularly. At nine each morning, Jessie Chase Fenton reviewed and presented case studies of genius, and the group discussed them. At ten, Dr. L. L. Burlingame of the Department of Biology and Dr. J. Harold Williams of the California Bureau of Juvenile Research presented the principles of heredity and described the methods of collecting field data. At eleven, the four assistants went over the forms that were to be used and decided on the best wording for questions. In the afternoon, they reviewed testing procedures so all four would go about the task in the same way. Sometimes the day was broken by a long ride with Mrs. Terman to San Jose, passing through fruit orchards dotted with trays of drying prunes. At the end of the training period, Terman took the four assistants to the Stanford Bookstore and equipped them with everything they needed or asked for, including fountain pens and Kodaks.

Miss Marshall worked chiefly in San Francisco. She met the Superintendent of Schools and convinced him that she could handle the project by following her first rule of business for women: "Let the other fellow do the talking; the more clever ideas he gets a chance to air, the brighter he'll think you are." It worked.

The basic plan was to sift the school population of one-quarter million in the larger cities of California for gifted children. Alameda, Berkeley, Oakland, Los Angeles, and San Francisco were the cities. In this population, Terman estimated that he was successful in locating ninety percent of the gifted in the grades studied. Each teacher was asked to name four pupils—the two brightest in her current class, the brightest in her class of the previous year, and the youngest child in her current class. Nominations were accepted only on overall brightness, not on special ability alone. Those nominated were then given a group intelligence test, either the National or the Terman Group Test, depending on the age level. If the child's IQ was above 140 on the group test, he was given the Stanford Binet. If the IQ on the individual Binet was still above 140, his parents were asked for consent for the child to become a member of the research group. A later check of other teacher nominations and group test results added about twenty percent to those first named, chiefly children who were shy and less good-looking than their fellows. The best criterion of giftedness proved to be age: the youngest child in the class was more likely to be gifted than those nominated as brightest by teachers.

In the interest of practicality, grades one and two were soon dropped from the study, unless a particular child was very outstanding. Teachers could not decide what the symptoms of intellectual superiority at that level were, a difficulty corroborated by later studies. And it was difficult to use group tests for screening such young children.

Things went well, or not so well, depending on the school. In Miss Marshall's first school of six hundred students, the principal had everything so well organized that the work was practically completed in less than a week. Of the forty children nominated, individual tests were given to seventeen, and two children were identified as gifted.

In the second school she visited, things went less smoothly. The principal decided that all parents must give their written consent for participation and that teachers could not spare time for a meeting, so each had to be interviewed individually. She also forgot to collect essential forms and assigned for the group testing a room where the only place the child could write was on his lap. Finally, she unearthed an order forbidding teachers to give tests without the permission of the city psychologist—a discovery which merely sent Miss Marshall up Telegraph Hill to the city offices for clearance. It was the story of field research anywhere.

In the third school of eighteen hundred students, Miss Marshall screened nominees but failed to find a single gifted child. In a fourth, again with a sympathetic principal and plenty of room to work, she tested twenty children, many of whom proved to be gifted. In some areas of town—the poor areas rather than those racially different or foreign—there were very few gifted children; in other, more prosperous districts, she found many more. All in all, Miss Marshall worked in San Francisco for nine months, identifying 350 gifted children.

The assistants kept in touch with Terman by correspondence, hasty visits, and more leisurely discussions each quarter. They corresponded with each other, working out better techniques and sharing them. By the end of the school year, they had located a total of 661 gifted students. Others were later added, including some tested prior to 1922, to make a group of 1528. The age range in the gifted group was from three through eighteen years, with most of the cases falling between five and seventeen, and the average age at eleven. The average IQ was 151, the range from 140 to 200.

Terman himself handled the problems implicit in research in such a sensitive area. Many people had little confidence in testing. Some were unwilling to have their children participate in the study because they refused to recognize individual differences as significant; if all received God's love, there was no question that all were completely intelligent. Others associated testing with mental disturbance or mental retardation. At social events, Terman talked with parents of superior children to secure their cooperation in the study; he also prepared suggestions for parents on handling gifted children (Terman, 1921j). He issued periodic summaries of findings as they were available (for example, Terman, 1946d) and made himself accessible for counseling. Within two years of the time he started, he was swamped with applications from parents who wanted a child included in the study, all of which were declined.

The initial data secured from the gifted group in 1922 were voluminous. For most subjects, they included two intelligence tests, the four-hour Stanford Achievement Test, a general information test, seven character tests, a test of interest in and knowledge of play, thirty-four anthropometric measurements, a one-hour medical examination, a sixteen-page home information blank including ratings on twenty-five traits, a school information blank including similar trait ratings, an interest blank filled out by the child, a two-month reading record kept by the child, ratings on the socio-economic status of the home, and a large amount of case history information supplied by teachers, parents, and field assistants.

The following year, 1922-23, Miss Marshall and Florence Goodenough stayed on at Stanford to help with the statistical work and the writing. It was a tremendous task in those precomputer days. Terman was ingenious in devising ways to quantify his data, and each facet of the study was examined in detail. The major account of the results was ready in 1925. It was reported in Volume I of the *Genetic Studies of Genius* (Terman, 1925e) and in part, in summary, or in elaboration in a number of other publications (Terman, 1924b; 1924d; 1924h; 1924j; 1925a; 1925b). Based largely on the original 661 gifted for whom the records were most complete, the report went into racial and social origin, anthropometric measures, health and physical history, medical examinations, educational history, school accomplishment, specialized abilities, interests, character, and personality. The overall results showed that the gifted child excels the average most markedly in intellectual and volitional traits; next in emotional and moral qualities; and least in physical and social characteristics.

Racially, every group present in California was represented, though Jews were the most numerous minority, and Mexicans and Negroes least often present. One Japanese-Caucasian marriage contributed four gifted, with a fifth too young to test. The homes of the gifted were somewhat above average in socioeconomic status in average neighborhoods. Two-thirds of the fathers were engaged in professional, semiprofessional, or higher business occupations.

The divorce and separation rate among the parents was less than average. A greater proportion of both parents and grandparents had completed high school than the population as a whole. There were more boys than girls in the group, a ratio of 116 to 100. There was little evidence of "pushing" on the part of the parents; when the child showed curiosity, however, they answered seriously rather than laughing or turning aside. They did not attempt to teach reading early, though many of the children learned to read at the age of four; instead, they simply gave words when asked for them.

The school achievement of the gifted was nearly as high as their intelligence. The average achievement quotient (ratio of achievement age chronological age) ranged from 137 to 152 in various subjects, compared with an average intelligence quotient of 151. Most had mastered the curriculum from two to four years beyond the grade in which they were enrolled. Nor were they one-sided in achievement. Yet their progress quotient, or ratio of grade assignment to age, was only 114. Eighty-five percent had been accelerated, but nonetheless, on the average they were placed two years below mental age by the age of eight, and three years below by the age of twelve.

On tests of personality and character, the gifted were as mature at the age of nine as most children are at fourteen. They were more than normally generous, honest, persistent, goal-oriented, conscientious, and socially concerned. They were less than normally conceited, nervous, and emotionally unstable. They were far from the stereotype of gifted children as smart alecks or eccentrics.

In social behavior, the gifted were near the norm, though they were above normal in social knowledge. They spent fewer hours playing, played alone more often, and preferred older playmates. They liked checkers, chess, and cards, and they read omnivorously—including the *Book of Knowledge*, dictionaries, and railroad timetables, as well as books. They had as much play information at nine as average children had at twelve. They had many hobbies and worked them hard. Gifted girls liked subjects and play preferred by boys, and gifted boys joined the girls in their preference for reading and quiet games of intellectual skill. Psychological sex differences were less apparent in the gifted than in the population as a whole.

In anthropometric measures, the difference between gifted and average was small but significant. According to hospital records, the gifted were taller and heavier at birth. They walked and talked early, and were more often breast-fed. They were normal, or above normal, on all medical tests with the single exception of a slightly higher proportion of eye difficulty. The visual problem might have reflected the greater amount of early reading, but it is equally possible that it simply showed the parents' greater awareness of the child and his problems.

Terman concluded that, since the gifted were markedly different and apparently neglected in school, something should be done for them. Teaching methods and curriculum should be modified to bring their talents to fruition. The single-track graded plan was a straitjacket for superior children. They should be accelerated enough to allow them to work at their own level and be given special work; they should have plenty of time for play with normal children, but no time to sit and daydream.

The complex findings were greeted by most reviewers as extensive, painstaking, and providing a wealth of new scientific data on individual differences (Freeman, 1925). Others granted that the study was significant and timely, but suggested that it was overambitious (Holzinger, 1926).

A byproduct of the initial study of the gifted was a book on children's reading coauthored with Margaret Lima, a graduate assistant (Terman, 1926c). Terman had earlier reported an extensive analysis of the reading of 2000 children, covering age changes from five to sixteen and outlining qualities appealing to the retarded and to the gifted (Terman, 1921i). *Children's Reading* (Terman, 1926c) first presented the point of view that children read to satisfy curiosity, to satisfy unconscious desires, and to find models to imitate. Children like direct action, human interest, imaginative appeal, plenty of specifics, humor and funny incidents, and most of all sincerity without preaching. Such tastes can be satisfied with good reading as well as bad; books read in the original may be more satisfactory than those written down for children. Terman therefore advised parents and teachers to put desirable books in the way of the child, link them to his interests, and talk with him about them. Gifted children should especially learn about nonfiction and biography (Terman, 1926b). Such suggestions were followed by an extensive classified, annotated bibliography. *Children's Reading* was very well received; it was characterized variously as "a guide, philosopher and friend," a list emphasizing nonfiction, a workman-like compilation, a carefully edited but heavy volume, and a list weighted unduly with the author's personal judgments (Terman, 1926c; Buswell, 1925).

Meanwhile, the publishers of Terman's *Measurement and Adjustment Series* had been disappointed that he did not publish the first volumes of the *Genetic Studies of Genius* with them. Terman replied that the material was too heavy with tables and research data for general reading, but that he would supply a popular volume on the gifted. That was doubtless the book on the education of gifted children written by Louise Stedman (Terman, 1924c). Miss Stedman taught a class for gifted children at the University Elementary School at the University of California at Los Angeles, in which she emphasized individualized, seminar-like work. The class pooled individual discoveries and joined the rest of the children in the school in play and school activities. Miss Stedman's book described Terman's ideal for the gifted in a graphic way. Later, in 1930, Terman further publicized his views by serving as chairman of the subcommittee on the gifted of the White House Conference on Child Health and Protection.

After the original study in 1921-23, the gifted group was systematically and comprehensively followed. As of 1970, contact was maintained with ninety-six percent of the entire group. For several years after 1922, information blanks were completed and mailed in annually by parents and teachers. In 1927-28, a grant from the

Commonwealth Fund made it possible to send out field assistants to retest most of the subjects and to obtain a large amount of additional information from parents, teachers, and the children themselves. The third follow-up was conducted chiefly by mail in 1936-37. In 1939-40 a fourth grant, this time from the Carnegie Corporation, made it possible to keep three research associates in the field for a year studying the group. Because of the intervention of World War II, the data were rechecked by mail in 1945 before publication of the results. The fifth follow-up, in 1950-51, was again conducted by mail. The resulting data were being processed at Terman's death in 1956, and the report was completed by his associate, Melita Oden, in 1959.

Melita Oden was Terman's chief reliance in the follow-up studies of the gifted from 1927 onward. She had served as director of the Psychological Clinic in Louisville in 1921-22, then returned to California as a psychologist at Sonoma State Hospital until her marriage in 1923. When Terman was looking for a research assistant for the gifted study in 1927, she decided that she could combine housewifery with a professional career, and joined his staff. Between the follow-up of 1927-28 and that of 1936-37, she assisted in the revision of the Stanford Binet as well. From 1936 onward, she served as research associate with the gifted study. After Terman's death in 1956, she remained with the study, carrying increasing responsibility until 1966, when she retired from full-time work, though she continued to participate in the program.

In the field follow-ups of 1927-28 and 1939-40, the field assistants retested the gifted; interviewed them, their parents, and their spouses; and brought case histories up to date. The mail follow-ups included questionnaires for the gifted, their parents, and their teachers. In 1940, all data were placed on punched cards, so processing thereafter was more easily done. In addition, Terman maintained a voluminous correspondence with the subjects and enjoyed personal visits with the many who called on him at Stanford. He wanted to hear firsthand every detail about them, personally or from his assistants; anything that bore on their welfare was welcome news to him. In turn, the gifted thought of Terman as their godfather; they often spoke of themselves as the "Termites."

The warmth of Terman's concern for those in the gifted group is illustrated by Robert Sears, who had known Terman since childhood. When Sears was an undergraduate at Stanford, he knew "Dr. Terman" as the highly respected chairman of the Psychology Department. When the two passed in the Quad, Terman would often stop for a chat, peering up through his glasses at the tall Sears, smiling and talking softly in a friendly, encouraging way, wanting to know what Sears was doing. Sears was embarrassed as only a late adolescent can be by such attention from a semi-stranger. Later, the awkwardness dissipated as Sears established his own career; when he visited his family at Stanford, Terman was always eager to see him. Terman invited him to lunch at a well-known spot on the highway, and they talked constantly, all about Sears, who was then an ambitious and achievement-oriented youngster. Terman was fascinated and asked questions. Sears felt that the lunch was part of Terman's assessment of the gifted group, and that Terman's interest in the doings of his subjects was a product of his strong identification with the group.

When Sears had children, Terman wanted their IQs. He and Sears continued to lunch together, and to talk in Terman's office for as much as an hour. Later, when Terman's health became more precarious and he tired easily, he would rise after ten minutes or so; that would be the end of the discussion. Between meetings, he sometimes wrote Sears, once asking for suggestions for follow-up. Sears suggested an inquiry on sources of motivation and on relations with parents.

The first field follow-up of 1927-28 is reported in detail in Volume III of the *Genetic Studies of Genius* (Terman, 1930c). It was written in collaboration with Barbara Burks and D. W. Jensen, from the work of Helen Marshall, Melita Oden, and Alice Leahy as field assistants. The data were compared with the original study item by item. For the group as a whole, the picture had not changed greatly in the six years between the two studies. The gifted averaged nineteen years of age; they maintained their intellectual superiority. Most of them were in college, liked study, and made good grades. Socially, they were active and dated normally. If they had academic difficulty, it was because they gave too much time to nonacademic pursuits, were too individualistic to follow a routine program, or tended to substitute daydreaming for work (Terman unpublished, 1934). Terman pointed out the significance of the findings for schools and for child-rearing (Terman, 1930d; 1932d).

The questionnaire follow-up of 1936-37, the field study of 1939-40, and the postwar questionnaire follow-up of 1945 blend into each other in Volume IV of the *Genetic Studies of Genius* Terman, 1947b). By 1940, the average age of the gifted was twenty-nine, and they were established in their occupations. Two-thirds were married, and five hundred children had been born (Terman,

1940e; 1947b; 1951c; Terman unpublished, 1941a). The mortality rate was lower than the average, as were the divorce, insanity, and arrest rates. The gifted had maintained their intellectual status; they were still in the top one percent of the population on the new Concept Mastery Test designed by Terman to measure the stratosphere of intelligence in adults. It was clear that the gifted individual could be identified almost as accurately in the third grade as at age thirty.

The average gifted individual had entered high school at thirteen and college at seventeen. Eventually, eighty-seven percent of the men and eighty-three percent of the women entered college, and seventy-one percent of the men and sixty-seven percent of the women earned at least one college degree. Though the gifted averaged nearly two years younger than their classmates, they engaged more often in extracurricular activities, received more student body honors, and more often graduated with distinction. Of those who graduated, two-thirds of the men and half the women went on for graduate studies. Of the men who entered graduate school, about one-sixth earned a Ph.D., another sixth a medical degree, one-fourth a law degree, and one-ninth a degree in engineering or architecture. Of the women, less than one-tenth earned a degree beyond the M.A. Overall, the proportion of the gifted who earned higher professional degrees was twenty to thirty times as great as in the general population (Terman unpublished, 1941a).

Income was varied in those years of the Great Depression; the average was $3000 for men and about half that for women. Many had secured positions in colleges throughout the country and were already finding their way to positions of responsibility. They published widely—hundreds of articles in professional journals, a vast number of short stories, popular articles, poems, textbooks, and scholarly treatises. They had patented more than eighty inventions as well. A few chose not to enter the conventional race for material success; they became policemen, gardeners, clerks, and other skilled workers.

For the male gifted, an extensive analysis was made of the factors leading to occupational success. Though the women equalled or exceeded the men in school achievement throughout, most of them married upon graduation from college and moved into domestic roles. Terman deplored such a loss of talent for society, attributing it to lack of motivation for occupational success in a male-oriented society and to lack of social opportunity for women to achieve full fruition. Yet he complimented the gifted women on their high capacity for contentment within limits set for them.

"Success" was defined in the study as the extent to which each man was making use of his superior ability; it was not based on income. Data from the follow-up of 1939-40 were analyzed by three psychologists independently, and an achievement index was assigned to each man (Terman, 1939a; 1940e; 1942c; 1947a). The most successfull one-fifth of the men were then compared with the least successful fifth, with the two groups arbitrarily matched on age. Comparisons covered test scores from 1922-23, 1927-28, and 1939-40; family records and home environment; and case histories, health data, trait ratings, field interviews, and many other items of information.

Terman found that the most successful group of gifted began to draw away from the least successful in the high school years, though differences in personality had been apparent even earlier. On maturity, the successful reported happier marriages, greater perseverance, more self-confidence, and less marked feelings of inferiority. They were rated superior in attractiveness, poise, speech, alertness, frankness, curiosity, and originality. They had much more often served as officers in World War II. Terman concluded that the difference between the relatively successful and unsuccessful gifted was largely determined by nonintellectual qualities such as social adjustment, emotional stability, and drive to accomplish. The one common denominator that appeared consistently among the successful was what Terman described as "integration toward a goal."

Looking to the future, Terman thought it unlikely that more than fifty to one hundred of his thirteen hundred gifted men and women for whom records were fairly complete would become "eminent" in Galton's sense of the term. It would be surprising if, in the year 2041, even one were among the thousand most eminent of recorded history. Perhaps one-fourth might get into *Who's Who* or *American Men of Science.* In sheer intellectual ability, however, he believed that his gifted overlapped Cattell's list of the most eminent in history. He contended that although his group probably contained no intellect equal to that of Newton or Shakespeare, it did include many who were the intellectual equals of Washington and Napoleon, and a number as well endowed with literary talent as Longfellow, Hawthorne, George Sand (Terman unpublished, 1941a).

Most reviewers of Volume IV of the *Genetic Studies of Genius* (Terman, 1947b) were by this time convinced that there is something in the idea of giftedness—that it is better to have a high IQ than a low one. They claimed, however, that environmental causes such as motivation and socioeconomic status were neglected in the follow-up; that minor conclusions that might prove embarrassing to the gifted were glossed over; and that the reason the gifted were successful was that positive traits go together anyway, but the association does not necessarily mean a causal relationship (Farrar, 1947; Faris, 1948; Sward, 1948). Still, the volume piled proof upon proof that high intelligence and overall adjustment go together. Popular authors took up the issue, over Terman's strenuous objection to the sketchy and misleading nature of their interpretations (Silverman, 1952).

While working with the data from the field follow-up of 1950-52, Terman became concerned with the increasing social pressure for schools to produce scientists (Terman, 1945d; 1955a). The Office of Naval Research requested him to undertake research to identify superior ability in science and engineering, a study which Terman carried out with Office of Naval Research funds. He searched the records of the gifted group for scientists and nonscientists, and found 51 in physical science research, 104 in engineering, 61 in medical-biological research, 68 in physical-biological fields of work, 149 in social sciences, 83 in law, and 95 in the humanities. Then he compared the scientists with the nonscientists in pattern of abilities, occupational interests, and social behavior. He found that the scientists and engineers were at the opposite pole from the businessmen and lawyers in measures of ability and interest; he suggested that such basic personality differences contribute to a basic lack of understanding between equally gifted scientists and nonscientists in their attitudes on public issues.

The analysis of the follow-up of 1950-52 was interrupted in 1956 by Terman's death. Melita Oden completed the report, published as Volume V of the *Genetic Studies of Genius* (Terman, 1959). The findings were based on results of a revised form of the Concept Mastery Test, personal interviews, and questionnaires. The gifted then averaged forty years of age, and still maintained their intellectual superiority. Some eighty-six percent of the men were in the professions, higher business categories, or semiprofessions; eleven percent were in smaller business, clerical, or skilled occupations; two percent were in agriculture or related occupations; and one percent were in semiskilled work. More than one hundred were listed in *American Men of Science* or *Who's Who in America*. Their social adjustment was generally good, the divorce rate low. Over ninety percent had married, and the typical family included 2.4

children. General health was good in ninety percent of the men and eighty percent of the women. The overall conclusion was that gifted individuals mature into adults who are not only more successful than the average, but who are also better adjusted socially and personally. There was a leading oceanographer, two up-and-coming men in the State Department, a successful writer of science fiction, several recognized American psychologists, and others. But their names were known only to Terman and his assistants. The files on the gifted were held extremely confidential since, in some cases, they recorded delinquency, mental breakdowns, homosexual episodes, marital infidelity, sexual impotency, and suicides, along with all the more positive data. Terman would open them to no one. He was alarmed at a friend's suggestion that the records might be accessible to congressional subpoena in the days of the Un-American Activities Committee. He asked that on his death the records be kept in the Department of Psychology rather than going to the University Archives, because he wanted the data to be available for legitimate scientific study, but wanted no irresponsible person to have access to them. His will transferred custody of the documents to Stanford University under these conditions.

Terman wanted his work to go on beyond his death. He left half the royalties on the Stanford Achievement Test toward the cost of maintaining the files and toward subsequent follow-ups. Even after substantial expenditures, the fund had a balance of approximately $70,000 in 1973, and the annual amount from royalties was still rather large. Terman designated Robert Sears, who was not only the son of his School of Education colleague and a member of the gifted group, but also a psychologist of note and chairman of the Department of Psychology at the time of Terman's death, as the person to carry the official responsibility for the records. Sears, in turn, arranged for Melita Oden to complete the report of the 1950-52 follow-up and to maintain continuing contact with the group. In the fall of 1972, the thirteen hundred surviving members of the gifted group, then averaging sixty-two years of age, were sent questionnaires chiefly concerned with their retirement years, in a study directed by Sears and Lee Cronbach, another prominent psychologist and member of the gifted group. Sears and Cronbach hoped to explore the current concerns and activities of the group members, changes they had made in adjusting to later maturity, and particularly the problems gifted women faced in shaping their careers and utilizing their talents. The study of the gifted was the research of which Terman was most proud. It goes on as a living monument to him and as an increasingly valuable source on the life histories of able people.

Terman urged others to carry out follow-up studies of the gifted as well, as with the children at the Hunter College Elementary School. In fact, Terman wanted full study of gifted individuals wherever they might be found.

Through the busy years of launching his studies of the gifted, Terman found time for the gifted college students at Stanford as well. Beginning in 1922, he served for six years as chairman or member of university committees which introduced intelligence tests as a partial basis for admission to Stanford University, and which worked out the Independent Study Plan for gifted students there (Terman, 1923d; 1925g; 1925h). Terman felt that the usual compartmentalized courses offered in college were not what the gifted needed. Such courses gave little sense of adventure to the alert mind; there was little intellectual competition, since the able students were skeptical of the objectives stated for the courses; and the result was that the gifted scaled down their achievement to the level of the average student.

Instead, the gifted needed more student-faculty contact, more freedom to explore, and more responsibility for carrying through on their own. Their intellectual interests should be aroused and fed. They should be taught to reason inductively, form their own generalizations, and deal critically with ideas. They should learn to think independently, without spoon-feeding or propaganda. They needed to attend seminars rather than lectures, and to have a chance to work side by side with professors on research.

In the 1920s, independent study plans for able students were beginning to emerge in such colleges as Swarthmore, Smith, Barnard, and Rollins. Terman's committee recommended a plan for Stanford which was adopted by the Academic Council in 1925 for juniors and seniors, and extended to freshmen and sophomores in 1931. Each department might choose or not choose to offer such a plan for its majors. Under the plan, students with a B average who were recommended by their major department might be freed of course work for independent study. They were to meet with their advisors once each week, mark out an individualized plan of study, cover it as they wished, attend classes as they pleased, and read and discuss ideas with anyone they pleased. Their work was evaluated by comprehensive examinations at the end of each year.

A number of departments began to offer tutorials and honors programs for their majors: Biological Sciences, Education, English, Germanic Languages, History, Mining and Metallurgy, Philosophy, Physics, Political Science, Psychology, Romance Languages, and a general Social Sciences major. Social Sciences proved to be the most popular. The plan attracted the attention of the Rockefeller Foundation's General Education Board, which allotted $159,000 in support over a period of nine years. In the early years, when the plan was limited to upper division students, only thirty-nine students were graduated under the plan over a period of six years. But by 1935, when the plan had been extended to lower division students as well, 465 of the 3157 undergraduates at Stanford were working under independent study; it had attracted nearly one-seventh of all undergraduate students, many of whom went on to graduate work.

Terman dreamed of an endowed university that would concentrate its efforts on a handpicked group of gifted students, taxing itself to support fundamental research on the needs and achievements of such students (Terman, 1939c; Terman unpublished 1940c). But the demands of World War II on faculty and students, together with the withdrawal of foundation grants in 1940, put an abrupt end to the Independent Study Plan in its original form, although it was revived after the War in modified form.

Through all the research summaries and interpretations, Terman's point of view on the gifted and their education emerges (Terman, 1914g; 1931d; 1933a; 1950b; 1953a; 1954b; 1956b; 1958; Terman unpublished, 1947).

First of all, Terman defined the gifted as the upper end of the normal distribution of intelligence, the top one percent in ability to acquire and manipulate concepts. He differentiated giftedness from talent or specialized ability in a limited field; talent promises unusual productivity only if it is combined with giftedness (Terman, 1953d). And he distinguished both giftedness and talent from creativity, a personality factor independent of both. Lack of precision in defining the three terms later led to a good deal of confusion in professional groups (Albert, 1969).

Terman thought that the gifted should be identified in childhood, given guidance in finding and developing their talents, encouraged to learn the art of problem-solving, and helped to become creative. Only with such help and guidance would they become adults who would implement major innovations on behalf of society. He once told a seminar that the gifted should learn to see a problem where no one else had seen it; to develop hunches about how it could be resolved; to devise ingenious ways of checking out whether each hunch was right; and to be unbiased enough to weigh the pros and cons carefully before publicizing a discovery. It was a rigorous demand.

In the second place, Terman talked constantly of the social importance of developing the talents of the gifted on behalf of society as a whole. In the usual educational system, he claimed, the intelligence of the nation is squandered, because of popular compassion for the fellow at the foot and an assumption that the foremost could take care of himself. Instead, true democracy means a shift from providing the same education for all to an emphasis on equality of opportunity, to enable every individual to develop to the fullest extent of his potential, including the gifted. Such a change, Terman claimed, was essential to the welfare of society as a whole.

In addition, the gifted should be permitted to develop in whatever direction their talents and interests dictated, and not forced into a narrow mold set by society. They may find solutions society had not envisioned. Individuals of superior ability in all fields should be treated alike and encouraged equally as a long-range policy. In an article written before his death in 1956, but published in 1958 shortly after Sputnik, Terman wrote prophetically:

> The current *Zeitgeist*, under the influence of the cold war, is pointing up the need for many more scientists and engineers than we have, with the result that a desperate effort is being made to increase their number. Granted the great need for such increase, that fact should not lead to the neglect of other kinds of talent. What I propose is that education of the gifted should be planned not merely to satisfy the felt needs of a given time but also to prepare the way for future appreciation of needs not yet recognized. By encouraging the development of all kinds of special talent and of aptitude for every kind of leadership and scholarly achievement, the *Zeitgeist* itself would, in time, be molded along more liberal lines and to the appreciation of whatever enlarges the spirit of men (Terman, 1958, p. 17).

He urged understanding of the gifted as human beings, pointing out clear evidence of a popular prejudice against the gifted. Parents consider them difficult to rear. Teachers are pleased to have bright children in their classes, but when a child is so superior as to be termed *gifted*, they are not so sure: such students ask questions, disrupt class routine, and demand logic and pertinence. College students think of the gifted as "grinds," "bookworms," and "egg-heads," and recommend that they scale their efforts down to the gentlemen's standard of mediocrity. The gifted learn to hide their abilities for the sake of social acceptance; the more gifted the student, the greater the problem he meets in finding such acceptance (Terman, 1927b; 1942a; 1944b). Perhaps the prejudice is a defense against the different, particularly the potentially stronger; perhaps it rests on each individual's sense that his own possibilities are un-limited, despite his limited abilities. At any rate, Terman did much to show the fallacy of the stereotype that the gifted are odd in a less than desirable way. But he pointed out that emotional acceptance is something else. Only when people meet gifted children face to face can their social value be demonstrated and social prejudices lessened.

In the third place, the gifted child should be identified as early as possible—certainly not later than the first two or three years of schooling. Systematic screening should take place in schools through teacher nomination and group testing. This should be followed by individual testing on a measure stressing concept formation, as well as by a full case study. Early identification of gifted children would permit acceleration in the early grades and better planning for their total education.

In the fourth place, the gifted should receive systematically differentiated instruction throughout school, because their way of learning is different. Although the objectives for the gifted are the same as for other children, the ways of meeting them differ. The gifted need an emphasis on creativity, intellectual initiative, critical thinking, social adjustment, responsibility, and unselfish leadership. They need instruction through concepts and principles rather than through concrete facts. They often learn inductively rather than deductively. They respond on the basis of logic and reason, not social custom. They should have a maximum of new ideas, a mini-mum of review and drill. They work best independently, with self-direction rather than constant supervision, but with continuing understanding support. They need to build self-confidence and a desire to excel. They should associate with other gifted children to extend their horizons and to identify with those who share their kind of difference, as a bridge to understanding people of all sorts. They need to associate with older children and adults to find others with their interests, but they need also to play with children of their own age.

Parents should see to it that the gifted child spends ten to twenty hours a week in play with other children (Terman unpublished, 1947; 1948a). They should not overpraise him for what he does, but neither should they belittle him. Calling attention to his difference through any sort of publicity should be avoided. The gifted child should be taught to judge himself in terms of his own high standard, not the standards of other children. He should learn habits of industry, including home duties, early to keep him profitably employed. Parents should undertake no early intensive training. Instead, the child should be given information and help when he asks for it, even if it means that the parents must look up the answers. He should be encouraged to develop hobbies and should have access to the best books in great variety. He should not be pressured into an early choice of vocation, for he is versatile, his interests change rapidly, and the educational road ahead is long.

For the highly gifted, the need for differentiated instruction is particularly acute. They need an even higher level of concept impact, still more independence, and still more help in social adjustment. Yet for the normal child to receive such instruction would be disastrous. He needs many of the same things, but with a different approach. Too often high schools in particular become class schools, failing to serve the less academic half of the population while shaping the curriculum for the college-bound. Or they apply to all an idea useful for a small number of students. Instead, each child's instruction must fit his talents and needs. The gifted are no exception.

In the fifth place, administrative organization for teaching the gifted should be adapted to conditions in the school system as a whole. In small districts, a special teacher might be employed to help identify the gifted and set up individual programs, providing extra materials, assisting teachers, planning field trips, and discussing individual projects. But when the size of the district permits, some form of grouping or special class is the best way of meeting the needs of the gifted.

Acceleration is one of the most common ways to meet the needs of able students. The gifted child who is reasonably mature personally and well adjusted socially may well skip from one to three years before completing high school; he may well drop two or more additional years between his freshman year in college and his doctorate. Such acceleration adds from one to five years to the individual's productive life. Yet the gifted are seldom accelerated as much as they should be.

Enrichment is desirable as well, but it is very difficult to provide appropriately. Teachers should be alerted to the need for special assignments for the gifted; they should be instructed in the kinds of enrichment desirable. Specially-trained supervising teachers are essential to aid the classroom teacher in meeting the variety of demands gifted children make. Standard enrichment units imposed on the child seldom capture his interest or meet his individual needs. Instead, a program must be designed around the needs and concerns of each gifted child.

At their best, special classes are very good indeed for the gifted. For the highly gifted they are essential, no matter how much acceleration or enrichment may be available. In special classes, the gifted find their first real intellectual competition, lose any conceit they may have developed, and learn to adapt to others through identification with those who are like themselves. The regular classroom benefits from removal of the child who seems to have too many of the answers first. Though special schools are possible in large cities, special classes have many of the same advantages, together with ready access to other kinds of children. Special classes should be established wherever it is possible.

Special classes were popular during the 1920s, but they were largely abandoned during the 1930s under the pressure for reducing school costs during the Great Depression and during the subsequent egalitarian thrust. Small classes, modified programs, and supervision are expensive. And the perennial nature-nuture controversy discouraged any special provisions. Yet in the late 1940s and early 1950s, interest reawakened, even before the advent of Sputnik and the intensification of the Cold War. Through all the years, however, Terman's philosophy of maximizing the use of all kinds of talent remained firm. He repeatedly asserted that it is no more undemocratic to maintain special classes for the intellectually gifted than to provide coaching staffs for the physically gifted.

Finally, Terman believed that teachers need special training to work with gifted children. They must know how the learning of the gifted child differs, how to individualize instruction, what kind of discipline is appropriate, how to find materials and special opportunities, how to modify the curriculum, and how to stimulate interest and independent problem-solving. Such teaching is not easy.

Like other deviants, the gifted need more adequate counseling than the normal. In addition, because of their versatility, the gifted face more varied and complex choices. Their place in school and in

105

society is not ready-made; it must be carved out. As a result, some of the gifted settle for mediocre and perhaps comfortable lives. The sensitivity of the gifted to social rejection requires greater than usual adult support until they attain a high degree of self-reliance.

This, then, was Terman's vision for the gifted. In a century concerned strongly with the care of the weak and the welfare of the common man, he turned resolutely to the positive side of man's existence.

CHAPTER VIII

The Fruits of Eminence

For certainly it must be admitted that no final answer to the nature-nurture question has been attained or even approximated. The most that can be justly claimed is that the bounds of our knowledge have been in some measure extended. . . . It is conceivable that the elusive nature of the problem is such as to preclude for a long time to come, if not forever, a complete and final solution (Terman, 1928e, p. 6).

THE 1920s were perhaps the busiest years of Terman's life. He launched his major study of the gifted, built the Department of Psychology to national prominence, served as president of the American Psychological Association, and met the nature-nurture challenges of Bagley, Lippmann, and the National Association for the Study of Education. It was a grueling pace.

If Terman was restless at Stanford on his return from the war years in Washington, it was only because his own renewed identification with psychology on a national level was not fully matched in his professorship in Education at Stanford. But he was optimistic about the future at Stanford, and he was recognized and appreciated by his colleagues.

With his growing prominence, Terman was inevitably sounded out on other positions. In 1920, he was particularly interested in an inquiry from the University of Minnesota, asking him to consider directing the Department of Educational Psychology there. Terman replied that his decision would depend on the financial support for the department and on its relationship with the Department of Education. He suggested that Education and Educational Psychology might well be united under a single administrative head, though any such organization must consider educational psychology as a branch of psychology as valid as any other subdivision of that field. In 1921 he declined, saying that the outlook at Stanford itself was growing ever better—that his long-cherished plan for close liaison between education and psychology might well be realized there, in a reorganization similar to that at Minnesota, Columbia, Chicago, and Ohio State. In 1922 he declined a similar invitation from New York University, saying that it was very doubtful that he would ever leave Stanford.

Then came Terman's great opportunity. Frank Angell, chairman of the Department of Psychology at Stanford, retired in 1922. Angell was an introspectionist, a follower of Titchener, and an advocate of the "brass instrument" psychology with which Terman felt inept and which he considered unpromising for psychology as a science. The Psychology Department at Stanford was moribund: only one Ph.D. has been granted in all of Angell's thirty years as chairman. The departments of Psychology and Education had no common interests and little more than a speaking relationship. The liberal Terman thought Angell incompetent if not reactionary, which students agreed he was, and criticized the direction of the whole effort in the Department of Psychology as hopelessly wrong.

On Angell's retirement in August, 1922, President Ray Lyman Wilbur of Stanford did the unexpected; he moved Terman from Education to the chairmanship of the Department of Psychology. Although Terman had known that Angell was due to retire, his own appointment came without warning. He had not even been asked whether he would accept the assignment; one day he simply received a note through the mails from President Wilbur notifying him of the appointment. Terman had no administrative ambition and found administrative work somewhat of a chore, although he did it exceptionally well. He had no thought of himself as potential successor to Angell and had not run any kind of undercover campaign that would encourage the lightning to strike him.

Terman wondered how the faculty of Psychology would react to his appointment; he heard only positive comments, but had doubts about their completeness. For himself, he was delighted with the open recognition of his worth as a psychologist, and with the chance to remodel the program in Psychology to his own liking.

The first business was to establish a satisfactory relationship between the departments of Psychology and Education. Terman retained his title as Professor of Education along with his new title of Professor of Psychology. Appropriate courses were cross-listed in both departments. Truman Kelley in Education and Maud Merrill in Psychology were given joint titles similar to Terman's. It became possible for a student to obtain a graduate degree in educational psychology in either the Department of Psychology or the Department of Education, although after 1922 all were in the Department of Psychology except four M.A. and two Ph.D. degrees in educational psychology, chaired by Terman. The joint arrangement worked well.

Terman's second step was to remodel the Department of Psychology. He had a rare opportunity, for Thomas Welton Stanford had just left half a million dollars to Stanford. Thomas Welton Stanford was Leland Stanford's younger brother, who had gone to Australia as a young man and achieved considerable wealth from sheep ranches and agencies for oil. He had become interested in spiritualism and, since he was a childless widower, had originally planned to leave most of his fortune to Stanford University for "psychical studies." However, David Starr Jordan, Stanford's first president, persuaded T. W. Stanford to modify his will by inserting the phrase "and psychological" after the word "psychical." Thus money became available to develop a Department of Psychology.

There were two gifts in the T. W. Stanford bequest. The psychic research fellowship funds went first to J. E. Coover, already on the Stanford staff, who devoted part of his time to the subject. Coover's approach was conservative; ghosts must clearly indicate their presence before they would be recognized. The result of Coover's studies was a voluminous book on the research; it was clearly critical of the evidence and, in agreement with Terman, of the emerging studies of extrasensory perception as well. In the years since Coover's retirement, the funds have supported an intermittent series of short-term appointments of fellows and visiting scholars concerned with such matters.

The second and larger portion of the T. W. Stanford gift was designated for psychic *or* psychological research. President Wilbur allotted the entire fund to the Department of Psychology, to the distress of many parapsychologists. Though Thomas Welton Stanford had died in 1918, the money from his estate was not transferred to the United States until about 1922. Ostensibly, this was because of an unfavorable exchange situation immediately after World War I in transferring money from Australia to the United States; but according to conjecture, it may have been because President Wilbur wanted the funds to go to a new chairman rather than to Angell in expanding the Department of Psychology. Thus the foundation was laid for converting one of Stanford's weakest departments into what, in another decade, became one of its strongest. A $600,000 endowment would accomplish a lot at a time when $5000 was an excellent salary for a full professor.

Terman's initial staff, appointed during Angell's chairmanship, consisted of himself, Coover, and Maud Merrill (James) from the Psychology faculty, and Truman Kelley, whom he brought in from Education. To these he added Walter Miles in experimental psychology, Calvin Stone in animal psychology, Edward K. Strong in vocational psychology, and the young Paul Farnsworth, whose interest was aesthetics, but who as a beginner was assigned to teach whatever the older men did not want to each. That included the introductory courses, social psychology, modern viewpoints, and supervision of the laboratory. As time went on, Farnsworth managed to squeeze in classes in experimental aesthetics, where his research enthusiasm lay. At the time, experimental aesthetics was on the very fringe of psychology,. while experimental, animal, and vocational psychology were central.

Terman was as proud of his near-misses as of his appointments. He tried to persuade E. G. Boring to join him at Stanford, but Boring chose what he considered the more difficult position at Harvard. He barely missed getting Karl Lashley in the latter's early years. He wanted the best in his appointments; his tolerant appreciation of scholarship and his zeal for excellence drew such men to him, and then his permissive democracy led them to flower. His strategy was strangely like his son's later policy in a similar situation, building what his son called "steeples of eminence" around which the instruction in all fields might be upgraded.

In retrospect, Terman discussed his strategy in building the department in a letter to Don Marquis, who was faced with a similar situation in 1945. Terman felt he had been successful in building a strong department within five years because he started almost from scratch, and because he sought only the best of young psychologists for his faculty. As for endowment and research funds, they were secondary. A staff of the highest caliber was the most important requisite for building eminence.

As an administrator, Terman created an atmosphere in which personal relationships were good and work of a high level was accomplished. On his retirement in 1942, he wrote President Wilbur that the basic traditions he had tried to establish were to recruit the ablest appointees available, to use democratic administrative procedures, to encourage teamwork, to foster close relationships with other departments, and to guarantee academic freedom combined with personal responsibility. All these things he did quietly and unobtrusively. Terman came to his office at ten each morning, spent half an hour with his secretary, had half an hour free for appointments with students and staff, taught a seminar at eleven, and left at noon. That was the only visible aspect of his administration. In the afternoons he did a certain amount of committee work or consulted with administrative officers on matters such as admission testing or the Independent Study Program for able students. The rest of his time was devoted to his research, done largely at home.

Under Terman's direction, the Department of Psychology at Stanford quickly assumed a position of national leadership in psychology. Terman commented:

> Although I dislike doing work of an administrative nature, I think that nothing I have accomplished has given me a stronger or juster sense of pride than my part in helping to build up an outstanding department at Stanford (Terman, 1932f, p. 326).

His pride was justified. Between 1909 and 1918, Stanford had ranked last among the sixteen universities offering the doctorate in psychology. By 1925—three years after Terman assumed the Chairmanship— it was rated seventh among those in the United States by the Committee on Graduate Education of the American Council on Education. It received the highest rating of any of the sixteen Stanford departments on the same report. In the Kenniston ratings, made in 1957, Stanford's Psychology Department was ranked fifth in the country, again the highest rating received by any department at Stanford. In the American Council on Education's rankings of 1964, Psychology at Stanford rated second in the country, tying Electrical Engineering as the highest-ranked Stanford department. The momentum gained in the first three years of Terman's administration has been sustained; and his wisdom may have rubbed off on his son, who made a parallel administrative contribution to Electrical Engineering, first as dean, and later as provost of the university.

Evidence of the quality of faculty and students in Psychology under Terman's chairmanship is found in the number later elected president of the American Psychological Association. Three of the fifty-five Ph.D. degrees granted during that period led to that office (E. L. Kelly, 1955; H. F. Harlow, 1958; and Quinn McNemar, 1964). Three other students who began their work at Stanford but took doctorate degrees in psychology elsewhere might well be added to

111

the list (D. G. Marquis, 1948; R. R. Sears, 1951; and Neal Miller, 1971). In addition, three members of the Stanford faculty selected by Terman achieved the same honor (W. R. Miles, 1932; C. P. Stone, 1942; and E. R. Hilgard, 1949). All these followed in the steps of Terman's two mentors (G. Stanley Hall, 1892 and 1924; and E. C. Sanford, 1902) and of his two closest professional friends (R. M. Yerkes, 1917; and E. G. Boring, 1928), as well as of Terman himself (1923). Since Terman's own election, no decade has been without a president whose life was touched by Terman's at Stanford, and three decades have seen three or four such selections. It is a proud record.

With his chairmanship, Terman continued his activities in national organizations. He had been made psychological representative of the Division of Anthropology and Psychology of the National Research Council in 1919; he had been invited to membership in the Eugenic Research Association in 1920; he joined the International Council for the Education of Exceptional Children in 1923, and became a member of the Advisory Council for the Eugenic Committee of the United States in 1924. He continued to be active in the Association for Child Health; the sage nature of his advice is illustrated by an interchange with that organization's leadership in 1925. Terman opposed plans for an international conference designed to strip psychoanalysis of its aura of omniscience. Terman argued that it would be poor Freudian psychology to repress any tendency, that the degree of truth in psychoanalysis would gradually become apparent, and that to start a fight would certainly mess things up and might injure psychology as a science.

Terman had joined the American Psychological Association in 1917, during his war service; he had been elected to its council for the term 1919-21. In 1923 he was elected president. Psychologists who had worked with him liked him and respected his ability. His shift from the periphery to the center of American psychology was complete.

His election as president was one of the highlights of Terman's life. He had never been a joiner or convention-goer at heart, although he attended the meetings of educational organizations his professorship required and went to the more research-oriented psychological meetings by choice. In his early years, he had felt like an outcast among psychologists because of his practical point of view and his orientation toward education. Now he was welcomed in the company in which he felt he belonged. His election confirmed his eminence in psychology and made his sense of acceptance complete.

Terman's presidential address in 1923 clearly showed his orientation toward the applied in psychology, and particularly toward mental tests (Terman, 1924g). Historically, he pointed out, mental testing was an integral part of experimental psychology. The psychological test is a method of sampling mental processes, just as is any other method of psychological experimentation. Mental testing studies equally complex processes, and cannot be distinguished on either logical or psychological grounds from experimental psychology itself. Further, mental testing is central in the study of individual and race differences, the interrelation of mental traits, mental growth, the limits of educability, and the psychology of genius, mental retardation, and insanity. Such a method of psychological testing could even be used in the assessment of temperament and character. It permitted important new research, broadened and intensified public support, and attracted a host of new investigators.

His support of applied psychology as a field had already been expressed (Terman, 1921h). He produced evidence that at least half of American psychologists at that time were doing essentially applied work—a kind of work that had developed almost wholly since 1900. He predicted that standardized tests would exert a major influence on education, affecting not only pupil placement and instruction, but even educational aims (Terman, 1928g; 1931a). In an atmosphere of remote, theory-oriented endeavor in psychology, he pleaded for a return to people and their problems—in part for practical benefit, but even more as a way of pointing out new insights and new hypotheses for building viable psychological theory (Terman, 1924a).

Just before Terman assumed the presidency of the American Psychological Association, an outbreak of the perennial nature-nurture controversy occurred. Terman felt obliged to enter it, because of his impending office and his work with Army testing. Professor William C. Bagley of Columbia University, long a champion of the conservative point of view in education, had already disagreed with Galton's "fatalistic conclusion" that heredity is all-important. The publication of the Army test results in 1922 aroused Bagley's fear that the whole ideal of democracy might be threatened by the implications of the testing movement (Bagley, 1922). He did not deny differences in native mentality, but he claimed that test data such as the IQ could be significantly changed by social environment; he felt that native individual differences could be overcome and the functioning intelligence level raised through education. He saw himself as the champion of the common man, a rational equalitarian, and accused the hereditarians of being openly inhumane and blatantly antidemocratic.

Bagley's article provoked a controversy with a number of psychologists, including Terman (Terman, 1922g; 1922i). Except for what Terman called "one timid glance at reality" in granting differences in native ability, he accused Bagley of being guided wholly by sentiment and fighting a straw man. Psychologists had never suggested that native ability alone determined adult achievement. They proposed not an elitist educational system, but an individualized and adapted one. The published interchange between Bagley and Terman was short, but it created a continuing animosity which led to later revivals of the controversy and to mutual avoidance by the two men whenever possible.

In the fall of 1922, the battle moved to a larger theater. Walter Lippman published a series of six articles on mental testing in the *New Republic*, from October 25 to November 29 (Lippmann, 1922, series of six articles). Citing the Army results, Lippmann claimed that there was no evidence that such tests really measure intelligence or anything related to the problems of real life. They merely classified men for military service. Lippmann agreed that tests do identify a certain kind of ability, but to call that ability intelligence in the broad sense is absurd. The very process of group testing imposes conditions that blur the meaning of the tests; and though the results may show group differences, such generalizations should not be applied to individuals. Above all, the assumption that intelligence is fixed is wrong—it is not hereditary or unchangeable.

Tests were all right for classification in the Army or even in schools, according to Lippmann. But if the classification leads to categorization without a subsequent adaptation of instruction, such examinations become an "engine of cruelty," leading ultimately to a hereditary caste system. After all, he said, if intelligence is hereditary, its influence should diminish with common experience; but psychologists had demonstrated that this was not the case. Any claim to a heredity factor represented only a will to believe, not scientific truth.

In fact, Lippmann fulminated, the concept of a static IQ was a revival of the doctrine of predestination. The idea might lead to having psychologists decide who might go to college and who must go into manual trades. It was a new snobbery, a new chance for quackery in a field where quacks breed like rabbits..

In a postscript to his last article, Lippmann summarized his point of view. The idea that the intelligence of the nation is measured by the Army intelligence tests is without foundation. There was reason to hope that tests would prove of practical benefit to schools if they were administered with skepticism and sympathy. But there was a grave danger of abuse from tests if examiners were not purged of the fundamental assumption that tests measure an intelligence fixed by heredity. That concept was scientifically unsound and dangerous. The efforts of psychologists should be directed to preparing a multitude of specific tests for particular purposes, not to developing tests of so-called intelligence.

Of course Terman had to reply; he was incensed at the whole idea. He had little personal experience with the jungle of competitive society and its betrayal of social and ethical values. He had always been able to hold his own in a tolerant, understanding way when others differed. But this was too much. Here was a journalist who knew nothing about statistics or experimental procedure, daring to wipe the floor with a new psychological movement.

Terman's reply (Terman, 1922b) was a masterpiece of satire. He pointed out the impassioned tone of Lippmann's articles, denied that Lippmann had even a rudimentary knowledge of what the testers had done, and accused Lippmann of drawing the wrong deductions and presenting as facts ideas that had not been proved. Norms on the Army tests had been developed independently, not with reference to the Stanford Binet. Time limits affect results very little, as studies with unlimited time had shown. That the symmetrical distribution of the IQ is no proof of the measure's validity was true, but perfectly irrelevant. That tests would be useful in classifying school children but did not measure intelligence was possibly true, possibly not. That they would stamp a permanent sense of inferiority on the children could be true, but it was not. The argument about the inheritability of mental traits was difficult to prove; it was also destructive in that it pitted psychologist against psychologist, just as the controversy about evolution had pitted biologist against biologist. That intelligence tests do not measure pure intelligence is true: they measure native ability plus a variety of other factors. There was no final verdict yet on how much environment affects scores, though psychologists believe that native ability counts heavily.

That was Terman's only reply. Lippman returned to the assault for the final word (Lippmann, 1923). He admitted that he had an emotional complex about the whole business. He did not deny the existence of a hereditary factor in intelligence, but he did not believe that Terman had isolated one. Terman was insensitive to the importance of the early childhood years, and his claims were impudent, pretentious, and abusive of the scientific method. Still, mental testing might have a considerable future if it were approached with caution.

Terman's article triggered many congratulatory letters and comments in the press and from colleagues. They stated that what he did to his critic was "a sight," humorous instead of savagely cruel, but nonetheless calculated to give pain. The article was perfect in form, substance, and presentation; it should go to all those who dwell in darkness. He had laughed Lippmann out of court with his light, deadly cherubic charm and precise surgical skill. Just to look at Lippmann's mangled literary remains reminded his friends of school-days when a classmate got a well-deserved spanking. Terman was delighted.

The controversy brought forth one additional *New Republic* article, from Boring, who disagreed with both Lippman and Terman (E. G. Boring, 1923). Boring presented an operational view which was relatively new to psychologists at that time. This disagreement in no way lessened the long-standing friendship between Terman and Boring, though Terman never warmed to Boring's operational position.

The controversy was only beginning. The prestigious National Society for the Study of Education decided to devote its twenty-seventh yearbook to the nature-nurture issue; Terman was asked to chair the editorial committee. Reluctantly, he accepted. He issued a call for manuscripts, pointing out that no one really knew to what extent so-called intelligence scores were measures of achievement rather than intelligence, and citing studies supporting both sides of the issue (Terman, 1926i).

Selection of papers for the yearbook was based on the quality of the research and its relevance to the nature-nurture question (Terman, 1926h). Terman was carefully neutral in his editorship, and when the time came to present the yearbook at the annual meeting, he tried to avoid a place on the program, and even to avoid attending. He was overruled. Bagley was similarly reluctant to speak, but Terman urged him to remain on the program and to speak with whatever warmth he might wish, even though it was primarily a scientific discussion. Bagley agreed to some degree of objectivity despite his usual habit of injecting sentimental issues into educational discussions, and the meeting was arranged.

Terman's contributions to the yearbook were an introduction and an evaluation of the evidence presented (Terman, 1928d; 1928e). His conciliatory, practical point of view was apparent.

> The theoretical as well as the practical nature-nurture problem that faces us deals with human beings as they are—not as an experimenter might rear them in a nurture-proof laboratory. We are interested in the child or adult as he comes to us—with his unique complex of ancestry, associates, home training, schooling, and physical and moral attributes. We are interested, not in finding out how he would have developed if he had had no environment at all; rather we wish to discover whether or not he can be made a more intelligent individual or a more learned one by improving the conditions of his milieu within the limits found in reasonably good social communities. More generally, we wish to find the relative potency of all types of human endowment, and to know the limits placed upon achievement by endowment (Terman, 1928e, pp. 2-3).

Terman urged the reader to divest himself of emotional bias and predilection in order to consider the evidence. Terman felt personally that the yearbook contributed a mine of valuable information.

Terman tried to close his involvement with the controversy by resigning from the board of directors of the National Society for the Study of Education and turning back to his research. But the issue was as hardy as the doctrine of infant damnation. It surfaced again in a symposium on intelligence testing in 1939 (Terman, 1940b), in which six of seven contributors vigorously attacked the use of intelligence tests as measures of individual differences, citing them as a threat to the democratic ideal. The democratic ideal, Terman replied, can never alter the biological facts of individual variability, and the essence of democracy is that each person should have the maximum opportunity to develop his capacities, whatever they may be.

In 1939, too, the National Society for the Study of Education produced its thirty-ninth yearbook, again devoted to the nature-nurture issue. This time most of the studies came from the University of Iowa (Skeels, 1940; Stoddard and Wellman, 1940; Wellman, 1940). The contributors reported that institutionalized children adopted into superior homes gained significantly in IQ and came to resemble thier foster parents; that orphanage children who attended a preschool showed a permanent gain in IQ as a result; and that low-testing orphanage children placed with older feebleminded girls changed from apparent feeblemindedness to normalcy. The upshot was a theory of intelligence that permitted a large cumulative change in the child's degree of intelligence as a result of environmental factors.

Terman was asked to respond to the yearbook. After more than 100 hours spent reviewing the findings, he decided that the studies contained so many errors in experimental design that they were worthless. In the twelve years since the earlier yearbook, research methods had apparently regressed: he found careless formulation of problems, unsound technique in testing hypotheses, neglect of control groups, misinterpretation of data, and unwarranted conclusions (Terman, 1940c). The intelligence test data were not valid because comparisons were made between different tests at different ages, which were given with questionable rapport by inexperienced examiners, often at such an early age that any test was of doubtful validity. Sampling errors in choosing subjects were blatantly apparent. There was gross statistical blundering in a fanatical zeal to prove something; percentile scores rather than raw scores were correlated. The number of cases was inflated, and normal regression was neglected (McNemar, 1940). The evidence was bent and distorted toward a preconceived conclusion in the discussion, with bland disregard of published tables. The original scores were not published, so others could not verify the results. Only in Iowa could such things occur, said Terman.

As a matter of fact, Terman felt that the previous twelve years had weakened the case of the environmentalist, both through positive evidence of the importance of heredity and through bringing to light the errors of the environmentalists. Not that environment was negligible: intelligence tests had no meaning in cases of extreme deprivation or isolation from human contact. It was simply that environment had less effect on IQ than commonly thought, not only in his opinion, but also in that of the majority of American psychologists, according to Terman.

Further, it was an error to limit the nature-nurture controversy to studies of IQ constancy; the problem was much broader than that, and considerably different. Of course, there were numerous special abilities with little relation to general intelligence, but all the evidence pointed to an important general factor. Intelligence tests to measure that general factor predicted with moderate success the individual's ability to deal with the general culture. They had real utility even though they did not disclose the fundamental parameters of the mind-factor theorists.

The heat of Terman's feeling is clear in an unpublished manuscript prepared for the NSSE meeting (Terman unpublished, 1941a).
Terman quoted results from studies of animals, twins, foster children, and children attending preschools to further refute the Iowa
claims. The IQ could be lowered by many factors; the trouble was
to raise it.

It is true that Terman reacted very strongly to the Iowa claims.
He disliked controversies, and when he took a course of action
which was likely to get him into one, it was only because he felt very
strongly about the issues involved and believed he had an obligation
to be a spokesman for what he felt was right. He was sure that many
of the conclusions drawn were not substantiated by the background
data published currently; he felt obviously justified in raising serious
questions because of his earlier involvement. Perhaps, being human,
he over-reacted.

The reaction from Iowa was equally stormy. Terman's remarks
were intemperate, without any real justification, almost petulant.
The controversy smoldered, and continued to flare anew in succeeding decades.

Later, Terman took a similar point of view toward the work of
Allison Davis. Even more recently, since Terman's death, the racial
tensions of the late 1960s precipitated a whole new outbreak of the
controversy strangely reminiscent of earlier years. Arthur Jensen was
the psychologist at the eye of the storm this time, with his claim that
the variance in intelligence is about eighty percent hereditary in
nature, including differences of fifteen points in IQ between blacks
and whites (Jensen, 1968; 1969 (three articles)). Results of current
compensatory programs were showing little gain in IQ from intensive training. Jensen reviewed the pertinent material from genetics
and psychology, and then devised measures of various sorts of
learning ability. He found that associative learning of a relatively
rote nature is characteristic of the Negro child, whereas cognitive
or problem-solving learning is more often found in the white child.
Since the difference in learning style had developed through generations of separation, Jensen felt that difference should be reflected
in the way in which the two groups were taught in schools.

A tremendous outcry arose against Jensen. He, like Terman, was
accused of being antidemocratic, if not un-American and un-
Christian. Few psychologists and geneticists agreed with Jensen's
racial views. Many educators and members of the general public
accused him of making inappropriate generalizations and mathematical assumptions, limiting the size of his group of subjects,

119

advocating rote learning for some children when society can use few such individuals in its new technology, and ignoring the significance of infant training. The Society for the Psychological Study of Social Issues of the American Psychological Association even issued an official statement calling for alternative explanations of Jensen's findings (Albee, 1969). And personal harrassment of Jensen became so acute that, for a time, his college classes were shifted to unannounced places for his protection.

Jensen replied that all findings must be published, wherever the axe might fall—a contention in which he was supported by other academicians (Scriven, 1970). He replied to specific criticism, outlining areas of agreement and disagreement between the contenders and charging that the SPSSI statement was simply propaganda. He even analyzed a follow-up of the Skodak and Skeels data on adopted children (Jensen, 1973), applying his own genetic formulas and finding the results consistent with his own point of view.

Jensen contended that environment serves as a "threshold factor" essential for a hereditary tendency to develop. He pointed out the need to define the situation in which each competence can express itself, and then to recognize different needs by modifying teaching to fit each kind of learning style. Only then can learning be truly relevant (Cole and Bruner, 1971). Others suggested a critical look at the use of mental tests rather than an attack on them in toto. And sociologists and social psychologists defended the relationship between IQ and social structure, claiming that the racial differences were accounted for by such factors as family ideas about achievement, linguistic barriers, the mother's involvement in the community, the child's level of anxiety and familiarity with testing procedures, whether the family lived in a segregated or nonsegregated neighborhood, and the strength of family ties.

There was a major difference in emphasis, however, between the controversies in which Terman was involved and those surrounding Jensen. Terman spoke only of *individual* differences; Jensen discussed *individual and racial* differences. The major heat was generated over Jensen's racial emphasis, which, according to the evidence, the Terman of the 1940s and 1950s would not have supported.

In 1972, shortly before his death, Cyril Burt summed up the nature-nurture controversy by referring to current research on genetics, from the perspective of a Britisher watching the argument from a little distance (Burt, 1972). After a painstaking analysis of the data, he concluded:

120

The two main conclusions we have reached seem clear and beyond all question. The hypothesis of a general factor entering into every type of cognitive process, tentatively suggested by speculations derived from neurology and biology, is fully borne out by the statistical evidence: and the contention that the differences in this general factor depend largely on the individual's genetic constitution appears incontestable. The concept of an innate, general, cognitive ability, which follows from these two assumptions, though admittedly a sheer abstraction, is thus wholly consistent with the empirical facts (Burt, 1972, p. 188).

Terman would have applauded. A given genetic endowment is compatible with a whole range of developmental reactions and, consequently, of acquired attainments. All the endowment does is to set the limits of development and of achievement. The controversy had come full circle.

Through all the heat and lightning of succeeding tempests, Terman's basic point of view stands out clearly. He deplored most of the argument as fruitless—for when people get into the mysterious region of the mind, they believe that what they want to be true is true. His own thinking, defended courageously in his own era, began with individual differences.

Children, said Terman, are simply not all alike (Terman, 1924i). He had been a teacher. His own early work and that of his students had demonstrated some of the ways in which children differ. The sociologists and anthropologists who claimed that members of a single culture had little individuality were simply mistaken. Full recognition of cultural and educational influences need not blind anyone to the existence of large individual differences in intelligence and personality.

Therefore, the democratic ideal must make room for the fact of individual differences (Terman, 1934b; 1943a). As a liberal, Terman had a strong faith in the common people who, despite ignorance on specific issues, were more often right than Congress or the president. He opposed those who would have the nation run by an aristocracy of the intellectually able as trustees for the people. But democracy must square itself with the demonstrable facts of biological and psychological science. The idea that all are born biologically equal and should therefore have the same experiences, must be replaced by the notion that each individual is different, and that his environment should therefore be manipulated to recognize that uniqueness and bring it to its fullest fruition.

121

Further, intelligence tests measure one difference between individuals which is of great significance to society. Given environments that are fairly comparable, the ability represented in the IQ is reasonably constant; it predicts future behavior similar to that measured by the test with a small and known degree of error.

Because the IQ is relatively constant under a wide variety of life experiences, intelligence probably depends more on heredity than on environment (Terman, 1924a). Terman had been inclined toward environmentalism in his early work on *school health*, yet in his work on *intelligence testing*, he held to Galton's hereditary of view, and joined Goddard in his contention that feeblemindedness was a recessive Mendelian trait. Many of Terman's students—Kimball Young in particular—later differed and argued with him. Gross differences may have a biological foundation, said Young, but thought patterns, habits, and personality are acquired through social learning. Terman responded that they disagreed only on the question of balance and relative impact, and on the nature of the social learning. As the years went by, Terman's belief in the importance of heredity in explaining racial differences diminished, as he told his friend Paul Farnsworth, and as he wrote to Young only a year before his death.

Because intelligence is largely hereditary, Terman claimed, it was roughly reflected in social class structure. As a rule, brighter children came from homes higher on the educational, occupational, and economic ladder. Terman was concerned that, because there is a hereditary factor in intelligence and because less privileged social classes tend to have more children, the future of civilized nations of the present might be in doubt. Even the results of large testing studies in Scotland, which showed a slight rise in intelligence, he interpreted as meaning simply that students had become "testwise." In any case, the question of a national intelligence level was all a matter of inference.

Though Terman always emphasized the great overlap in scores between races, he clearly believed in 1932 that the evidence showed that whites were superior to blacks. In his autobiography, he stated one of his beliefs to be:

That the major differences between children of high and low IQ, and the major differences in the intelligence test scores of certain races as Negroes and whites, will never be fully accounted for on the environmental hypothesis (Terman, 1932f, p. 329).

Eleventh of fourteen children: Lewis as a young child.

At the time of entering Central Normal College at Danville: Lewis at 15.

Teacher of a one-room country school: Lewis at 17.

Five years of teaching and three baccalaureate degrees: Lewis at 20. A year later he entered Indiana University on his master's degree program.

The Ph.D. at Clark University completed in 1905 with a dissertation based on intelligence testing: Terman at 28. He went to California as principal of the San Bernardino High School.

Anna Minton became Mrs. Lewis Terman in 1899. She wanted for Lewis, then 22, what he wanted for himself.

In 1906 Terman became Professor of Psychology at what is now UCLA. He built a home for his family in the suburbs of Los Angeles, where they lived until he went to Stanford University in 1910. The children are Fred and Helen.

Major on the Surgeon-General's staff compiling the account of psychological testing in the army in 1918. Here Terman's lifelong friendships with Robert Yerkes and E. G. Boring began.

The psychologists who designed the Army Alpha and Army Beta tests at Vineland in 1917. *Upper, left to right:* Wells, Whipple, Yerkes, Bingham, Terman. *Lower, left to right:* Doll, Goddard, Haines.

Terman at his Stanford home in the 1920s. There he worked, gardened, golfed and held his seminars.

Anna Terman in the early Stanford years. She kept the home going and became prominent in the activities of faculty women.

Lewis and Anna Terman in mid-life.

The Stanford Psychology Department about 1930. *Upper, left to right:* Q. McNemar, M. M. James, E. K. Strong, Jr., P. R. Farnsworth, M. Campbell. *Middle, left to right:* K. Murray (secretary), R. T. Storey, C. C. Miles. *Lower, left to right:* W. R. Miles (succeeded by E. R. Hilgard), L. M. Terman, C. P. Stone, J. E. Coover.

Terman the eminent psychologist in the 1930s. Among other honors he held the Presidency of the American Psychological Association early in his career (following two of his teachers and preceding three of his colleagues and three of his doctoral students).

"If there's anything as nice as children, it's grandchildren." Lewis and Anna Terman in their later years. *Upper, left to right:* Terry Terman (grandson); Anna Terman; Fred W. Terman (grandson); Sibyl Terman (daughter-in-law); Fred E. Terman (son). *Lower, left to right:* Sally Briscoe (fiance of Fred W.); Lewis Terman; Lewis Terman II (grandson).

But in his personal copy of that article, there is a penciled circle around the mention of Negroes and whites, tied to notes in his handwriting in the margin and signed with his initials. The notes read, "I am less sure of this now (1951)!," and, "And still less sure in 1955!" He also wrote friends that, if his statement of belief had been written later, he would have omitted the dogmatic statement regarding the alleged inferiority of Negroes. Such was the measure of the man: he could be wrong and admit it. Though he still believed that an individual's potential is laid down largely by heredity, he had been convinced that if any racial differences exist at all in average hereditary potential, those differences are probably quite small. At any rate, each person should be judged as an individual and not by his race.

Most of all, Terman never regarded the nature-nurture controversy as closed. There were too many uncontrolled variables, too many emotional arguments, too little reason. The facts were simply not available, and the final solution would not come for a long time, if ever. The statement was prophetic.

During most of the tumultuous years of the 1920s Terman was well, but he was careful to use his energies economically. Though he claimed that he would like to travel, he found traveling more a chore than a pleasure. In particular, the long train ride across the United States wore him out, and he would usually return with a bad chest cold that would hang on for quite a while. As a consequence, he traveled less and less. Much later, after World War II, when one could travel easily by airplane, he made several trips east and found travel much less fatiguing. Nevertheless, he still stayed close to his hotel at night and tried to get plenty of rest.

When he was at home, Terman played golf fairly regularly at the country club and practiced on the putting green behind his home every day in good weather. His form was far from perfect—though he did once make a hole-in-one—but he was more interested in the exercise than in the game. He was not a sportsman, and was never intrigued by Stanford football or baseball contests.

He used his frailty as a defense against formal social obligations, and was seldom seen at purely social gatherings. He was embarrassed when the audience rose to applaud at professional meetings: his modesty disliked aclaim, although his need for acceptance clearly enjoyed it.

He declined invitations to teach at other universities, preferring the quiet, scholarly atmosphere of Stanford. He avoided demands he felt were a waste of time, even using a roundabout route to his second-floor office when he saw people conversing casually on his usual path. His achievement motivation made him utterly unwilling to waste a minute of time by getting caught up in what he would consider trivial. To some he seemed aloof, but to his freinds he was simply a man who wanted to control his own time and energy output.

Terman's sense of humor was strong, and at times unusual. When Marx brothers movies came to town, he would call Farnsworth to go with him to chuckle through them. He would even laugh at himself. Once, when he invited an ardently religious couple to dinner, he picked up a magazine of quite dirty cartoons that he claimed he could not understand and asked them for enlightenment. The couple went through agony trying to respond, and left convinced that Terman was an evil-minded old man. But Terman's eyes twinkled; he had only wanted answers.

With the advent of radio, he listened in his free time to news, Amos and Andy, and sometimes to music. When there was a prize-fight, he called men in the department to come over and listen to it with him. He did not care for bridge or other card games, and though he liked art he felt incompetent as either artist or critic. Most of all, Terman was a voracious reader. He bought all books of current general interest in addition to the professional publications, and there was always something at hand to read in case he had a moment of leisure.

He built a cabin among the redwoods in the mountains behind Stanford, about twenty miles away. There the family and lucky students broiled steaks and held picnics in youthful jubilation. He took groups of students with him to Carmel for an Easter work-vacation, and even dabbled in real estate investments there.

Anna continued to adapt to the life Terman was making for himself. She carried the burdens of household management, including gardening, with great efficiency. She handled the children; if they went to their father, he would only say, "Do what your mother says." She made it easy for Terman to hole up and work, a protection that helped him a great deal. She knew he needed rest, and could not be constantly interrupted. She took care of relationships with his Indiana relatives as well as her own, releasing him from family demands except for one memorable visit in 1926. On that visit he found his childhood haunts unchanged. Not a house had been repainted, but Campbell's pasture had succumbed to a housing development. And his former friends seemed terribly old.

Anna established more independence for herself as the children grew older. In her first ten years in the big house at Stanford, with two children living at home, she did all the housework. Yet she was so well-organized and efficient that one never had the feeling that she was tired. Then, for a few years, the only help she had was a Japanese cleaning boy who came in once a week. By the mid-1920s the Termans were in comfortable financial circumstances, the children were self-supporting, and Anna employed a live-in housekeeper. This gave her a degree of freedom she had never before possessed. At the same time, it released a great deal of energy for which she found a variety of outlets.

One of Anna's interests was travel. She made a trip about every second year to Indiana to visit her father, sister, niece, and nephews, as well as to visit the Terman clan, with whom she maintained close contact until she was in her seventies. Once or twice she picked up a car and drove it back to California alone; on one occasion she made a trip to Florida with her sister, just to see that part of the country. At another time, in the early 1930s, Terman was invited to an international congress in Copenhagen, but declined to attend. Anna decided that she would like to see Europe. She went alone by steamer through the Panama Canal, did quite a bit of sightseeing on the Continent and in England, and then attended the Copenhagen meeting as surrogate for her husband. There she renewed her acquaintance with the wives of psychologists she had known over the years and had a marvelous time.

Anna became increasingly involved in community affairs on the Stanford campus. She took a personal interest in the wives of the psychology students and was one of the founders of the Stanford Dames—a club for the wives of married students—and of the Stanford Mothers' Club. She helped run the annual rummage sale of the Senior Auxiliary of the Stanford Convalescent Home and was active in women's relief activities during the Great Depression. She made many close friends among the faculty wives and served a term as president of the Stanford Faculty Women's Club. She carried more than her share of the social responsibilities—not only for her family, but also among old friends, faculty wives, and graduate student wives.

Although she did not share her husband's professional and intellectual interests, Anna was an intelligent woman who established a place for herself among the women in the Stanford community. In addition, she was an important factor in Terman's successful career. She provided him with the working conditions he needed; looked after stray students and wives; and, through her social and service activities, extended his influence on the Stanford campus as a whole.

Meanwhile Helen, who characterized herself as the "uncertain" child, was establishing her own life. In 1925, after completing her degree at Stanford and teaching for a year, she married a budding young lawyer and moved to Los Angeles. She soon became the mother of Terman's two beloved granddaughters.

Fred, too, was establishing his independence. Terman was proud of Fred's scientific interest, and encouraged him to continue his explorations both in school and at home. Fred completed his work for the baccalaureate and for the E.E. degree at Stanford, and was ready for advanced graduate work.

The summer of 1922 illustrates the diversity of family life for the Termans at that time. Fred was off investigating the piling up of voltage on power lines in the Sacramento Valley. Anna spent nearly two months in Indiana visiting relatives. Helen was busy riding horses and hoeing potatoes on a ranch near San Luis Obispo. Terman was teaching and keeping his research moving at Stanford. Then, late in the summer, the family came together for their one major expedition since going to Stanford—a trip to Tahoe, Yosemite, and the Mariposa Big Trees. That was a critical summer, for it ended with Fred's departure for advanced graduate work at the Massachusetts Institute of Technology, a parting which gave his father quite a wrench.

Terman's health was good; finances were no longer a source of worry; Helen was establishing her own life; and Anna was enjoying a new independence. Fred went to the Massachusetts Institute of Technology in 1922, where he obtained the Sc.D. degree in electrical engineering in 1924, doing his dissertation with Vannevar Bush, later a leading figure in the national scientific research effort associated with World War II. In the spring of 1924, Fred accepted an appointment as instructor at MIT for the year 1924-25, and returned to Stanford to spend the summer with his family. Then the blow fell.

A few weeks after arriving home, Fred had a lung hemorrhage and was promptly put to bed. Within a few more weeks, he suffered a second hemorrhage; thereafter, he barely put his foot on the floor for a number of months. In time, his fever subsided and he began to gain weight, then to do a little work. But early in the spring of 1925, just as things were looking promising, he developed a tubercular appendix which ruptured and required a nasty operation. Again he pulled through and slowly regained his strength.

When Fred had arrived home in June 1924, the Electrical Engineering Department at Stanford had an unexpected vacancy, which was offered to him. In view of Fred's commitment to MIT, Stanford indicated a willingness to defer the appointment a year in the future. When MIT learned of Fred's illness, they also offered to postpone his arrival for a year. The result was that while ill, Fred had the comfort of having two attractive positions available upon recovery. As his illness progressed, he decided to decline the MIT position; like his father, he felt that his prospects for permanent recovery would be much better in California than in Massachusetts.

Because of the setback from his appendix, Fred was unable to undertake a full-time assignment at Stanford in 1925-26. Instead he arranged for half-time duty consisting of teaching one course each term at the graduate or advanced senior level, getting a research program started, and supervising three theses for the master's degree. During his two years of illness and convalescence he was able to read a great deal, particularly research that related the electrical circuit theory he had learned at MIT to what is now called electronics. From its origin in his early ham radio work, this interest had gained momentum from a very challenging summer job in 1923 at what is now the Bell Telephone Laboratories, and was reinforced further by the broadcasting boom that was just getting started. During the long period when he was bedridden, Fred amused himself by attempting to pick up broadcast stations from all over the country on an improvised homemade radio.

During Fred's illness, Anna dropped all her other activities to nurse him patiently and cheerfully, always confident of his ultimate recovery. When he was finally free of fever and able to do light work, she took a two-month vacation in Indiana. Terman spent some time in his mountain cabin and used other devices to escape the demands of casual summer session students. Though Fred's parents were still deeply concerned about his health, they were careful to avoid the worried parent act. He must have his independence.

In the spring of 1927, Fred met Sibyl Walcutt, a graduate student in psychology, and the two were married in 1928. Again his parents were accepting and approving, without any great fuss over the transition. Within the next few years, they welcomed Fred's three sons to the family circle.

Fred responded to his parents' supportive and nondemanding attitude by throwing himself into his work. He gained a reputation as a clear, well-organized lecturer, and began a program of research and publication that gained him eminence in his field. Early in his career, he prepared a textbook that became the leading text in his field for thirty years. He became an Assistant Professor in 1927, Associate Professor in 1930, and Professor and Executive Head of the Department of Electrical Engineering in 1937. Terman had every reason to be proud of his son.

The fruits of eminence were bittersweet. They held the final accolade his university could give in building a Department of Psychology to his own liking, and national recognition of the highest order. They held the controversy which such visibility invites. And they held deep anxiety in Fred's encounter with Terman's old illness.

CHAPTER IX

Pioneering in Personality Research

He sat toward the back of the room in an easy chair while a student presented his own experimental work, or reviewed a new book or a development in the field. He entered the discussion quietly, often warmly appreciative of an able job, but then raised a few trenchant questions that left no doubt of his skill, breadth of knowledge, and critical acumen. If the student was shoddy or in any sense bluffing, the ordeal could be a punishing one. Mrs. Terman usually invited a few of the students to dinner before the seminar, and both of the Termans soon were calling all of the graduate students by their first names, and taking a personal interest in their wives and children (Hilgard, 1957, p. 477).

B Y the late 1920s Terman's place in the history of psychology was assured. The department he headed was recognized as outstanding, and he was nationally and internationally recognized as a leading psychologist. Then illness again appeared, and he withdrew from such an active public life. He became once more the teacher and scholar, the pioneer at the frontiers of research.

In 1925, during Fred's illness, Terman had decided he should have a physical checkup himself. It included his first X-rays, which showed his lungs filled with scar tissue from past tubercular activity. In 1926 he suffered an attack of influenza; in 1927 a bout of pneumonia. When his doctor advised four months of bed rest Terman refused, saying that it would make him an invalid. Instead he stayed up, claiming he recovered faster that way. Then, in 1928, he had a light hemorrhage, without any elevation in temperature or positive sputum; it was diagnosed as a recurrence of the tuberculosis. Terman spent a week or two in bed, then gradually returned to his research.

The illnesses of 1926 to 1928 coincided with the first followup of the gifted group and with the preparation of the yearbook for the NSSE. Terman kept his research and writing going, but withdrew as completely as he could from traveling, which he found tiring, and from group activities that he found tiresome. At home he worked with his students and assistants, enjoyed his own circle of family and friends, or went into seclusion on the desert or elsewhere, as his health and work demanded.

In 1936, X-rays taken after a severe cold were interpreted as indicating renewed tubercular activity, so he entered a tuberculosis sanitarium for six weeks. He found the experience pleasant, the dry air bracing, the food superb, and the patients interesting and not too despondent. He was away from work only six weeks, but he again cancelled all organizational responsibilities.

Then, late one night in 1937 after working at his office, Terman stepped off the University's outer arcade ... into space. The result was a minor fracture, muscles and tendons that seemed to have gone through the third degree, and another beautiful rest combined with work.

In 1940, he encountered a new difficulty. His eyes were troubling him; their condition was likely to lead to cataracts. Golf, his favorite exercise, was out for the time being, for hitting the ball was no fun if he could not see where it went. His friend Yerkes advised him not to be too unhappy about things he could not help, but Terman accepted such simple advice only to the extent that it did not cut down his reading too much.

Fred was now married, and along with his son's growing success, Terman enjoyed his three grandsons and their apparent brightness and their interest in science. By the middle 1930s Helen had moved to Stanford following separation from her husband. There she obtained a position that quickly became administrative assistant to the director of women's housing, a position of responsibility that she held for many years until she took an early retirement in the 1960s. Terman enjoyed her two daughters, bright and full of initiative, climbing into bed with Anna in the mornings to learn the old songs from her. On holidays, Terman sent the girls rhyming telegrams, such as:

Nana's gone to Mexico
Where she hadn't ought to go.
Because they're having many quakes
And everything just shakes and shakes.
Merry Christmas!

In turn, his granddaughters loved their Daddy-Lew's sense of humor and searched for messages that might interest him. Small wonder that Terman felt that if there is anything as nice as children, it is grandchildren.

Meanwhile, Anna was traveling more and more. Terman approved her independence, as a part of his philosophy of individual self-fulfillment for every human being. Perhaps her more frequent travel was related also to rumors, common between 1925 and 1935, of Terman's relationships with other women. There was supposedly an affair with a very attractive young woman one summer, as well as two or three other liaisons. Terman's friends noticed that, instead of writing at home, he worked more and more in his office evenings and weekends. They mentioned the cabin in the hills, the outside entrance to his study at home, and his plan to build a new study in a Los Altos golf tract, where he would be pretty much secluded. Yet, to his friends, Terman's personal life was his own. They met inquiries with silence.

Gossip speculated widely on the cause for the alleged liaisons. Perhaps Terman's marital life was not entirely happy. His children were grown; but Helen had never shared his intellectual life, nor Fred his elfish humor. Anna was an exceptionally supportive wife, but she had never pretended to share his intellectual interests. His friends saw few hints of marital unhappiness, but only personal distance.

Or perhaps Terman was just a typical man of the midwestern culture from which he came. He had always professed a strong interest in sex, learned from his early farm years among neighbor boys for whom it was the prime quality in life. Perhaps he was itching a little. Sexual intercourse was a natural activity of man, and in a rich life it was to be promoted, provided harmful effects were avoided. Certainly extramarital affairs were common in the Stanford of the 1920s; with the number of women on campus limited to five hundred out of the thirty-five hundred students, sexual competition was exaggerated out of all proportion.

Or perhaps it was that Terman, a fundamentally shy person, found mature women who were intellectually stimulating to be particularly sexually attractive. His reserve meant relatively few close relationships, but he could really have those few in totality. His introversion, coupled with his need for closeness, in an atmosphere in which social restraints were loose and status and virility were closely bound together for the male—all made for such involvements.

Whatever the answer, Terman's professional productivity did not suffer. He was so work-oriented that he was never deeply involved with anyone other than Anna. Even his growing distance from Anna was more a withdrawal from a close relationship than an expression of a need to draw near to someone else. He wanted his time for his own work. If he became impatient with Anna, it was the same as becoming impatient with a caller who overstayed his allotted fifteen minutes.

At any rate, Terman confided in no one. Anna met the situation with tolerance and maturity. If their man's-work-woman's-work division of labor carried them apart, that was inevitable. When she sought out their mutual friends on her travels, Anna showed her loneliness only in an increased warmth and an apparent desire for closeness. She never complained or gossiped.

The early 1930s were busy years for Terman. The Psychology Department enrolled about twenty doctoral students, two to six of whom completed their degrees each year. To these students were added postdoctoral fellows, such as Keith Sward, who worked on the intellectual abilities of younger and older professors, and Harold Carter, who investigated the resemblance between identical twins in mental abilities and personality traits. It was a brilliant group.

Everyone wanted to take a class with Terman, and admission to his classes was highly restricted. Yet Terman's daytime seminars were casual, hardly systematic or textbookish. He liked to work with ideas that held psychology in a large setting, so students would ask questions and seek their own answers. At the first one or two meetings of a class, Terman would set the stage for the quarter by presenting a series of possible topics for reports and give any guidelines he thought necessary. He would ask each student to select a topic and arrange dates for reports. The class would then adjourn until the date of the first report. Terman knew he had good students, and he trusted them to educate themselves. The more rigid students were horrified by the apparent lack of prearranged organization, but the more self-directing found it highly stimulating. At any rate, Terman lectured only during summer sessions; he said simply, "The more experience I have with the pouring-in method, the less I think of it."

The class reports were prepared with care and presented with considerable tension. The quality of the papers was high. During the reports, Terman made occasional notes but offered no corrections. After the class, the student was invited to Termans office for private discussion—an illustration of Terman's sensitivity to people. Terman then corrected the pronunciation of technical terms and suggested other topics of interest.

The highlight of many a student's career, however, was Terman's Monday evening seminar in his home, reminiscent of that of G. Stanley Hall. Open on invitation only, the seminar was religiously attended by the entire faculty and by all graduate students in the Department of Psychology. The topics were varied, though usually related to one of Terman's wide-ranging interests. After the report, Terman was quick to express warm appreciation, or to rescue a novice whose work was criticized unduly by pointing out that the study was preliminary and basically sound. Because he valued originality, he was kinder to a student fumbling with a new idea than to one dealing meticulously or pedantically with a trivial concept.

Often Terman would invite the student who had reported to remain after the evening seminar for private criticism; he did that in the case of Lowell Kelly. Kelly had once hitchhiked from Greeley to Cheyenne in order to confer with Terman at a meeting; when Kelly explained that he had no money for graduate work at Stanford, Terman offered him a part-time research assistantship on the spot. In the private conference after Kelly's first seminar presentation, Terman turned to Kelly and said, "Lowell, your performance this evening was quite satisfactory—in fact from the substantive point of view it was superior. But where in the name of God did you learn to speak the English language the way you do? Your diction and grammar are atrocious, and to be a professor you will have to learn to talk respectable English." The effect on Kelly, who had grown up on a midwestern farm as Terman had, was profound. He began a valiant program to improve—talking to himself in the mirror, asking his fellow students to correct him when he made errors. At Kelly's second report for the seminar, Terman congratulated him on the improvement, but told him there was still a long way to go. Kelly kept at it, and in a few years overcame the handicap completely.

Those who wrote dissertations or books with Terman found his demands rigorous. Margaret Bennett, who taught an orientation course for freshman in 1922 while enrolled in independent study with Terman, wanted to incorporate her materials in a book. His reply was, "You are not yet ready to write, just keep going." A few years later she received a terse note: "Where is that manuscript?" Still later, when she found that someone else had published much of

133

the mimeographed material in her first draft, Terman replied laconically, "Just do it over again. You're bound to do a better job with extra effort."

Another student seemed unable to get his dissertation written. Terman told him that he should get out his materials and sit at a desk or table with them before him for an hour every day. He made the student promise that he would do that and nothing else during that hour each day. Within a month, the student brought in a finished document.

When Robert Bernreuter went to Hawaii for a year during his graduate work, he was determined to get his dissertation done during that time. Terman quietly told him that no graduate student had ever been able to meet Stanford's requirements while working away from the university. Bernreuter persisted, only to find on his return to Stanford that he must begin all over again. Terman told him, "Suppose Thorndike, Spearman, and Thurstone were here in the room with us. What do you think would be their evaluation of your work?"

And Lowell Kelly, who had planned a longitudinal study of marital happiness, was advised by Terman that it would take too long. He should choose a simpler, more restricted problem for his dissertation and save the marriage research for later. Kelly subsequently saw the wisdom of the advice.

Terman's standards for writing style were as demanding as those for research; in this he anticipated many of the principles later popularized by Rudolf Flesch. Of course a manuscript must be free of errors, whether statistical, spelling, typographical, punctuation, or grammar. Semicolons should not replace periods; commas should be used sparingly; the hyphen must be used accurately; "per cent" must be written out. Underscoring and parentheses within parentheses were forbidden. Sentences should be simple in structure; they should not begin with "but," "and," "with," "so," or "then," and they should not end with "however." The writer must find the most apt word, use the term "data" properly, and simplify his phraseology to make it less stuffy. Repetition of words and phrases must be eliminated. Length must be sacrificed to clarity and force, sometimes to the extent of deleting eighty or ninety percent of a manuscript. Curves must be trimmed and placed with statistics and supporting data in the appendix. Footnotes and bibliographical references must be consistent in form. Quotations must be kept to a minimum; the writer must use more of himself instead. Old material, fulsome praise, and exaggeration were equally forbidden.

But despite his rigor, Terman tried to avoid unnecessary detail in criticism, lest he destroy the original language of the author and risk mutilating his thought. For himself, Terman was impatient with what he considered his slow rate of writing; every time he picked up a chapter of his own, he wanted to rewrite it.

Yet Terman was far from rigid in the formalities of academic requirements. Whenever a student brought a registration form to him for signature, he carefully placed a blotter over the list of courses the student had selected. Any student who did not know what he needed to study was not worthy of being Terman's student. And when Lowell Kelly, who had a good background in Latin, Spanish, and French, failed his reading examination in French because of an error in interpreting a double negative, he went to Terman, who was the French examiner for students in psychology. Terman pulled out a volume of Binet from his bookshelf, opened it to the beginning of a chapter, and asked Kelly to translate. Kelly did so at sight, without error. Terman looked up and said, "You have just passed your French reading examination."

At the same time, Terman's intimacy with his students varied. Some relationships were formal, as in the case of John Kennedy. As a Fellow in Psychical Research, Kennedy found Terman friendly and thoughtful in listening to questions, but somewhat abrupt in making it plain when the student should depart and let Terman get back to work. With other students, the distance was temporary. When Miles Tinker arrived at Stanford he had been warned to expect a formal relationship, but the Termans soon called at the Tinkers' little apartment and the ice melted. Later, Tinker went on a work excursion to Carmel, where Terman loaned him money for a speeding ticket he had picked up on the way.

Students found Terman consistently sensitive and warmly helpful. When Anne Roe accompanied her first husband, Cecil Brolyer, to Stanford for his oral examinations in 1927, she became ill with brucellosis. The Termans took her in for the first few months of her nine-month illness. So it was with students; there was always someone who needed looking after.

Terman encouraged Curtis Merriman to take an assistantship with Cubberley, even though the tie between Terman and Merriman was close; later, Merriman treasured the memory of Terman's stopping to talk with him at a national meeting. On another occasion, when Terman overheard a student talking with his secretary about taking a drive to the redwoods, he stepped out of his office to offer the use of his own cabin for the weekend. And during Prohibition, when Terman stopped by his office with two bottles of wine after a visit to his bootlegger and found the wine leaking out on the table, he joined the laughter at a student who was lapping up the wine. Students stranded at the university over long holidays often found themselves quietly included in the Terman family celebration. So it went.

Even to the point of a change of name. Harry Harlow, born Harry Israel, had always been a maverick. Shortly before he finished his second graduate year, Terman called him to the office to say that the staff found Harry able, but he would never be able to speak effectively in public and should therefore seek work in a junior college instead of going on to the doctorate. But, according to Harlow, the junior colleges had standards, too; he failed to find a job, so he returned to Stanford. That fall in Terman's seminar, Harlow gave a thoughtful research report, then added a totally outrageous one all his own. Terman was entranced. He concluded that Harlow had the stamp of genius, and Harlow tried to live up to that designation.

After Harlow had received the Ph.D., Terman again called him in, this time to say that he should change his name. Terman had known anti-Semitism at Clark University: there, a fellow student named Josiah Moses had found no work for two years following his doctorate despite his obvious brilliance. But with his name changed to Josiah Morse, he had quickly obtained a university position and ultimately made *Who's Who in America*. Terman's sensitivity was heightened by the experience of Samuel Kohs in college work. Now here was Harry Israel—culturally a gentile, with less than one sixty-fourth Jewish ancestry, facing the strong anti-Jewish prejudice of the early 1930s.

Terman offered Harry an assistantship for the next year to tide him over until a better position could be found. As Harry left the office, the secretary handed him a telegram offering a position at the University of Wisconsin, which he immediately accepted. But ten days later, Terman again called Harry to the office, voiced his pleasure in the appointment, but said he still thought Harry should change his name. Harry asked Terman to name him. Terman suggested that he take some name that had been in his family, and Harry replied that either Harlow or Crowell would do nicely. Terman chose Harlow. Harlow claims that, as far as he knows, he is the only scientist ever named by the chairman of his major department.

136

Terman kept in touch with his students even when things went wrong. An able student who had been admitted despite a history of personal difficulties, and to whom Terman had even loaned money, was arrested for a series of crimes ranging from gambling and writing bad checks to burglary. The judge asked Terman for advice on the disposition of the case. Terman replied that he was unable to judge whether the man was responsible for his acts, but whatever the situation, the man should not be set free until his chances for rehabilitation could be assessed. More tersely, if the man were a psychiatric case, Terman felt he should be handled accordingly; if not, he should take his punishment.

For his students, Terman was a one-man placement and public relations officer, too. During the Great Depression, this quality was perhaps as responsible for the later successes of the psychology students from Stanford as the training they received there. Terman worked diligently in placing his students, and was critical of department heads at well-known institutions who made little effort to find jobs for the students they had trained. His efforts were so successful that often, after all his own students were placed, he would pass on his knowledge of remaining vacancies to friendly rivals.

As each student neared completion of his degree, Terman wrote to influential friends, discussing the good qualities of the candidate. He was especially helpful to women psychologists, for he felt they got the short end of things all along, from admission through graduate work and finding a position, to winning awards and offices. When a student took what Terman regarded as a dead-end job—as when Kelly went to the University of Hawaii, then small and remote—Terman warned him to consider the position temporary. He wrote to Kelly repeatedly, reminding him of the importance of returning to the mainland. Kelly left Hawaii for a year's fellowship in Europe, then went to Connecticut State College as department chairman.

Terman was tolerant and understanding with his students, accepting diversions from a vocational route or a research area with the attitude that unconventionality merely makes a person interesting. His students were young enough to afford a plunge off the beaten track. They could be specialists of a sort; after all, any graduate student had a divine right to great gaps of ignorance as long as he knew *something*, and knew it well. To those whose work he approved, he was helpful, appreciative, and sometimes lavish in praise. To those he disapproved, he could administer a rebuke in such a friendly, sympathetic way that it was accepted without resentment.

To his assistants he was particularly generous. They shared credit with him for the authorship of monographs, even if the publications represented work for which they had been paid. Terman was careful always to credit ideas to those who originated them.

Terman's dedication to work was a compulsive force, and it brought an underlying toughness and ambition to his work with students. He set the highest possible standards for himself and his associates. In the 1930s he was busy writing in his office many of the evenings, but never too busy to be interrupted for a few minutes by a student. His objectivity and experience counterbalanced their enthusiasm and naivete. He advised Kelly not to publish his early material on homosexuality until he became an established psychologist, lest the social bias against homosexuality interfer with his career. He complimented Don Marquis on finding a problem and staying with it rather than jumping from field to field. He had no faith in cooperative research among psychologists, thinking they did not work well in teams; instead, he advised getting together to talk over problems, and then going back to work alone.

He congratulated his students on their productivity and on the honors that came their way. He told professional acquaintances of the students' achievements and wrote letters of appreciation to those who helped his proteges. Many former students sent reprints of their publications to Terman routinely and stopped by Stanford for a visit when they were in the vicinity. When Kelly was elected president of the American Psychological Association, he made a beeline for a telephone to let Terman know. In return, Terman made a special effort to attend the national meeting to hear Kelly's presidential address in September, 1955, only a few months before Terman's death.

It is no wonder that graduate students almost universally loved Terman. He had tremendous faith in his students; he expected their best effort and got it. He transferred to them his own faith in the unique worth of every individual. He was proud of their careers and delighted with their devotion.

To these students and to many others who did not go so far as the doctorate, or for whose theses I was not primarily responsible, I am enormously indebted. All, in one way or another, have influenced my

138

interests, and some of them have led me to extensive modification of my views. I think I can truthfully say that I have always tried to encourage the graduate student to do his own thinking, and that, other things being equal, I remember with most satisfaction and gratitude those who held out most strongly for their opinions (Terman, 1932f, p. 328).

In addition to his teaching, Terman had the usual professional chores. He reviewed Kurt Lewin's work favorably (Terman, 1935f). He commended E. L. Thorndike's three-and-one-half-pound volume for its emphasis on the social significance of individual differences, though he differed with Thorndike's proposal for a benevolent aristocracy of the able (Terman, 1941b). He commended E. S. Conklin's book on adolescence as an extension of the work of G. Stanley Hall, but with a strong emphasis on research rather than on theoretical issues inaccessible to a scientific approach (Terman unpublished, 1935).

He wrote introductions to books on testing, statistics, individualization of instruction, higher education, the gifted, and personality (Terman, 1930a; 1930b; 1931b; 1932a; 1932b; 1935e; 1941a; 1942a; 1946a). He hosted such visiting professors as Kurt Lewin and John McGeoch. He served on faculty committees, such as one to find a successor to President Ray Lyman Wilbur. Terman found the first ch oices unavailable and the second ch oices wholly unexciting. It was too bad the Good Lord had not bestowed a brand on the type of person they were seeking.

He continued to bring in distinguished colleagues to the department, such as Ernest Hilgard. As an administrator Terman was easygoing, almost casual. He did not want to spend much time on routine, so he disposed of such matters quickly. In the sense of full faculty participation in all decisions, he was perhaps not a very democratic chairman. He held faculty meetings regularly, but increasingly delegated work to committees. He was careful not to infringe on the time of his newer colleagues. Occasionally his enthusiasm led him to make a decision alone, but that was not unusual in the college administration of that day. He was adamant in defending his colleagues and was a benevolent dictator dedicated to the welfare of his faculty.

Terman's correspondence with Robert Yerkes and Edwin G. Boring formed a deepening intellectual triangle. With Boring, the letters contained a wide-ranging discussion of common aspirations, ideas, and interests; they had an impersonal quality which Boring attributed to his own personality rather than to Terman's. In turn, Boring's devotion to Terman is apparent in the long, encouraging, and informative letters he dictated during his last illness as an aid in this biography.

With Yerkes the letters were more personal. The two men had worked together during World War I. Terman admired the psychological work Yerkes directed later at Yale, and still later in Florida. The letters ranged from discussions of promising young psychologists to mutual illnesses and family events to a discussion of the biographies they exchanged in support of their mutual enthusiasm. When Yerkes rambled too much, Terman warned him that he should spend his time on issues with which he was better acquainted. Yerkes had his own reciprocal warnings for Terman.

During the early 1930s, Terman supplied an autobiography for the Murchison series (Terman, 1932f). He found writing it a tremendously hard thing to do. Copy was delayed several times, by Anna's surgery, by his own illness, and by the pressure of preparing other documents. Perhaps his own reticence about himself and his perfectionistic demand for appropriate content and pleasing style also contributed to the delay.

Terman's enthusiasm for the biographical approach to psychology never wavered. He pointed out the importance of psychological-biographical study for historians, claiming that they deal with fundamentally the same concerns as psychologists in analyzing the causes and consequences of human behavior (Terman, 1941d). Terman taught a course in the psychology of biography; he was pleased when Robert Sears, who had taken the course as an undergraduate and found it dull, initiated his own at Yale. He wrote to others who made a similar effort. He followed the Murchison series, *History of Psychology in Autobiography*, with interest and care. He criticized his friends' contributions for failure to share personal reminiscences, or for revealing too much and being too self-centered. He even wished he could find time to write a book on the psychology of biography.

One section of Terman's autobiography is especially pertinent for the early 1930s. The editor had asked each contributor to state his position on psychological issues and movements then current, and Terman did so explicitly.

To begin with, Terman felt that mental testing was in its merest infancy—that it would mature within the next fifty years to include measurements of special abilities and personality. Children from kindergarten to the university would be subject to hours of testing;

public testing bureaus would be established for adults. In many of these predictions Terman's words proved prophetic, though psychology has gone through several "anti-testing" phases and will doubtless go through more.

Terman felt that testing would affect such social problems as the identification of delinquent and prepsychotic individuals, marital counseling, and even economic theory, industrial methods, politics, and the administration of the law. Today, industry uses tests, politics relies on public opinion polls, and the law admits testing in evaluating evidence, but Terman's broad prediction still lies in the future.

For the development of related fields, he gave other predictions. Psychiatry would not be "pulled out of the mire" until it required instruction in psychobiology, mentality and personality testing, and statistical methods. A new type of biographical literature would emerge, based on quantitative measures of ability, personality, interests, and attitudes. Psychology would become almost the sole basis for a science of education. Changes have occurred in the directions he predicted, but they are small. Psychiatry has admitted psychology as coworker in mental illness; education has admitted school psychologists for diagnostic functions; and psychobiography has formally arrived.

In psychology itself, Terman predicted that associationism had about run its course, that Watsonian psychology would finally be seen as a cult, and that emotional conditioning of infants was ridiculous as a theory. Introspection would never become obsolete regardless of the growth of objective psychology, Gestalt psychology was a wholesome influence, both in experimental work and in theory. Animal psychology was important because of its attack on problems closed to human experimentation. And Freudian concepts were one of the two most important contributions to modern psychology—along with mental testing. In such predictions, Terman showed his inductive and cognitive bias. The primitive associationism of Watson is gone, but operant conditioning thrives. Introspectionism is still in disrepute. Gestalt psychology has come and gone. But Terman was right in his prediction of the importance of animal experimentation, of aspects of the Freudian approach to psychotherapy, and of mental testing.

Terman gave some illuminating facts about himself in his autobiography as well. On the Goodwin Watson Test of Fair-Mindedness he rated as an extreme radical in his attitude toward the church and problems of social ethics, and as a liberal on political and economic issues. He was pessimistic about the trends in a democracy which endorsed prohibition and censorship. On the Strong Test of Vocational Interest he rated A— compared with psychologists and educators, B compared with personnel managers and journalists, and C compared with artists, chemists, engineers, architects, farmers, and salesmen. On his own test of mental masculinity and feminity he rated average for men. On the Bernreuter Personality Inventory he stood at the ninetieth percentile in introversion, at the thirtieth percentile in dominance. As for psychologists, he disliked those who exhibited overmuch zeal in defending their pet systems. His favorites of all time among psychologists were Galton, whose work he greatly admired, and Binet, whose originality, insight, open-mindedness, and rare charm shone through all his writings.

Terman was not content with teaching, administration, updating tests, and following the gifted. In his fifties, approaching the end of his career, he still had a tremendous creative urge. He expressed an interest in projective tests, in undertaking a series of studies on the last third of human life, in having a qualified person do a psychoanalytic study of Freud, in evaluating studies of feral children, in studying the sex life of apes in their natural habitat, and in studying identical twins reared apart in Communist Russia. He needed a new field for pioneering.

The study of psychological sex differences appealed to him. He had touched on developmental differences between boys and girls in his early work on child health, and in 1925 he was already working on a measure of masculinity-femininity. He hoped to find out, once he had such an instrument, how masculinity-femininity is affected by age and by physical maturing at adolescence; how it differs in opposite-sex siblings; how it relates to the cross-sex parent; how it is modified by the preponderance of women teachers in the early grades; and whether it distinguishes between the divorced and the happily married.

He reviewed the experimental findings on sex differences in the association of ideas (Terman, 1919d), concluding that women tend to be slightly more subjective and evaluative in response, whereas men are more objective and judgmental. He was quick to point out that such differences may well reflect social custom rather than innate tendencies.

By 1928, he had a preliminary form of his M-F test ready. In it were reflected the early "Plays and Games" questionnaire used with the gifted in 1922, as well as his review of the association of ideas and items based on the masculinity-femininity scale for the Strong Vocational Interest Test. He tried out the measure on a small sample of his gifted group and on fourteen homosexuals in a state prison.

After several years of intensive work with a number of groups totaling fifteen hundred subjects, and after two to three years of delay in getting the materials in form for publication, the results came out in *Sex and Personality*, coauthored by Catherine Cox Miles (Terman, 1936c). Terman first presented the test of psychological masculinity-feminity. The bulk of the volume then described relationships between the test and physical measurements, trait ratings, personality and achievement measures, age, education, intelligence, and occupation. The findings showed characteristic differences between the sexes, decreasing with age after maturity and with greater mental ability and education. Included were 134 cases of male homosexuality, which led to a tentative scale for measuring sexual inversion in males. Extensive case studies supported the Freudian doctrine of the Oedipus complex. Yet despite all his data, Terman was unable to decide whether sex differences were primarily the product of nature or nurture.

Reviewers credited the volume with reducing opinion to quantitative fact in a new field (Reuter, 1937; Wechsler, 1937). None challenged the validity of the data. But they did find the masses of facts without the structure of overall theory wearisome. The plethora of data, they said, would relieve investigators of glib and biased generalizations. They underlined Terman's caution that the scale should not be used by the uninformed because of the possibilities of misinterpretation.

Terman also published the results of a study of the validity of the M-F test (Terman, 1936a). He concluded that the individual student can shift his score enormously in either direction if he wishes to do so, and warned that subjects should not be aware of the purpose of the test if the results are to be valid.

True to his primary concern with individual differences, Terman also summarized the literature on physical and psychological sex differences in variational tendency (Terman, 1936d). He found girls more variable in physical measurements between ten and fourteen years of age, and males more variable in physical measurements beyond the age of fifteen. At all ages, males were more variable on tests of musical talent and of verbal intelligence. There were no apparent sex differences in physical measurements before the age of ten, or in artistic ability at any age.

Terman was critical of less careful work in the field, particularly that done with homosexuals (Terman unpublished, 1938). He criticized Kahn's book *Mentality and Homosexuality* as rambling, largely anecdotal, lacking a statistical base, containing errors in statistics and interpretation, naive in diagnosis and design, redundant, and ambiguous. In sum, it made no contribution to either the scientific or the practical aspects of homosexuality.

Terman summarized sex differences in social attitudes and emotionality, based on research ranging from laboratory studies and time sampling to clinical data (Terman, 1940f). He covered the scholarly literature from 1920 on sex differences in interests, personality, social behavior, and environmental influences (Terman, 1946b). And he aided and endorsed Leona Tyler's similar chapter for the next edition of Carmichael's *Manual of Child Psychology* eight years later (Terman, 1954c).

While his book on psychological sex differences was in its final stages, Terman launched another research project, the search for psychological and psychosexual correlates of marital happiness. Terman's interest in the study of sex had roots extending back to his childhood; it was reinforced by the work of Arthur Banta, a fellow student with Terman in an early one-room school, who had become a noted biologist. From his reading and his correspondence with Banta, Terman concluded that sex in mammals is determined by the sex chromosomes at conception, but that sexual development is affected by endocrine substances and by psychological and environmental factors.

Terman's choice of sex in marital happiness as a research field was doubtless affected also by Yerkes's chairmanship of the Commitee for Research on Problems of Sex of the National Research Council. The Council had given funds for Terman's research on psychological sex differences; now funds were available for his studies of marital happiness as well. In 1939, the first grant came for working up the marital happiness data on his-most recent followup of the gifted; after that he tailored successive new research proposals to fit both the topic and the source of funding.

For Terman was one of the earliest psychologists to seek and find large grants for research. Terman had always been a good businessman, canny in judging what was marketable in tests and books. Grantsmanship was simply good business in research.

Terman's first major grant of $45,000 had come for the study of the gifted in 1921. That and each succeeding grant was renewed and supplemented from time to time. Terman's files hold letters of solicitation to many agencies, including the California State Bureau of Juvenile Research, Carnegie Corporation, Columbia Foundation, Commonwealth Fund, Federal Inter-Departmental Social Hygiene Board, General Education Board, Haynes Foundation, Kellogg Foundation, Japanese-American Association, Josiah Macy Foundation, Laura Spelman Rockefeller Memorial Fund, Manpower Branch of the Office of Naval Research, National Institutes of Health, National Research Council, and the Rockefeller Foundation.

Terman's technique was impeccable. He kept a correspondence going with influential friends in key places. He kept a "hope" list of topics which might well be financed, including his own grants on the gifted, the revision of the Stanford Binet, and research in human development, child welfare, and later maturity. Every few months he reported to each donor on the progress of the funded study, mentioning previous grants in related fields, referring to friends doing similar research and their comments on the project, and offering to meet the donor to acquaint him with the aims and plans of the program. Terman often embedded a reference to the use of his own funds as well, for he characteristically declined all royalties and plowed the funds back into the research. He could thus point out that a grant would in no way obligate the donor for the future. He congratulated his influential friends on their achievement, thanked the foundations for their encouragement, sent small gifts and autographed copies of publications, and looked after donors and members of their families who found themselves at Stanford. All these relentless courtesies paved the way for grants and grant renewals.

Terman's interest in studying marital happiness had been intensified by his association with Lowell Kelly, who had wanted to explore marital happiness through a longitudinal study, but was dissuaded from using it as a problem for his dissertation. Kelly never regretted the postponement. He had planned to devote seven years to the project, but found himself summarizing the data not seven but thirty years later.

When the grant for Terman's study of marital happiness came through, Terman wrote Kelly a long letter. He had been certain that Kelly would find no academic opening during the depths of the Depression, so he had applied for funds with the hope that he could offer his former student an assistantship to tide him over until better placement was available. But Terman had not told Kelly of the application, for he knew the young man was attached to Stanford and might turn down other and possibly better offers elsewhere. Then Kelly went to Connecticut.

Terman was embarrassed that he had proposed and been funded for research in a field so close to Kelly's major interest. Terman suggested that Kelly either undertake a joint project with him at Stanford during the summers, or work independently on some preliminary phase with Terman during the year, and then apply for his own grant the following year. Terman would then drop his own research if Kelly wanted to reclaim the field as his own.

Kelly's feelings were mixed; he was naturally annoyed at not having been told of Terman's plans. But he made a counterproposal for a division of labor. Terman was to use his grant at Stanford for a short-term cross-sectional study involving a detailed comparison of happily and unhappily married couples. Kelly would plan his work around a longitudinal assessment of a large group of engaged couples, following them through several years of marriage. Terman accepted the proposal and, in the following year, helped Kelly secure a relatively large research grant. He specifically requested that Kelly's request be given priority over his own for more funds. From that point on, the studies continued in parallel, with occasional exchanges of letters.

From 1934 to 1937, Terman was hard at work on the data on marital compatibility. He found it a trying undertaking, possibly because of his health, possibly because of the sensitivity of the research field. He used a variety of tests to study 334 couples divorced for a three-year period and controls drawn from various clubs in the vicinity. He compared the 100 most happily married with the 100 least happily married couples. By 1935, he had a preliminary report ready (Terman, 1935c; 1935d). He found that age and the desire for children had little effect on marital happiness. Instead, the happily married seemed to have more outside interests in common, more agreement between husband and wife, more parental attachment, more emotional stability, more social adaptability, and greater conservatism. The unhappily maried were more often neurotic, introverted, and intolerant. Divorced women showed more self-reliance, independence, tolerance, and initiative than either the happily or unhappily married.

The major report, *Psychological Factors in Marital Happiness*, came out in 1938 (Terman, 1938b). It was based on a study of 792 married couples and covered personality, background, and sexual adjustment. Precautions were taken to assure the anonymity of subjects, and a scale for the prediction of marital happiness was drawn up. The most important predictor of marital happiness proved to be a combination of personality and background factors; sexual adjustment took a less prominent role. In happy marriages, the spouses came from happy childhoods, found partners of similar ability and of happy temperament, and formed marital relationships emphasizing tender intellectual and emotional qualities. Unhappy marriages reflected unhappy childhood and unhappy temperament; they were characterized by nagging, failing to show affection, selfishness, lack of consideration, touchiness, and quick temper. There was no evidence to support popular beliefs about early marriage, brief premarital acquaintance, petting in adolescence, inadequate sex instruction, income, religious training, or differences in age or education.

Reviews were cautiously accepting (Berle, 1939; Cottrell, 1939; Hollingworth, 1938; Klaiss, 1939). Reviewers agreed that the study was a pioneer research, a valuable addition to knowledge, rich in concrete findings and suggestions for further research, well done despite controversial points in design, clearly and concisely written. Yet they found it essentially atomistic in interpretation, with a tendency to joust with such "straw men" as social scientists and philosophers. But after all, the author was modest, claiming neither finality nor perfection. It was a major study, to be used with caution, but highly useful to those working with marriage research.

Terman took a careful second look at the validity of his data (Terman, 1939b). He went on to present a critical comment on six of the leading studies of factors influencing marital happiness, pointing out the need for joint approach by a number of disciplines (Terman, 1939d). And he found corroboration of his conclusions about sexual aspects of marital adjustment in the work of Carney Landis (Terman, 1941c) and in other studies in the field (Terman, 1939e; 1952).

When Kinsey published *Sexual Behavior in the Human Male*, Terman's criticism was scathing (Terman, 1948). Terman agreed on the importance of the topic and on the plethora of data, but that was about all. He claimed that Kinsey had inflated the number of cases, had misrepresented the work of others, and had authorized highly subjective interviews, loosely conducted by a carelessly selected staff, on content subject to errors of memory. Terman also stated that Kinsey's sampling was anything but random, that he was impervious to criticism and uncooperative when asked to describe his procedures, and that statistical expertise was lacking in the treatment of the data. Kinsey's sweeping factual statements, said Terman, were not facts but rather Kinsey's own subjective evaluations.

This was Terman the enthusiast speaking, from emotion as well as from his concern for careful research design in a field near his heart. It was the same emotion and concern that had reacted so strongly when his work on child health was attacked by medical and religious groups, and when his work on intelligence testing embroiled him in the Iowa controversy.

Terman continued his research on marital adjustment into his retirement. He summarized the data in the field (Terman, 1947c), and analyzed the validity of marriage prediction and marital adjustment tests and discussed the methodological questions involved (Terman, 1949c). He used the marital adjustment test in his 1950-51 follow-up of the gifted, for comparison with similar data gathered in 1940 (Terman, 1950a). In this way he found that the instrument predicted pending divorce, though not accurately enough to be used for individual prediction. He also pursued in painstaking fashion the question of sex in marriage, with a study of orgasm adequacy in wives (Terman, 1951a); he again concluded that sex is only one of many factors influencing marital happiness.

Terman also prepared other papers that did not find their way to publishers. He analyzed the problems in marriage research and presented a concise, well-organized review of findings in the field (Terman unpublished, 1946). And he reviewed the relationships among marital happiness, marital aptitude, and sex adjustment in a report for the American Association of Marriage Counselors (Terman unpublished, 1949).

On the whole, Terman was deeply disappointed with the reception both his M-F tests and his marriage studies received. The tests proved valuable chiefly in stimulating additional research by others. Yet Terman had pioneered in another field, and his contribution led to significant development in the area of marriage satisfaction. He could not foresee that his research lay in a field that was to be greatly affected by rapidly changing mores in marriage, divorce, and sexual adjustment, so that his techniques could only yield less than lasting results.

In the decade before his retirement, then, Terman developed two new research fields, psychological sex differences and marital compatibility. All his characteristic imagination, zeal, and creativity were harnessed in that effort to his expert knowledge and meticulous methodological rigor. His findings set the pace for research in those fields for a number of years following.

CHAPTER X

Public Affairs and the Social Conscience

Whether our new ballot is evasive of the main issue depends, I suppose, on what one conceives that to be. As I see it, the issue boils down pretty much to whether Hitler or Roosevelt is the greater menace to the future of this country. ... I can see only one answer to that question.

Perhaps the best we can do is to agree to disagree. The matter can rest there without affecting my personal feeling toward you. ... There is one thing, I am sure, on which we can agree; namely that the greatest peril that could confront a university would be the discouragement of free expression of opinion among the faculty. (Unpublished letter from Lewis M. Terman to President Ray Lyman Wilbur, October 15, 1941)*

T ERMAN'S concern for individuals reached out readily to embrace the problems of society. His rejection of anti-Semitism extended from Morse, Kohs, and Harlow to the University in Exile in the early years of Nazi influence. His zeal for school health reform stood firm before the League for Medical Freedom and the Church of Jesus Christ, Scientist. On the Goodwin Watson Test of Fair-Mindedness, Terman reported himself as scoring as an extreme radical on problems of social ethics, and as a liberal on political and economic issues. He was a social reformer, ready to battle for what he considered to be the right.

As his retirement approached and as the European situation became critical, Terman turned increasingly to larger social issues.

---

*Documents cited in Chapter X are in the personal files of Frederick E. Terman, through whose courtesy they were made available.

He sponsored the regional Council on Intolerance in America as well as the Consumer's Union. He had nothing but contempt for the Dies committee. He donated to the Spanish loyalist cause. He even sponsored a new civil liberties organization in San Francisco, until he learned it had been infiltrated by Communists; then he promptly resigned. Perhaps that is why he warned other psychologists to be careful what they sponsored (Terman unpublished, 1941). Each generation seems to enjoy its own particular variety of social neurosis. Terman would have none of it.

He enthusiastically supported his candidates in presidential elections, sometimes coming nearly to blows with his dearest friends. Though he always registered as a Republican, he voted for Wilson in 1912, Hoover in 1928, Roosevelt in 1932, 1936, and 1944, and Willkie in 1940. He favored Stassen or Vandenberg in 1948. Though at first he was eager to see Eisenhower nominated, he did a complete about-face before the convention and supported Stevenson. When Eisenhower ran again, Terman gathered statistics to show that Eisenhower would probably never finish his second term. For Truman and Nixon he had no use at all, though he respected Nixon's political skill.

Long before World War II came to Europe, Terman was concerned with the trend of events there. As early as 1934 he promoted the University in Exile, helping to bring to America able German psychologists like Kurt Lewin, whose work he found extraordinarily original and significant. And as early as 1940 he recorded his belief that the United States was headed for war with Germany within a year or two. He analyzed the basic social reasons leading to the war (Terman unpublished, 1942). Terman considered war to be the result of rapid progress in applied science, reflected in profound changes in industrial production and transport—all of which made ineffective the kind of democracy that worked smoothly in a nation of artisans and farmers. He thought the machinery of democracy should be altered so it would work in the new social milieu.

Terman was appalled by the ignorance of presumably intelligent persons about the critical European situation. In 1941, he suggested that the Fight for Freedom Committee appoint a group of scholars to compile a list of twelve to twenty books for Americans to read. Each reference would be briefly annotated, and the composite pamphlet of perhaps ten pages would be mailed to thousands of influential individuals and groups. Terman's list of books included Hitler's *Mein Kampf* and *My New Order*; Rausch-ning's *Voice of Destruction* and *Revolution of Nihilism*; Taylor's *Strategy of Terror*; Tolischus's *They Wanted War*; Miller's *You Can't Do Business With Hitler*; Shirer's *Berlin Diary*; Reimann's *Myth of the Total State*; Reveille's *Spoil of Europe*; Harch's *Pattern of Conquest*; and Stowe's *No Other Road to Freedom*. He urged more frank and forthright national leadership from a vacillating president (Terman unpublished, 1940) to stir the United States to a more positive effort.

In the latter half of 1941, a year before his retirement, Terman spearheaded a movement at Stanford which illustrates his active concern and his astuteness in handling a critical social issue. During the summer of 1941, fifteen prominent Republicans, including Stanford Trustee Herbert Hoover and Stanford President Ray Lyman Wilbur, joined in the Alexandria Bay statement protesting that President Roosevelt's foreign policies were leading inevitably toward involvement of the United States in the European conflict.

Terman believed that full participation in the war was the only way of preserving the American system; he had committed himself to this view in a paper he had circulated (Terman unpublished, 1940a). Late in the summer of 1941, several members of the Stanford faculty became concerned that the signatures of Hoover and Wilbur to the Alexandria Bay statement might give Stanford an isolationist image in the public mind. They prepared a statement on foreign policy to correct that impression and circulated it to the academic faculty for approval or disapproval. The statement read as follows.

Stanford University
August 21, 1941

We whose names appear below have prepared the accompanying statement on OUR NATION'S FOREIGN POLICY for submission to members of the Stanford faculty. In taking this step we have been influenced by the patently increasing confusion of thought in regard to the nature and meaning of the present world conflict and by the evidence that Germany's attack on Russia is having some of its intended effect in the promotion of doubt and disunity. The issues involved are so momentous and so fraught with possible tragedy that we think the time has come when all who believe that the future of our country is endangered by a policy of isolationism should say so publicly and emphatically. If the statement we have prepared expressed substantially or approximately the views you hold we respectfully urge that you give it your signature.

Eliot Blackwelder	*Albert Guérard*	*C. V. Taylor*
E. A. Cottrell	*Emile Holman*	*L. M. Terman*
Gordon Ferris	*Graham Stuart*	*David Webster*

OUR NATION'S FOREIGN POLICY

In the belief that the present international conflict seriously jeopardizes the future of our democracy unless unity of purpose and decision in action are achieved, we wish to indicate our support of the following principles:

1. Inasmuch as the President of the United States, under our Constitution, is Commander-in-Chief of the Army and Navy and is responsible for the conduct of our foreign relations, we as Americans, regardless of party affiliations, should accord him our unified support in this period of national emergency.

2. Opposing aggression, we heartily support the Hoover-Stimson Doctrine which refuses recognition to changes in the territorial status quo in violation of treaty commitments.

3. As a logical corollary, the United States must assume its share of responsibility for a world order based upon international law and justice, and recognize the utter futility of a policy of economic and political isolationism.

4. Recognizing the fallacy of the idea that a passive defense is still possible, we support a more dynamic policy of action as the most effective means of security against the totalitarian menace.

Signed _____

In response to the faculty action, President Wilbur wrote to Terman that they were not far apart in their understanding of the situation, but that they differed in their degree of faith in the Roosevelt administration. For Wilbur, to think of a war run by such a group filled him with terror; the only practicable program under the circumstances was to supply, as completely and rapidly as possible, everything Great Britain or China might require.

Matters were well in hand in circulating the faculty statement when Terman left campus for ten days on August 30. Already, 120 signatures had been received, and plans were complete to release the report to the press on the afternoon of September 2, marked for release on September 5. Seven newspapers, press agencies, and representatives were named in plans for a news release.

By September 5, the statement had been endorsed by 176 Stanford professors—nearly eighty percent of those responding. It was a large return for a time when most of the faculty was away from home for the summer or for the between-quarter break. A number of newspapers carried the statement in full; the *Palo Alto Times* even added the names of the 176 signers. The resulting flurry of correspondence ranged from congratulatory letters from two who regretted that they signed too late for their names to be included on the press release, to some who signed with the reservations professors usually have to signing anything they did not themselves write. Two others wrote that they did not sign because they did not wish to risk war, although they deplored America's tendency toward isolationism.

Hoover, long an acquaintance and neighbor of Terman's, disapproved of the faculty statement. He thought it misleading and set about composing a questionnaire of his own. He knew that such questions were difficult to formulate, and just as difficult to answer and interpret. He tried to phrase each question in terms of a concrete action then under debate—an action which would follow upon adopting the policies implied in OUR NATION'S FOREIGN POLICY. Four questions were related to the call for "dynamic action":

(a)   Do you think we should carry munitions to England in American flagships?

(b)   Do you think we should convoy them the whole distance?

(c)   Do you approve complete naval action against Hitler in all waters?

(e)   Do you think we should send a land force to the Continent against Hitler?

One question referred to the Hoover-Stimson Doctrine, which was first applied to Japan in 1932:

(d)   Do you believe we should demand Japanese retirement from China and declare war if she refuses?

The final question asked for an interpretation of the president's authority as commander-in-chief of the armed forces:

(f)   Do you think Congress should be asked to authorize such steps before they are taken?

Hoover's questionnaire was released on September 22, 1941. It was sent to the "whole faculty," which was presumably the roughly eight hundred individuals connected with the University, including about four hundred visiting and part-time faculty, instructors, librarians, secretaries, and clerks. It was sent out with a short, individually typed covering letter to each recipient, stating that Hoover had read the declaration by members of the Stanford faculty with much interest; that everyone was searching for a wise course; that he agreed a "dynamic policy" rather than a "passive defense" was needed; but that he differed in what he thought to be appropriate national action. He simply wanted information on the conclusions of the faculty on a matter in which all were deeply concerned. The questionnaires were to be filled out anonymously and returned in an enclosed envelope to avoid embarrassment.

Fuel was added to the flames by President Wilbur's address to 1700 students and faculty on September 25, 1941. Wilbur urged that America remain out of war, which he called the greatest of all human stupidities. He warned against actions which would lock America into war without declaration by the Congress. He felt the nation must hold back, oppose hysterical thinking, and deny arbitrary leadership through the process of representative government. America must look for solutions other than another AEF; there was more to be gained with a loaf of bread than by looking down a gun barrel.

On September 26, 1941, four days after it was mailed to the faculty, the Hoover questionnaire was released to the press. Ten days later, on October 2, the results were announced by *The Stanford Daily*. Briefly, the Hoover poll reported the following results:

(1) On the issues of "dynamic action," forty-seven percent of the respondents favored carrying munitions to England in American flagships; forty-four percent convoying the whole distance; thirty-nine percent naval action against Hitler; eight percent land action against Hitler now; and nine percent land action later. On those same issues, a tally for the 176 signers of the earlier faculty poll gave percents respectively of seventy-three, seventy-three, sixty-seven, sixteen, and twenty-four.

(2) On the Hoover-Stimson Doctrine as applied to demanding Japanese retirement from China at the risk of war, six percent of the respondents favored the action, while for the 176 previous signers the figure was nine percent.

(3) On the question of the authority of the commander-in-chief and the statement that such actions should be authorized by

Congress, sixty-six percent of all respondents were in favor without qualification, and twenty-three percent with qualifications. For the 176 previous signers, the comparable figures were twenty-three percent and forty percent.

Hoover's conclusion was that sixty percent of the Stanford faculty agreed with him in opposing the foreign policies of the Roosevelt administration. His report was fair and good-humored, though many newsmen found his conclusions neither clear nor logical.

Terman's own reply to Hoover's questionnaire was dated September 24, 1941, the day before the general results were released. It read in part:

> . . . I would unhesitatingly answer your first three questions in the affirmative, but I think it would be more misleading than clarifying to give a mere yes or no answer to the remaining questions. Perhaps the following statement on these questions will make my position clear:
>
> *Question (d).* I favor giving every possible aid to China and continuing or even extending our embargo against shipments to Japan. I think we should face squarely whatever risk of war such a policy may involve.
>
> *Question (e).* This question seems to me quite pointless at the present time since we do not have any armed force to send and probably shall not have before 1943. I believe that as rapidly as possible we should raise and equip a large army and that when it is ready we should not hesitate to send it to any place in Europe, Asia or Africa where it could contribute to the destruction of the Hitler regime.
>
> *Question (f).* With my very limited knowledge of constitutional law I do not know how far the President can go with any semblance of legality in carrying out the policies I have indicated. I believe he would be justified in stretching his constitutional powers to the very limit, as several other Presidents have done, including Jefferson and Lincoln. My personal conviction is that this country should not only repeal the neutrality act but should formally declare war against Germany and Italy. I recognize, of course, that Congress could not be led to declare war at this time, and I can only hope that some incident will occur which will jar that body out of its political-mindedness and into a clearer realization of what this country is up against.
>
> To go ahead with our small efforts on the assumption that Hitler is on his way out and will succumb to the hatreds he has engendered, or to refuse aid to any country that is fighting Hitler, is, to my thinking, terribly and tragically wrong. If Britain falls, as I fear she

may unless this country does far more than it is now doing, I have little hope that either we or our children will live to see the establishment of any real peace in the world.

Two weeks later, on October 10, 1941, Hoover replied to Terman in conciliatory fashion. The two of them differed, he said, not in opposition to dictatorships but in the method of keeping free of them. Only time would tell who was right and who was wrong, possibly within five years.

Press coverage was general. The San Francisco *Chronicle* picked up the Hoover report on the day it was released. An editorial the following day characterized the inquiry as a dubious cross-questioning of the faculty by a Stanford trustee. The editor himself answered all the questions with a spirited "yes," and called for Congress to authorize all steps that required its approval. An editorial comment on October 4 pointed out that only in countries outside Axis control could there be the complete freedom of expression that marked the responses to the questionnaire.

The San Francisco *News* drew parallels between the plight of the Stanford faculty and that of the protagonist in *The Male Animal*, then playing in the city. The *News* did not question Hoover's sincerity, but expressed doubt about his judgment. His action in trying to expose the attitude of the faculty posed a threat to academic freedom and economic security. *The People's World* was more critical, interpreting the poll as an attempt to intimidate the faculty, destroy independent opinion, aid America First, and sell out to the Fascist Axis.

On October 13, 1941, *Newsweek* published a report claiming that Hoover had been angered by the preceding faculty statement, citing two national surveys showing that 70 to 80 pecent of the American people believed that Hitler's defeat was more important than keeping out of war. *Time,* on the same date, reported that Stanford students, though mildly isolationist, blasted the Hoover faculty poll. *Time* set the Stanford report against polls showing strong anti-isolationism at Princeton, Chicago, and Northwestern, and milder versions of the same attitude at Harvard, Wisconsin, Missouri, and Minnesota.

Only one report—a speech by the Chairman of the Executive Board of the America First Committee of Northern California, presented over radio station KQW on October 5—favored Hoover's point of view. It called Roosevelt's foreign policy a "slipping into war by the back door" and a "betrayal of public trust."

Correspondence to Terman was almost uniformly congratulatory, despite Hoover's action. A letter from President Sproul of the University of California was typical; it said Terman would be amused at how much of Sproul's correspondence advised him to go to Stanford to learn something about American participation in the war before making any pronouncements.

Meanwhile, the third phase of the controversy was already under way. On September 23, 1941, the day after Hoover's questionnaire was mailed to the "faculty," a conference of about seventy-five signers of the original faculty statement of August 21 was called to discuss how to respond to the questionnaire. Terman was unanimously requested by those present to chair the meeting. His old friend Jesse Sears served as secretary.

Terman and others objected strongly to the manner in which the polling process on the Hoover questions was conducted. Including all Stanford University employees was a clear violation of the academic definition of "the faculty," which includes only individuals with the rank of professor, associate professor, or assistant professor. There was no segregation of academic faculty from others in the report, and no information on how the 176 signers of the previous statement had been identified in a presumably anonymous poll. The total number of responses was not reported, only characterized as "generous." There was no information on who had counted the ballots or how they had categorized doubtful or qualified statements. Some members of the faculty believed the poll had been sloppily done by employees in the Hoover Library, whose loyalty to "the chief" was more intense than their respect for the integrity of their results. Yet the faculty was also convinced that if anything unethical was going on, Hoover was its innocent victim. The wisdom of a trustee's polling the faculty of his university might be questioned, but no one who had any personal contact with Hoover questioned his personal integrity.

Most of the discussion in the meeting focused, however, on the nature of Hoover's questions. It was the consensus that categorical answers, particularly to the last three questions, would not clarify the faculty position, and might well be misleading. New questions should be formulated, directed precisely to existing issues without reexamining old problems. The meeting agreed that a committee, chaired by Graham Stuart and including the other eight men who had prepared the first statement and one other, should prepare a statement to be submitted to the faculty.

Terman served the faculty committee not only as a member, but also as its expert on matters of questionnaire formulation and the data gathering process. He went about the poll meticulously. The questions were carefully drawn up, selected, and formulated by the sponsoring committee; they were brief, direct, and unambiguous. The questions were designed to reveal the true attitude of the respondents on a policy of isolationism, as well as their approval or disapproval of measures either already taken or before Congress for meeting the national emergency.

The poll was confined to active and emeritus members of the Academic Council and to other members of the regular teaching staff in the three professorial ranks. There were 483 such names in the current catalog; to each, a ballot and a return envelope were mailed. All ballots were accounted for, both in distribution and in return. The number who gave some response to one or more of the questions was 341, an unusually heavy vote for a poll conducted by mail. Of the 142 who did not reply, 41 were on leave and presumably away from campus; several were officers in the armed services and not permitted to express their opinions; and others were faculty members who disapproved of faculty polls on controversial issues.

Ballots were opened and counted by four tellers—two isolationists and two interventionists, a precaution to avoid bias in tallying. As it turned out, the four agreed unanimously on all responses. No member of the sponsoring committee was present during the count, and the ballots were left open to inspection in the Department of Political Science.

Terman served the committee also as liaison member on other fronts. He maintained contact with the Medical School faculty in San Francisco to keep it informed of the proceedings. He notified Hoover and the 176 previous signers of the actions taken at the meeting which led to the new poll, and suggested that respondents to Hoover's questionnaire send copies of their responses to Graham Stuart to guide the committee in formulating the new inquiry. Terman also released a statement to the San Francisco *Chronicle*, giving some of the criticisms of the Hoover poll and suggesting that little significance should be attached to the statistics given there.

Meanwhile, President Wilbur did what he could to quiet the controversy. The whole affair was painful to him, for Hoover had been a close friend since his college days. Wilbur could only wish that the whole thing would miraculously disappear. On October 4, 1941, he wrote Terman that since everybody had had a turn at self-expression, he hoped the debate could be dropped. He offered to see that the matter was dropped at the other end as well.

Terman replied on October 6 that, though he recognized the delicacy of the situation, he felt that the harm had already been done by the fact the Hoover poll was taken at all, by the nature of the questionnaire used, and by the questionable interpretations in the summary given to the press. At any rate, Terman argued, he was only one of nine who sponsored the first statement of the faculty, only one of its 176 signers, and only one of about seventy-five signers who met to decide what to do next. He had no authority to call off the next step.

On October 9, the committee formulating the new inquiry met to consider Wilbur's note. It was agreed that the committee must go ahead with the new ballot authorized by the meeting of September 24, 1941. A copy of the proposed new ballot was sent to Wilbur for his information.

On October 11, Wilbur replied, thanking Terman for the proposed list of questions and expressing the hope that they might never come to light. He thought that they were opportunistic in character and evaded the fundamental question of the responsibility of the legislative arm of the government to declare war. But he did nothing to interfere with the taking of the poll.

Terman's reply on October 15 pointed out that whether the new ballot evaded the issue depended on what one conceived the issue to be. For Terman the issue was whether Hitler or Roosevelt was the greater menace to the future of the United States. He assured Wilbur of his personal friendship and of his appreciation of the president's service to Stanford. But he also pointed out the peril to the university inherent in any attempt to limit free expression of opinion among the faculty.

On October 15, Wilbur replied that free expression of opinion was important, but that such expression should be clear-cut enough to wear well with the passage of time. He agreed that there was no personal feeling on his part engendered by the difference of opinion, adding that unanimity would be strange indeed, in view of the crisis in which the country found itself.

Nor were the pressures of President Wilbur the only ones on the Stanford campus in October and November 1941. The America First Committee was trying to establish a chapter there. Terman wrote of his revulsion for that organization, saying that not even

Goebbels could direct the activities of America First more to Hitler's advantage than its leadership was doing. And a student wrote in the Stanford *Daily* of attempts on the part of America First to enlist her leadership; she stated vividly her sense of insult and her rejection of the invitation.

The second faculty questionnaire was released in early October, with October 22, 1941 set for announcement of the results. It read as follows:

> In order to obtain further clarification of the attitude of the Stanford faculty in regard to the foreign policy of the United States, the following questions are being submited to members of the academic council, the emeritus members of the academic council, and to all other members of the teaching staff of professorial rank. Will you please answer the questions promptly and mail your reply to Box 3004, Stanford University. It is hoped that the results can be tabulated and announced by October 22. No signatures are required.

Eliot Blackwelder	*Emile Holman*	*L. M. Terman*
E. A. Cottrell	*R. V. A. Lee*	*D. L. Webster*
Gordon Ferris	*Graham Stuart*	
Albert Guérard	*C. V. Taylor*	

Yes   No

1. Do you support the foreign policy of our government in the measures which have already been taken against the Axis powers? (Food and munitions to enemies of the Axis; the Lend-Lease Act; the exchange of destroyers for military bases; the military expedition to Iceland; the North Atlantic patrol; embargo on war supplies to Japan.) _____ _____

2. Do you favor the measures now proposed to defeat the Axis powers, namely: revision of neutrality legislation and further lease-lend legislation? _____ _____

3. Would you favor stronger measures if they should be needed to defeat the Axis powers? _____ _____

Results were released to the news media on October 23, 1941. They were reported in percents of the 341 who answered one or more questions. Briefly, they showed the following findings.

(1) Supporting the foreign policy of the government in measures already taken against the Axis powers was 86.51 percent of the faculty: 83.87 percent without qualification, 2.35 with qualification, and 0.29 a little on the yes side. The percent opposing was 11.15: 8.80 without qualification, 1.76 with qualification, and 0.59 a little on the no side. Of the respondents, 1.47 percent gave answers which were not classifiable, and 0.88 percent failed to respond to the question. The overall ratio of yes to no answers for the unqualified responses only was 9.53 to 1.

(2) Supporting the measures then proposed to defeat the Axis was 82.70 percent of the faculty: 80.94 percent without qualification, 0.88 with qualification, and 0.88 a little on the yes side. The percent opposing was 15.25: 14.08 without qualification, 0.88 with qualification, and 0.29 a little on the no side. Of the respondents, 1.47 percent gave answers which were not classifiable, and 0.59 percent failed to respond to the question. The overall ratio of yes to no answers for the unqualified responses only was 5.75 to 1.

(3) Favoring stronger measures if needed to defeat the Axis powers was 78.30 percent of the faculty: 75.37 percent without qualification, 2.64 with qualification, and 0.29 a little on the yes side. The percent opposing was 17.01: 12.61 without qualification, 3.23 with qualification, and 1.17 a little on the no side. Of the respondents, 1.17 percent gave answers that were not classifiable, and 3.52 percent failed to respond to the question. The overall ratio of yes to no answers for the unqualified responses only was 5.98 to 1.

Terman concluded that more than eighty percent of the Stanford faculty approved the Roosevelt Administration's current foreign policy, and that seventy-five percent favored the use of even stronger measures if they should be needed to ensure the defeat of the Axis powers. It was clear the faculty stood with President Roosevelt on his foreign policy, not with Hoover, Wilbur, and the other signers of the Alexandria Bay declaration.

Terman sent a copy of the committee report to Hoover the day it was released. Hoover replied on October 30 that policies such as those the Stanford faculty innocently supported would lead to sending millions of American boys to Europe, and that he saw no point in continuing such a discussion with friends who apparently did not know what they were doing. Hoover said he would file the whole set of papers for review ten years later in light of the wisdom of the proposals, the intellectual honesty of the policies promoted, and the fidelity to the spirit of the democratic process of such

161

proposals. He predicted that forces greater than any individual would save or destroy the foundations of freedom in America long before that time, so there was no need for friends to spend those years in quarreling.

Terman's reply, dated November 10, 1941, was conciliatory. He agreed that it was inevitable that friends should differ, but that friendships should not be broken over such differences. He only questioned whether more American boys would be lost by entering the war while there were still allies than by taking a chance on what would to happen if there were none.

While Terman and Hoover were corresponding, the news media were carrying the story of the new poll. The Stanford *Daily*, Palo Alto *Times*, San Francisco *Chronicle*, *News*, and *Examiner*, and Los Angeles *Herald-Express*, carried an immediate report. The New York *Times* and the *Christian Science Monitor* carried later accounts. Most of the releases were factual only, although some of the earlier caustic comments on the impropriety of a powerful trustee "picking the brains" of his faculty were revived.

Correspondence within the faculty supported Terman's handling of the poll and the reporting of results, with only a single exception. There were small donations covering committee expenses; expressions of indebtedness of faculty to Terman for taking the poll at all, in view of the pressure exerted to get him to drop the matter; and congratulations on his forbearance in the correspondence with Hoover.

Off campus, the response was similar. The chief editorial writer of the Oakland *Tribune* congratulated Terman on his leadership in injecting a little intelligence into the controversy. Former students and public figures expressed their appreciation of his position. Terman's old friend Boring wrote in a philosophic vein that war is a wonderful object-lesson on the motivational determiners of opinion. Each side thinks the other is blind. The whole war experience had increased Boring's distrust of the possibility of human objectivity; each faculty luncheon seemed to boil over into reactions predictable according to predetermined attitudes. Boring missed the sympathetic weighing of an opponent's point of view. Though people in psychology were fairly tolerant, the war seemed to have got them. He congratulated Terman on his activities, knowing that they took time, but knowing also that they formed an outlet.

Late in December 1941, a professor of philosophy at another university asked permission to quote the Hoover and Terman

162

questionnaires and their divergent results in a book he was preparing, as a telling illustration of what can be done with statistics if the right questions are asked. Terman sent full information on his poll but withheld consent to quote. He pointed out that the enormous difference between the Hoover poll and the faculty poll was due not only to the questions asked, but also to the differences between the permanent faculty alone and the aggregate of university employees, to the time allowed for replies to be submitted, and to the method of tallying.

The whole incident stands as a model of restraint as well as effectiveness in the field of action on a controversial issue. The faculty, scattered for the late summer vacation, was called to action by a dedicated few. It rallied together to stand up for academic freedom and to oppose being used for partisan purposes. The university, as represented by Wilbur, behaved very properly despite the painful position in which it was placed, making no real attempt to muzzle faculty expression. Despite the strong feelings, all actions taken by the faculty, by Hoover, and by the University administration as represented by Wilbur were fairly announced and in good taste. In contrast to recent campus controversies, this one featured no sit-in, no picketing, no rushing to the press with strong denunciation. Even though the affair was fully reported by the national press as well as by the local papers, there were no radio interviews of campus figures. Even the Stanford student paper concentrated on reporting the facts rather than promoting a partisan view. The handling of the matter typified the democratic process at its best.

Though Terman, Hoover, and Wilbur had agreed that only time held the answer to where the right lay, it was not necessary to wait ten years or even five for the answer. Less than a month after the last letter from Terman to Hoover—December 7, 1941—was Pearl Harbor Day.

When World War II broke out, Terman went to work doing what he could. He planned a course on Military Psychology, devoted chiefly to personnel techniques, propaganda, and morale. By summer 1942, he had an outline ready. Unfortunately, the manuscripts were lost in a fire at his home and the project was never completed.

After World War II, Terman shifted his efforts to opposing the activities of the McCarthy committee. He suggested a psychiatric study of McCarthy, pointing out the man's similarities to Hitler. Perhaps Terman's feeling was made more acute by the thought that he might well be in the committee's files because of his mistaken involvement with the civil liberties group in San Francisco, his sponsorship of Consumer's Union, and the five dollars he had given the Spanish loyalists. He actually disliked Communism intensely, less as a system than because of its aggressive attempt to destroy other ideologies.

Though he had little sympathy for professors who gave too much of their time to political activities, Terman opposed the California loyalty oath when it was extended to teachers, and particularly when it was extended to professors at the University of California (Terman unpublished, 1950a). Since students who were considered politically doubtful were dismissed from universities in Iron Curtain countries, and since the University of California had a loyalty oath for its faculty, he suggested that the next logical step would be to require a similar oath for university students. And, since teachers in public schools must take such an oath, the parents of school children should file a similar document, either at the time of taking out a marriage license or possibly when they reached the age when they might produce offspring.

Terman opposed censorship and the Ban the Books movement. He was invited to join the Council of the Atlantic Union Committee in 1951, and he lent his name to its activities. He accepted an invitation to membership on one of the official boards of the United States Federation of Justice as well.

Terman's letter to Nicholas Pastore sums up his special attitudes over the years. Pastore was doing a dissertation in which he claimed the advocates of "nature" in the nature-nurture controversy were inherently politically and socially conservative (Pastore, 1949). He sent the first draft to Terman, whose response was vehement. Terman said he was *not* a free-enterprise advocate of the National Association of Manufacturers variety. He favored social and economic planning, would like to see the nation blanketed with Tennessee Valley Authorities, and supported federal soil and forest conservation and federal aid to education. He advocated stiff inheritance taxes, old-age pensions, and social security measures. He believed in unemployment insurance, minimum wage laws, fair employment practice regulations, federal price controls within limits, and labor unions, as long as they did not try to influence elections.

Most of all, he believed in civil liberties and in the Bill of Rights. He felt it a national disgrace that minority groups were not protected and that widespread racial discrimination existed. He favored complete freedom of speech, limited only by national security.

He hated the Dies committee, and detested even more the witch-hunting and character-smearing activities of other federal and state committees as the most un-American thing in the country. If he were called before such a group, he would go to jail rather than answer any questions about his political beliefs and affiliations.

In addition, he disliked every form of national totalitarianism. He had favored stopping Mussolini in 1935 and Hitler in 1938—by force if necessary—and had advocated an embargo on shipping oil and steel to Japan long before Pearl Harbor. He approved extending the European Recovery Plan to all needy countries no matter what their trend toward socialization.

Terman said he was more of a New Dealer than a "social and political conservative." He had not previously aired his social, economic, and political viewpoint, because that was inappropriate for a scientist. But he did have Quinn and Olga McNemar, Melita Oden, and Anna Terman rate him on the social-political viewpoints scale he had devised for the gifted group. These close friends ranked him 2.5 to 3.5, or distinctly liberal on a scale between average and extremely radical; he ranked himself 3.0, or middle-of-the-road. He was far more liberal than the average of 5.9, or conservative, for his 667 gifted men and 543 gifted women.

Terman argued that it was a gross injustice to assume that because he thought intelligence tests were valuable meant that he was a conservative or worse. His approach had always been empirical—he had simply put together the most promising test items he could assemble and checked to see how the items and the scale as a whole were influenced by schooling and by the general experiences that come with age. His belief in mental inheritance, individual differences, and the value of intelligence tests as rough measures of such differences gave no basis for inferring social and political attitudes, either of liberalism or conservatism.

Pastore revised the section on Terman somewhat. He still clung to the idea that, since Terman's 1932 autobiography had voiced pessimism about trends in democracy, he had been a conservative until the beginning of the Great Depression, and then switched to liberalism. He conceded that Terman was an exception to the trend toward conservatism among advocates of the "nature" point of view.

165

It would be more fair to say that Terman was a man of strong social conscience. The ethical and religious influences of his childhood and his sensitivity to individuals bore fruit in a concern for all mankind—a concern which had for him the driving force that more conventional forms of religious belief had for others. In "My Faith" (Terman unpublished, 1948b), he expressed the belief that man's divinity rests upon two things: his ability to think and his capacity for love. Though differences in intelligence are important, differences in conscience and moral outlook are more largely susceptible to social and cultural control. If man is to keep pace with the increasing tempo of cultural change, the tempo of his social and moral evolution must be increased as well. In Terman's own words,

> ... From my point of view, the wholehearted dedication of one's life to the promotion of social justice, mutual understanding, racial tolerance and equalization of opportunity, is as good evidence of a truly religious spirit as any beliefs one might hold about miracles, immortality, or a personal God. (Terman unpublished, 1948b)

CHAPTER XI

Retirement

We will not cultivate the illusion that our most important achievements are probably ahead of us. . . .

We will emulate especially those members of our emeritus group who have shown that age is no bar to zest for life and for service. . . .

We will not refuse the little services we can render, because we are no longer equal to the bigger things we could once have done (Terman unpublished, 1942b).

A⊤ Stanford, retirement came at age sixty-five, with no nonsense about who is able to continue and who is not. And Terman was sixty-five on January 15, 1942. He knew that some men are less senile at seventy-five than others are at sixty-five, and that psychologists could easily determine the intellectual ability of any individual facing retirement. But he could not imagine a university making use of such a method to reach an individual decision.

Terman anticipated his retirement as early as 1940 in seeking relief for his overloaded bookshelves. He began looking for an appropriate college to which he could give his large library. He talked with the Stanford Director of Libraries, who discussed the matter with a number of librarians at a national meeting; the recommendation that emerged was the Joint University Libraries at Nashville. A survey of college libraries made by the American Council on Education in 1934 had found no adequate research library available in its field from North Carolina to Texas and from Illinois-Indiana to the Gulf of Mexico. In 1938 and 1939, two educational foundations had endowed a top-notch joint library for Vanderbilt University, George Peabody College, and the Scarritt College for Christian Workers in Nashville. The Director of the Joint University Libraries was a man of unusual energy and ability; the building and its equipment were especially adequate and well financed; and the library had only a small collection in Terman's field of interest. In addition, there were able psychologists in the participating institutions, and there was no other library nearby with an important collection of this kind. Such a library was essential to the participating institutions in preparing graduate students as guidance specialists and college teachers, and in fostering research on such matters as Negro-white differences and the significance of isolation of segments of the native white population.

Terman was enthusiastic at the prospect. He liked the idea of having his library serve the South; he was happy that the more technical part of his library would be used by graduate students, and that the more general and elementary books find use also. His collection was strong in the fields of mental tests, individual differences, and educational and child psychology, with sizeable sections in general, comparative, abnormal, social, and industrial psychology. In addition, there were numerous publications in mental deficiency, delinquency, personality, genius, and the psychology of sex. Most important of all for research, there were complete files of nearly all psychological journals published since 1905; Terman proposed to continue having these sent to the Joint Libraries.

Late in 1940, Terman shipped the thousand volumes he needed least. He sent most of the remaining three thousand from time to time as he could spare them. With characteristic orderliness, he included in each box a packet of three-by-five cards giving the authors and titles, and prepaid the shipping charges as a part of the gift.

When the Joint University Libraries proposed some announcement of the gift, Terman demurred. He preferred no credit. Besides, any announcement would give the impression that his professional career was about over, and he was certainly not bowing off the stage so early in the game. He asked that for the time being, the gift be listed simply as "Anonymous." Later he agreed to a bookplate indicating the source of each volume, but he adamantly opposed housing the collection as a special library. Terman's library thus became the first large gift to the Joint University Libraries, and a significant foundation for the growing study of psychology and educational psychology in the south-central United States.

Also around 1940, a group of Terman's former students set in motion a plan to show their affection for him and their appreciation of his work. Over a period of two years they prepared a memorial volume for his sixty-fifth birthday, *Studies in Personality*, published in 1942. The preface states their intent.

Lewis M. Terman, servant of psychology, has labored untiringly to extend the boundaries of our knowledge of human behavior. His achievements and personality have been an inspiration to psychologists everywhere and especially to those who have had an opportunity for work and study under his guidance. It is fitting, therefore, that this series of papers on a topic about which so much of his own research has centered should be prepared for the occasion of his sixty-fifth birthday.

The authors of this book are but a small proportion of his many former graduate students who have been quickened by his leadership and who join with us and with his colleagues everywhere in the hope that his work may be continued for many years to come. (Woodworth, 1942, p. vii).

Florence Goodenough was chairman of the group which planned the volume; she was assisted by Robert Bernreuter, Quinn McNemar, Maud Merrill, Catherine Cox Miles, Miles Tinker, and Kimball Young. Following a glowing introduction by Robert Woodworth, the volume presented sixteen papers related to Terman's wide-ranging interests, written by sixteen of his former graduate students. An annotated bibliography of Terman's publications was added.

Terman's surprise and delight were expressed in a letter dated January 19, 1942, addressed to his "incredibly devoted friends."

> *Studies in Personality* was as big a surprise as Pearl Harbor. No suspicion had crossed my mind: I was caught completely off the alert. Like Pearl Harbor too it left me overwhelmed and speechless.
>
> There the parallel ends, for the after effects are as pleasing as the event itself was surprising. No other conceivable token of your appreciation could have meant so much to me.
>
> But the thought of all the labors your gift cost makes me feel very humble. . . .
>
> Someone has said that the psychology of personality probably had its beginning in primitive man's love of gossip, long before the invention of back fences or front gates. If this is true, the fact that no breath of gossip about your plot ever reached me in the two years it was brewing would suggest that the science has progressed a long way from its origin.
>
> In accepting your splendid memorial I must beg leave to think of it as more than a personal tribute to me. . . . Both in scientific and literary merit *Studies in Personality* is vastly creditable to its authors and to Stanford. (Terman letter, Stanford Archives, 1942)

Seldom has such an illustrious group of former students shown affection to a mentor and friend so clearly and appropriately.

When retirement came the following August, it was an easy transition. For the next month Terman did little except loaf and reshuffle his collections of notes, reprints, and documents preparatory to moving into a new office. Then he settled down to fairly steady writing on the gifted data. There was no problem in adjusting to retirement. He had not enjoyed life so much for a long time. It was a tremendous relief to be free of administrative and teaching duties. Besides, he had his fourteen hundred gifted to look after as godfather, counselor, and father-confessor. And he had an office staff, with the help of foundation and government support. Small wonder that when his friends reached a similar milestone, he offered no condolences, but simply wished them the same joy in retirement that he had experienced.

His attitude toward retirement is reflected in his "Ten Vows of the Stanford Emeriti Graduates of 1942" (Terman unpublished, 1942). These ten commandments vowed humility, helpfulness, a reasonable philosophical detachment, an open mind to newer trends, and a sense of humor. They denied feeling sorry for oneself, condemning the younger generation, enlarging on one's accomplishments, and allowing oneself to believe friends who say he looks as young as he did thirty years before.

Terman's enjoyment of retirement was interrupted from the beginning by a series of illnesses and accidents. In November 1942, three months after his retirement, Terman suffered extensive second degree burns when his campus home caught fire. He had always smoked heavily, despite his tuberculosis; one evening when smoking in bed he noticed a small fire, which he put out by pouring water on the mattress. Then he fell asleep, awakening a short time later to find himself enveloped by flames. His home was extensively damaged, and Terman was disabled for eight months. For six of the eight he was confined to bed, with Anna nursing him. As the burns healed he underwent extensive skin grafting, and for a time he spent part of every day going from one orthopedic apparatus or exercise to another. For a long time the new skin was so sensitive to clothing he could scarcely tolerate anything heavier than light pajamas on his body.

Arthritis developed in his right arm, and writing by hand became difficult. His secretary replied to letters. He even bought a dictaphone and contemplated dictating most of Volume V of the *Genetic Studies of Genius*, but he soon went back to writing everything in longhand.

In addition, his cataracts became worse. He gave up movies, for he had no time in the afternoon, and at night he preferred to read in his den. In 1944 he had the cataract removed from one eye, with only a slight hemorrhage in the eye a few days after the operation. He spent the tedious days of recovery in a semi-darkened room at home, in the company of his radio. After two months, a lens gave him a vast improvement in vision. Then, in 1947, he had the cataract removed from the other eye, and was delighted to see the world in perspective again, rather than as if it were painted on a wall. He was amazed that colors were so bright—much brighter than he could remember.

Between the two bouts with cataract surgery, he had still another accident. In December 1946, Terman stumbled over a displaced wastebasket in his unlighted study one night and struck his hip against the corner of a wooden bench. In the hospital, he had to lie flat on his back for several weeks, with the upper femur nailed together and a pin through the lower femur attached to an apparatus to keep the leg stretched. The doctors said he might be able to sit up by February and walk with crutches two or three months later. It was an unpleasant business—having to lie still on the sensitive scar tissue from his burns, being able to read very little because in that position his one useful eye tended to fall out of focus. Yet Terman was amazed by his own adaptability. He listened to the radio: comedy, variety, and music from classical to hillbilly, even the soap operas. He had constant callers, and the general confusion of the hospital left little time for other activities. After the first three months he was able to work a little, completing three chapters on the marital adjustment of the gifted group. And after six months he could be about on crutches.

Then, nine months after his accident, he found that the wisdom of his body in maintaining homeostatis had been too much of a good thing. New bone had been poured out at such a rate that it irritated the surrounding flesh, and the screws, bands, and nails had caused friction in the joint as well. He must have the hardware in his leg removed and the extra bone formation chiseled out. He told his friends that he was saying his beads for luck. Fortunately, the surgery was successful. He went home only four days later and was soon able to walk around the house with two canes, thankful to be on his feet on any terms.

The following month he started going to his office again. True, one leg was a good deal shorter than the other, had a built-up shoe, and needed a stout cane. Terman chafed at needing help in getting the sock on his right foot; he found it difficult to climb stairs without a bannister and to get in or out of taxis and airplanes. He declined all invitations, even accepting an honorary degree from the University of Pennsylvania *in absentia*. Yet he went to his office daily, perky as ever, limping and wearing dark glasses.

All these illnesses were expensive. He estimated the cost of the fire, his hip injury, and his cataract surgery at around $20,000. His retirement income alone could never have covered such an amount; only the royalties from his books and tests made it possible to meet the expenses.

There were lesser illnesses, too. In 1947, the extraction of a molar led to excessive bleeding, which left him shaken and weak. In 1948, he had a severe, old-fashioned case of hives, something that had never happened to him before and that he hoped would never happen again. In 1949, he underwent prostate surgery, coming home within less than a week. Five years later, a bladder infection led to a prolonged series of treatments. Shortly before his death, Terman injured a vertebra from severe coughing and was fitted with stays for a few months. He truly learned, as he said, that the more things happen to you, the more can happen.

But he thought of the positive side of his health as well. His blood pressure continued low, and there were no signs of a recurrence of the tuberculosis. He could beg off from the dinner before he gave the Bingham lecture and decline to go to professional meetings. His associates kept him busy with all the work he could do when he was ill, and enjoyed with him the hours at the office and the long, conversational coffee break when he was well. On the rare occasions when he went to a meeting, someone would push a big easy chair to the foot of the receiving line for him, so he could talk with as many people as he would like without the discomfort of standing. His only regret was the time lost from work. He discouraged talk of his misfortunes, lest people think of him as an invalid—which he firmly claimed was untrue.

Fortunately, Anna's health remained good through all these years. She did a lot of waiting on Terman during the months following the fire, and again after his hip accident. True, she was embarrassed by an occasional inability to recall names, or to give both the common and the botanical name of each of the scores of kinds of plants on the home lot. But Terman told her that he too found himself groping for the right word occasionally when writing or dictating. She worked in the garden for an hour or two every day when the weather was good, raising tomatoes, corn, beans, and beets. Or rather, the gardener raised them under Anna's supervision, and left the harvesting to her.

In 1950, following a series of gallstone attacks, Anna had her gallbladder removed. She chafed, for she had never learned to enjoy being waited on as Terman claimed to have done. About this time, too, she was fitted with a hearing aid, which she had checked frequently as her hearing deteriorated all too rapidly.

Happily, the Termans seemed to draw closer together in their later years. Perhaps the most successful professional men use any defense they can find to prevent interruption in their early years, including illness. Their wives adjust, often with some discomfort, to the limited social life. Then, when success has eased the striving, husband and wife come together again and seem marvelously satisfied. So it seemed for the Termans. Terman voiced this feeling in a letter, saying that if he could live his life over he would give less of his time to writing books and more to his family and friends. Anna doubtless knew and was comforted.

Fred and Helen, and their families, were nearby. Helen became increasingly a part of the Terman family circle again, helping to manage the illnesses of her father and the increasing frailty of her mother. Her older daughter, married to a Navy man, lived some distance down the coast, where for twelve years as teacher and principal of a school, she put into practice Terman's ideas of how children with varying intelligences and interests should be taught. Helen's younger daughter, who had been trained in chemistry, was with her chemist husband who worked at a paper mill in Ketchikan; she was a housewife with three children, but found time to be active in community affairs, and hoped for more art and music lessons.

Fred was rapidly winning distinction. Early in 1942, he was asked to organize the Radio Research Laboratory at Harvard, where he eventually supervised eight hundred wartime researchers in developing countermeasures against enemy radar. For that work he received honorary doctorates from Harvard and other universities, as well as honors from both the British and United States governments. In 1945, he returned to Stanford as Dean of the School of Engineering. He introduced a plan to foster relations between industry and the university that benefited both and contributed to the growth of the high-technology industrial complex on the San Francisco Peninsula.

Terman lived to see Fred become Provost of Stanford University in 1955. He missed Fred's promotion to Vice President of the University in 1958 and his emeritus consultantships in building

173

similar relationships between universities and industry in a number of other places.

Terman was particularly proud of Fred's election to the National Academy of Sciences in 1946. He and Fred constituted one of only two father-son pairs ever to be elected to that Academy; his delight knew no bounds. Fred, in return, included a public acknowledgment of his pride in his father in his acceptance of the Herbert Hoover Medal for Distinguished Service to Stanford. In fact, to their friends, father and son seemed much alike.

Additional insight on Terman is provided by the very real effect he had on Fred's career. In Fred's own words, in a personal letter to the author in 1973, Terman

... talked fairly frankly around the family dinner table about the members of the Stanford faculty. ... He had clear perception as to what it was that counted in a university, who were the really important faculty members and what made them important, who weren't carrying their weight and what they lacked. I absorbed all of this in a matter-of-fact way, but the consequence was that by the time I was a sixteen-year old freshman I ... had a set of values that I could apply myself in judging faculty. The result was that as an undergraduate student I had a better understanding of what counted around a university than did most of the young members of the faculty. When I first joined the Stanford faculty I consequently had a very clear conception of how I should allocate my time, and how to establish myself both as a teacher and as a productive scholar. That is to say, I already knew how to play the game in a way that would maximize my personal success and simultaneously give me personal satisfaction, whereas I found that most of my ... colleagues of those days lived from term to term without any long-range career strategy. Later, as I got into administrative work, I began to appreciate that as a result of the values I had learned from Father I had sharper judgment and higher standards in the evaluation and selection of faculty than did most others among the younger administrators in the University, and I also had a better appreciation of those administrators around the University who were doing a really good job of building up strong programs, rather than being merely personally good in their own specialty.

Father also had a very profound effect on my career in another way. In the era in which I graduated from Stanford (1920) the typical engineering student took a job immediately upon graduation, and there was a widespread belief that one needed practical experience rather than more education. However, like many of the Stanford students interested in electrical engineering, I went on to an Engineer's degree (equivalent to an M.S.), specializing in high-voltage work. In those days no one, and I mean *just no one* went for a Doctor's degree. However, I was young and Father suggested it would be desirable for me to . . . work for a doctorate. I didn't have any feeling on the matter one way or the other, but since the family could afford to send me away to school. . . . I accepted this advice, consulted with . . . the department head as to which would be the most desirable school, and he recommended MIT. This turned out to be the most fortunate single thing that happened to my career. At MIT I fell in with Vannevar Bush who was then a young faculty member just making his reputation, and ended up by doing a dissertation under him. At MIT I had my horizons drastically broadened in directions that Stanford needed to go but had never heard about. The result was that when I joined the Stanford staff, all of my initial teaching was at graduate or high senior level. . . . In this connection it is to be observed that at that time the Electrical Engineering Department at MIT included only two men with the doctorate, and that my Sc.D. degree awarded in 1924 was the eighth Doctor's degree in electrical engineering that had ever been awarded at MIT, and the only Doctor's degree awarded to a U.S. citizen in the six years after the end of World War I. Thus Father steered me into what was then an unconventional direction, but one which certainly paid off as far as my career was concerned.

. . . In a very important way he was my teacher, too!

Fred increasingly took over the job as head of the Terman family. He kept an eye on his parents' financial affairs. When Helen traveled, Fred handled her correspondence and sent her photostats of the originals, lest they be lost. Helen had learned early that when she wanted to do something Fred might disapprove, it was best to do it first and tell him afterward. Then he could only say, "Well, if you had asked my advice I would have told you I thought it wasn't a good idea. But what difference now?"

Terman's pride in Fred included Fred's three sons, all so gifted that he hoped at least one might join father and grandfather in the National Academy of Sciences some day. By the time Terman was in his last years, the oldest was well along in his graduate work in physics at Harvard; the second had his baccalaureate in physics and had been accepted for graduate work at the California Institute of Technology; and the third was entering Stanford with a major in either physics or engineering. Terman spoke of all five of his grandchildren with devotion and pride; he boasted to Yerkes that he was pretty certain to beat him to the great-grands.

Terman became more interested in his boyhood family as well. In 1948, while on the way to professional meetings, he spent six

175

days around Indianapolis visiting with some forty relatives and numerous boyhood acquaintances. His brother John, who had helped with Terman's early education, was at eighty-one running a filling station in the town of their boyhood. On the other hand, some of his boyhood friends were terribly changed, obese, or lame.

Terman had a talent for lifelong friendship. He exchanged letters regularly with Arnold Gesell, most of them on such professional interests as feral or "wild" children. The lively correspondence with Yerkes continued as interest and whim dictated; they would write nothing at all if nothing interesting turned up, or at length if there were any new developments.

The letters to and from Boring went on. It was during this period that Boring characterized Terman as a man of ambition and friendly warmth—in the Sheldon classification, a "viscerotonic somatoton," somewhat like himself. They wrote about ideas and events with a mutually counterbalancing effect. When Terman solicited Boring's participation in support of a peace movement, for example, Boring advised him not to let the intensity of the need affect his judgment on what to do about the need. Enthusiasm, he said, is the friend of action and the enemy of wisdom.

Yerkes's death occurred shortly before Terman's own, but Boring lived until 1968—long enough to enter into one of his characteristically warm and enthusiastic bits of correspondence with the author regarding Terman as a man. From his hospital bed, he dictated thorough and free-ranging letters on the matter. He hated the drugs he had to use to kill pain, because they were soporific and killed productivity; but he, in turn, used talking and writing to kill the sleepiness.

Terman especially enjoyed the letters of Harry Harlow, such as the one announcing that Harlow's staff at Wisconsin had decided to start giving Stanford Ph.D.'s. They were organizing a Wisconsin in-group of the Stanford out-group in a big way, and they asked Terman's endorsement of the Land-Locked Branch of the Stanford Department Division of Graduate Studies. Terman replied in the same vein.

There were new friends, like the sprightly Betsy Bonbright, who asked Terman to diagnose the trouble with her typewriter. Terman replied that he got amusement out of erratic machines just as he did out of erratic people. He had a clock that either gained or lost from five to twenty minutes a day without rhyme or reason, and he would not trade it for a perfect timepiece. He even enjoyed earthquakes when they did not do too much damage; they stirred things up a bit.

Through all these peripheral events and personal relationships, Terman's work continued to be the central focus of his life. From 1942 on, he averaged three to four publications each year. In addition, he produced manuscripts which were not published on a number of social problems, as well as on marital happiness, the Stanford Binet, and his gifted children (see Appendix B). In 1948, a periodical solicited an article on "My Faith," which it later rejected as containing too little conventional religious feeling. And in 1953, Terman wrote, "I Was Lucky," the story of his bouts with tuberculosis, for inclusion in a book by thirty ex-tubercular patients who had recovered sufficiently to have successful careers. Many of these unpublished manuscripts provide insight into his thinking during the later years. When a publication allowed two years to elapse between accepting one of his articles and publishing it, Terman tartly requested a postscript stating the date of submission, so readers would not think he had overlooked the literature for those two years.

He was still active in university affairs as well. In 1945, he joined in a faculty protest on restrictions against consultantship work for faculty, imposed by Stanford's new president. And he defended educators against criticisms by psychologists, saying that although he had been in closer touch than most with the strictly professional literature in education, he would hesitate to express an opinion on the issues some of his colleagues were so certain about—divisions of the school period, content of the curriculum at various levels, level of professional training, vocational education, and freeing the schools from political influence.

He gave large public lectures. A 1947 lecture on the gifted, in Stanford's Tuesday Evening Series, drew an attendance of 1318, including 518 students, one of the largest ever. He was interviewed for radio and for shortwave broadcast to South America. And in 1954, when he was seventy-seven, he was chosen by a committee of distinguished psychologists to give the first Walter V. Bingham Lecture for the American Psychological Association. Though he dreaded the task, the lecture went over better than he had dared hope; one thousand people turned away from a hall which seated twenty-five hundred.

Honors had begun to come Terman's way as early as the 1920s, when he became a member of Phi Beta Kappa and of Sigma Xi. He was elected to the Eugenics Research Association in 1920, and later served as a member of its Consultative Council in 1952-53. In 1934, he was elected to the American Academy of Arts and Sciences, and in 1953 to the American Philosophical Society. His name appeared in *American Men of Science* and other biographical dictionaries too numerous to mention.

He was awarded the LL.D. in 1929 by Indiana University, in 1930 by Clark University (in absentia), and in 1945 by the University of California. In 1946, he received the honorary D.Sci. from the University of Pennsylvania (in absentia). And in 1949, he was awarded the LL.D. by the University of Southern California. In 1947, he was made an Honorary Fellow of the Educational Institute of Scotland, and in 1950, of the British Psychological Society.

In 1955, Terman presented a brief paper at the convention of the American Psychological Association (Terman unpublished, 1955); at the same time he received citations from two APA divisions, Old Age and School Psychologists, for his application of scientific methods of appraisal in the behavioral sciences. At that convention, President-elect Theodore Newcomb briefly congratulated Terman on establishing so many landmarks. Terman replied that luck had a great deal to do with it—that he had just happened to be in the right place at the right time on a few occasions. Newcomb quickly asked whether Terman had ever determined the probability that he was the man who happened to be at that particular place at that particular time so often. Terman grinned and chuckled.

In 1956, Terman received the Award of Merit given by the American Vocational Guidance Association. In the same year, he was selected to receive the Gold Medal given as the Distinguished Psychologist Award of the American Psychological Foundation, an honor previously conferred only on Robert Woodworth. Terman died between his nomination and the scheduled presentation in September 1957; since the Foundation gave no posthumous awards, the committee in charge honored him by finding no substitute. As late as 1959, when the American Psychological Association selected the ten most outstanding American psychologists, Terman was third on the list. All these honors must have gratified the humble farm boy and teacher who became a distinguished psychologist.

As retirement went on, Terman's interest in research began to wane. His reading narrowed somewhat. He read little psychology in languages other than English. Though he had been a member of the Book-of-the-Month Club for many years, taking one book out of three, he lost confidence in its recommendations. He became even less fond of poetry and lost most of the interest he once had in philosophy. He had never had a deep interest in painting, sculpture, or music. Most of his nonprofessional reading was still biography; his other interests were history, economics, and archaeology.

During his retirement years, Terman formulated his views on religion more explicitly. As early as 1929, he had pointed out that people are not all alike: some need religion and some do not. When friends urged him to include material on religion in his gifted follow-up, he agreed; he had neglected the field up to that point because so few of the gifted had mentioned it, and because psychologists lacked interest in studying religious phenomena.

For himself, he had never been especially religious, though he was not truly antireligious. He questioned whether any Catholic, even a liberal, could become a good scientist. Yet the twenty to thirty Protestant ministers he had known disgusted him with their sanctimonious speech, while the half-dozen priests he had come across were much less narrow and hypocritical. Terman opposed any kind of religious infiltration into the public schools, even excusing children for religious instruction. All theologies and dogmas seemed equally childish to him.

He congratulated friends who found a religious philosophy that gave them peace of mind. For himself, determinism and free will were opposing incompatibles. As a scientist, he leaned to determinism; as a person, he believed in freedom of will. Yet he was deeply religious in one sense. When he read the new cosmologies by leading astronomers, he was struck by the mystery of it all—what it is, how it began, what it might mean. Such ultimate questions would never be answered by science, and he doubted that the scientific way could even become a complete substitute for religion.

He wrote to Anton Boisen that of the four criteria of religious faith Boisen proposed, only one was valid for him, that of social consequence. Terman had spent some time among Mormons when he had visited Utah State College, and though he thought Mormon theology absurd, he would rate the religion very high on social consequence.

Terman's views on religion are best expressed in a manuscript solicited for a series in the *American Weekly* (Terman unpublished, 1948b). He contended that if God is a synonym for the universe of being, it is a semantic contradiction to deny His existence. Yet if God is taken as a personal entity, no logical, theological, or philosophical discussion could require the acceptance of such a definition as the *sine qua non* of faith. It is the spirit, not the dogma, of religion that is important. It is simply not given to us to know whether there is a life after death; it is better, instead, to live so that the good one does will continue to influence the minds and hearts of those who come after. Prayer as a petition for favors is childish, but prayer as communion with one's better self in taking stock of acts and motives and in searching for strength has great validity. Because science cannot reveal final causes does not make it incompatible with religious attitudes; science is simply another form of the quest for knowledge, more productive than blind faith. If one believes in ultimate Good, it does not matter whether one believes in a personal God. The wholehearted dedication of a life to the promotion of social justice, mutual understanding, racial tolerance, and equalization of opportunity is as good an evidence of a truly religious spirit as any beliefs one might hold about miracles, immortality, or a personal God.

Only a few years later, Terman faced his religious beliefs in a far more personal way. In 1954, Anna suffered a slight stroke; her only symptoms were an inability to focus her eyes, some dizziness, and awkwardness in one leg. She went to bed at once, the symptoms disappeared quickly, and her blood pressure returned to normal. During 1955 she continued to have dizzy spells; in December of that year she woke one morning slightly paralyzed on her right side, though less severely than in her previous attack. But she suffered a noticeable impairment of memory, so she needed a practical nurse with her constantly. Terman was disturbed about her future.

Late in March of 1956, death came to Anna. She had enjoyed a weekend with a number of visitors, followed by a visit from an old friend about eight o'clock in the evening. As the nurse was helping her get ready for bed, she dropped to the floor and was gone instantly. The doctor was there within ten minutes, but death had come without a struggle from a sudden, unexpected failure of the heart. Anna had often hoped that when her time came she could go in just that way—without a long period of invalidism. Terman, who was in the hospital for two weeks recovering from an injured vertebra from convulsive coughing, went home at once. As they had agreed, no formal rites of any kind were held for Anna.

With Anna gone the house seemed very big and lonely. Things could never be the same with her life permanently closed, her sympathetic understanding and adjustment to reality gone. Terman could not imagine why anyone would want to go through life unmarried. The memories of fifty-six years together made it easier to overlook the deterioration she had suffered during her last months. To his closest friends he admitted his loneliness, but consoled himself with the thought that if one can believe death is not the end, one can be reconciled to waiting. For himself, he could not imagine life simply stopping.

For a while, his life consisted of trying to do alone all the things he and Anna had done together. His children and grand-children were nearby, and the needs of members of his gifted group took his mind off himself. He still had the housekeeper who had looked after him and Anna so faithfully for many years. He arranged for a law student to live in his home to keep the house from seeming so lonely. He bought a television set and enjoyed it, though he made the purchase initially for the sake of the two graduate students or young instructors he hoped to have living with him. Each would have a private suite of study, bedroom, and bath, and one would pay no rent if he were willing to stay at home most of the evenings, just in case anything happened to Terman.

By this time Terman was seventy-nine. His old sixty-hour week had shrunk to less than the thirty hours he recommended to friends at retirement. The obituaries in science and elsewhere reminded him forcefully of the uncertainty of life; yet he did not worry about death. It was only that there were things he was anxious to get done before ill health, senility, or death stopped him. He still went to the office for three to five hours a day, and managed to get in four to five hours of reading each evening. As time grew shorter, he grew more and more eager to get some books read that he had not previously found time for.

Most of all, his attitude remained positive. Anything could happen to a man in his late seventies. The only thing to do was to keep going as long as one could and to avoid pessimism. He was fortunate that his eyes permitted so much reading and that he had not failed mentally. He felt lucky to be able to work, though it took far more effort than in the old days. He was fortunate to have lived so long, and to have had so many moments of happiness.

In his own words:

Approaching 77 now, I have lived more years than I dared hope for a half century ago and have accomplished more than I ever dreamed possible, probably as much as I would have accomplished if I had never had TB. From this distance it is possible to look back upon the threats of those earlier years without reviving the raw anxiety they caused me. Though I long ago lost my fear of death from tuberculosis (or anything else), I still find myself occasionally counting my pulse or reaching for the clinical thermometer that lies on a table by my bed. ... I want to finish another book and to watch for a while longer developments on the world scene. Besides there are my 1400 gifted "children," now at mid-life, who were selected by mental tests in 1922: I have already followed their careers for thirty years and should like so much to follow them for another thirty! (Terman unpublished, 1953).

Terman did not have long to tolerate his loneliness after Anna's death. Six months later, on September 27, 1956, he spent his last day at the office. He suffered a cerebral thrombosis, but recovered rapidly enough to plan a return to work in early November. On November 21 he had a second stroke, which left him in the hospital for a month, paralyzed on the left side, with only brief interludes of consciousness. Yet when he was conscious, his remarks indicated that his intellect was not affected. When Paul Farnsworth visited him, Terman's mouth was moving; when Farnsworth said, "Hello, Lewis," Terman replied, "Oh-oh, you caught me." Farnsworth asked what he meant. Terman explained, "Well, Paul, I can't imagine living without a decent IQ." Then: "I'm trying to recall things, to be sure I can recall.": "This really worries me terribly. So if you ever see me again with my mouth going, you'll know what is happening."

Still, the doctors did not give up hope. Because of his remarkable recovery from serious illnesses in the past, his friends hoped he would weather this crisis, too. As late as December, Terman roused himself enough to ask about topics discussed at a scientific meeting, and to learn that a new Palo Alto junior high school had been named for him. But his frail body could not rally from this final blow. Terman died on December 21, 1956, three weeks before his eightieth birthday.

As Terman had wished, there were no funeral rites. He had told his closest friends, as well as the Stanford Chaplain, that he did not want a memorial service in a church. In fact, if there were any rites at all for him at his death, and if he could possibly do it, he would come back and haunt them.

But Fred was Provost of Stanford University, and to have no service of any kind would be a source of embarrassment to his family and his friends on the faculty. So, three months after Terman's death, on April 7, 1957, a Conference on the Gifted Child took place, designed by Robert Sears as a day devoted to Terman and his work with the gifted. Melita Oden reviewed Terman's work, and Dael Wolfle and Nancy Bayley participated as representatives of the psychological profession. The Cubberley Auditorium at Stanford was filled, and the program was broadcast to other centers. Terman could have had no objections to such a meeting, and his friends were content.

The usual necrologies were arranged for. Fred asked Boring to write a biography for the National Academy of Sciences (Boring, 1959). Ernest Hilgard, who had succeeded Terman as Chairman of the Department of Psychology, summarized his career for the American Psychological Association (Hilgard, 1957). Robert Sears evaluated Terman's contribution for *Science* (Sears, 1957). William B. Lewis reviewed his life's work for the *British Journal of Statistical Psychology* (Lewis, 1957). There were many brief reviews in newspapers and periodicals (Beck, 1956, and others).

Even before the Conference, however, Melita Oden and the office staff were gradually getting back into stride. Terman wanted the follow-up of the gifted to continue after his death, and his will had allocated half his royalties on the Stanford Achievement Test for that purpose. By 1959, Volume V of the *Genetic Studies of Genius* was ready (Terman, 1959), documenting the follow-up of the gifted after thirty-five years. And under the supervision of Robert Sears (David Starr Jordan Professor of Social Sciences in Psychology) and Lee Cronbach (Lee Jacks Professor of Educational Psychology), two of the "Termites," the work still goes on—a living memorial to Lewis Madison Terman.

CHAPTER XII

Perspective

I am fully aware that my researches have not contributed very greatly to the theory of mental measurement. On problems of less theoretical significance, but of importance for the usefulness of tests and for the psychology of individual differences, I think I have made contributions of value. If I am remembered very long after my death, it will probably be in connection with my gifted children, and construction of mental tests, and the psychology of sex differences. I think that I saw more clearly than others the possibilities of mentality testing, have succeeded in devising tests that work better than their competitors, and, by the application of test methods, have added to the world's knowledge of exceptional children . . . (Terman, 1932f, p. 328).

HALF a century has passed since Lewis Terman launched mental testing on a large scale, focused attention on the gifted, and helped to introduce systematic empirical study of the psychology of sex differences and marital happiness. Other psychologists have taken up his work, extending, supporting, or opposing his points of view. Two questions remain: Just what kind of man was Lewis Terman? And what were his lasting accomplishments?

Lewis Terman was a man who loved learning. With the tolerance and encouragement of his pioneer family, he rose from an ordinary background to a position as one of the leading psychologists of his day. As a child, he learned easily and read omnivorously. As a young man, he used his every resource to continue his schooling to the doctorate. He sought and found a professorship in which his tremendous capacity for growth brought a formidable reputation for research. And in retirement, he continued his investigations and explored new fields.

Lewis Terman was thoroughly work-oriented; he was patient and tirelessly persistent in the pursuit of ideas. His farm boyhood taught him the importance of work early. He found things intellectual to be the way to achievement and status for him, and illness

184

and debt sharpened an anxiety that drove him relentlessly. He was a man of enthusiasms, ambitious for his interests, and an ardent defender of his conclusions once they were reached. Though eminence eventually relaxed his intensity, he never relinquished the quest for knowledge as long as he lived, and he left an endowment to assure the completion of his work.

Lewis Terman was a sensitive and friendly man, mature in the sense that he had found a good balance between intelligence and feeling. He was humble and unpretentious—sometimes almost naive. Many of his acquaintances found him more than a little shy, preserving a certain distance between himself and others. But others found him kindly and gracious, wise and tolerant and liberal. In those nearest him he engendered not only a dedication to knowledge, but also a rare personal loyalty. He seemed to develop a kind of protective facade behind which lived a gentle man who radiated warmth, but whom few ever really knew.

This was the man who became a pioneer in mental testing. Taking up a movement in disfavor, he developed a systematic and amazingly reliable method of measuring intelligence. Then he turned the same process to group testing of intelligence, achievement, and personality. As an innovator, he became the focal point of attacks on testing. He rested his case on the simple fact that when a sample of behavior is measured under standard conditions with a standardized measuring instrument, future behaviors of a similar kind can be predicted with a known degree of error. In the end, his efforts affected schools, industry, court procedure, and many other social organizations.

Most of all, this was the man whose landmark studies created a taxonomy of the gifted. He destroyed the common myth that the brilliant youngster is peculiar, unhealthy, and doomed to early deterioration. Himself a gifted child, Terman used his knowledge of childhood and of individual differences to illuminate; he pleaded the case for modifying the upbringing and education of the gifted, for the sake of the society whose strongest resource they might well become.

He applied his talents to the study of personality, particularly sex differences and marital compatibility. He gave a basic factual foundation to understanding psychological sex differences and to the theory on which marital counseling rests.

These contributions are enviable. Beyond them, Terman's point of view influenced others in more subtle ways. To begin with, he transmitted his own high research standards to his students. He kept them working near the limits of knowledge, raising new ideas, developing a respect for research and the feeling that they should do something about it. He permitted no superficiality, no guesswork, no sloppy technique. Instead, he fostered a dispassionate way of looking at things, a keen analytic ability, and a devotion to setting back the boundaries of the unknown. He infected his students with his own enthusiasm for resarch.

He was an excellent interpreter of his own ideas. Beginning with Binet as a model, he formed a writing style known for its clarity and simplicity. He reported facts, then brought out their implicit meaning through cases, parallels, and implications. Such clear and felicitous writing was important in making the kind of major breakthrough he sought understandable and acceptable to other psychologists and to informed individuals everywhere.

Terman advocated an inductive approach to research. He differed from the current deductive psychological fashion of beginning with a hypothesis to be tested. In his opinion, starting with a theory or hypothesis limited exploration; in addition, it smacked of the early introspective psychology which he thought utterly ridiculous. Establishing a theoretical framework only limited and warped the meaning of research. His curious and inquiring mind went after significant facts wherever they were to be found, without stopping to see whether they fit into a particular hypothetical system. He preferred to tease out facts, juggle and manipulate them looking for overall principles, and then bring principles into an overall theoretical order as a final step. His inductive approach was particularly suitable to the large-scale empirical research he chose to do in pioneering fields.

He understood the two-way relationship between education and psychology as few others have. As a teacher turned psychologist, he had rare insight into both fields. He defended educators to psychologists who were overeager for wholesale reform. He pointed out that a wholly theoretical attack on practical problems is often sterile, and that a more concentrated focus on immediate, practical problems more often leads to major theoretical advance. He argued that education is not simply a field in which psychology is applied, but one to which psychology might well turn for problems and hypotheses.

Lewis Madison Terman left his mark, as a pioneer in psychology and as a man. His influence broadened the understanding of many who now carry on their own work in fields where he turned the first furrow.

Publications of Lewis M. Terman

1904—"A Preliminary Study in the Psychology and Pedagogy of Leadership," *Pedag. Sem.*, 1904, *11*, 413-451.

1905—"A Study in Precocity and Prematuration," *Amer. J. Psychol.*, 1905, *16*, 145-183.

1906—"Genius and Stupidity: A Study of Some of the Intellectual Processes of Seven 'Bright' and Seven 'Stupid' Boys," *Pedag. Sem.*, 1906, *13*, 307-373.

1907—"Scholarship and the Professional Training of Teachers," *Educator-J.*, 1907, *7*, 375-377; 447-450.

1908—a "Child Study: Its Reason and Promise," *Univ. Calif. Chron.*, 1908, *11*, 145-158; *Educator-J.*, 1911, *12*, 117-134.

 b "Factors of Safety," *New Eng. Mag.*, 1908, *39*, 508-512.

 c "The Point of View, Confessions of a Pedagogue." *Scribner's Mag.*, 1908, *43*, 505-508.

1909—a "Commercialism: The Educator's Bugbear," *Sch. Rev.*, 1909, *17*, 193-195.

 b "Education Against Nature," *Harp. Wkly.*, 1909, *53*, 17.

 c "Pathology of School Discipline," *New Eng. Mag.*, 1909, *41*, 479-484.

 d "Waste on Phonic Drills," *Educator-J.*, 1909, *9*, 433-436.

1911—a "The Binet-Simon Scale for Measuring Intelligence: Impressions Gained by Its Application Upon Four Hundred Non-selected Children," *Psychl. Clin.*, 1911, *5*, 199-206.

 b "Medical Inspection of Schools in California," *Psychol. Clin.*, 1911, *5*, 57-62.

 c "Paradoxes of Personality, or Muckraking in the Psychology of Character," *New Eng. Mag.*, 1911, *44*, 371-374.

 d "Relation of the Manual Arts to Health," *Pop. Sci. Mon.*, 1911, *78*, 602-609.

 e "A School Where Girls are Taught Home-making," *Craftsman*, 1911, *20*, 63-68.

 f "Some Paradoxes of Personality," *Out West*, 1911, *1*, 201-204.

1912—a "Does Your Child Stutter?" *Harp. Wkly.*, 1912, *56*, 12.

 b "Evils of School Life," *Harp. Wkly.*, 1912, *56*, 24.

 c "A New Apostle of Childhood," *Educator-J.*, 1912, *12*, 585-588.

 d "Professional Training for Child Hygiene," *Pop. Sci. Mon.*, 1912, *80*, 289-297.

 e Review of "Normal Child and Primary Education," by Arnold Gesell. *J. Educ. Psychol.*, 1912, *3*, 526-527.

 f "School Clinics, Dental and Medical," *Psychol. Clin.*, 1912, *5*, 271-278.

 g "Survey of Mentally Defective Children in the Schools of San Luis Obispo, California," *Psychol. Clin.*, 1912, *6*, 131-139.

 h (With H. G. Childs) "A Tentative Revision and Extension of the Binet-Simon Measuring Scale of Intelligence. Pt. I. Introduction." *J. Educ. Psychol.*, 1912, *3*, 61-74. "Pt. II. Supplementary Tests." *J. Educ. Psychol.*, 1912, *3*, 133-143; 198-208. "Pt. III. Summary and Criticisms." *J. Educ. Psychol.*, 1912, *3*, 277-289.

1913—a (With David Starr Jordan) "The Contribution of School Hygiene to Human Conservation," *Dietetic and Hygienic Gaz.*, 1913, *29*, 489-490.

 b "Psychological Principles Underlying the Binet-Simon Scale and Some Practical Considerations for Its Correct Use," *J. Psycho-Asthen.*, 1913, *18*, 93-104.

 c "A Report of the Buffalo Conference on the Binet-Simon Tests of Intelligence," *Pedag. Sem.*, 1913, *20*, 549-554.

 d Review of "School Hygiene," by Fletcher B. Dresslar. *Science*, 1913, *38*, 625-626.

 e (With A. Hocking) "The Sleep of School Children: Its Distribution According to Age, and Its Relation to Physical and Mental Efficiency," *J. Educ. Psychol.*, 1913, *4*, 138-147, 199-208, 269-282.

 f "The Sleep of the Feeble-minded," *Train. Sch. Bull.*, 1913, *9*, 150-153.

 g "Social Hygiene: The Real Conservation Problem," *North Amer. Rev.*, 1913, *198*, 404-412.

 h "Suggestions for Revising, Extending, and Supplementing the Binet Intelligence Tests," *J. Psycho-Asthen.*, 1913, *18*, 20-33.

 i "Teacher's Health." *Riverside Educ. Monogr.*, 1913.

 j *The Teacher's Health: A Study in the Hygiene of an Occupation.* Boston: Houghton Mifflin, 1913.

 k "Tragedies of Childhood," *Forum*, 1913, *49*, 41-47.

    l (With D. S. Jordan) "World Congress for Child Welfare," *S. F. Call*, Sunday Mag., Aug. 1913.

1914—*a* "Concerning Psycho-Clinical Expertness," *Train. Sch. Bull.*, 1914, *11*, 9; *J. Educ. Psychol.*, 1914, *5*, 164-165.

    b (With Ellwood P. Cubberley) "Educational Work at Stanford University in Behalf of Backward and Feeble-minded Children," *Sierra Educ. News*, 1914, *10*, 501.

    c "The Effects of School Life Upon the Nutritive Processes, Health, and the Composition of the Blood," *Pop. Sci. Mon.*, 1914, *84*, 257-264.

    d (With E. B. Hoag) *Health Work in the Schools.* Boston: Houghton Mifflin, 1914.

    e *The Hygiene of the School Child.* Boston: Houghton Mifflin, 1914.

    f *Medical Inspection, Hygiene Teaching, Physical Training and Special Schools for Defectives in Portland, Oregon.* Report of the Survey of the Public School System of Portland. Yonkers: World Book, 1914.

    g "Precocious Children," *Forum*, 1914, *52*, 893-898.

    h "Recent Literature on Juvenile Suicides," *J. Abnorm. Psychol.*, 1914, *9*, 61-66.

    i "Review of Meumann on Tests of Endowment," *J. Psycho-Asthen.*, 1914, *19*, 75-94, 123-234, 187-199.

    j Review of "Problems of Educational Readjustment," by David S. Snedden. *Stanford Alumnus*, 1914, *15*, 174-176.

    k Review of "School Health Administration," by Louis W. Rapeer. *Science*, 1914, *39*, 725-726.

    l "The Significance of Intelligence Tests for Mental Hygiene," *J. Psycho-Asthen.*, 1914, *18*, 119-127.

    m "The Sleep of School Children," *Child*, 1914, *4*, 804-810.

    n "Teeth and Civilization," *Forum*, 1914, *51*, 418-424.

    o (With Ellwood P. Cubberley) "To Help Backward School Children," *Stanford Alumnus*, April 1914.

    p "A Vocabulary Test," *Youth's Companion*, 1914, *88*, 672.

    q (With J. H. Williams) *Whittier State School Biennial Report:* Psychological Survey of the Whittier State School, Preliminary and Final Reports. Whittier, California: Whittier State School, 1914.

1915—*a* (With E. P. Cubberley, J. H. Van Sickle, J. B. Sears, and J. Harold Williams) "Buildings and Health." In *Report of the*

Survey of the Public School System of Salt Lake City, Utah. Salt Lake City: 1915, Pt. 3, Pp. 221-298.

b "Earache, a Danger Signal," *Youth's Companion*, 1915, *89*, 10.

c "Impressions of the Eighth Annual Congress of the American School Hygiene Association," *Child*, 1915, *6*, 77-79.

d "Measuring Intelligence," *Calif. Outlook*, 1915, *18*, 4-5.

e "The Mental Hygiene of Exceptional Children," *Pedag. Sem.*, 1915, *22*, 529-537.

f "Protecting the Teeth," *Mother's Mag.*, 1915, *10*, 110.

g (With J. H. Williams) *Relation of Delinquency and Criminality to Mental Deficiency.* Whittier, California: Whittier State School, 1915.

h *Research in Mental Deviation Among Children: A Statement of the Aims and Purposes of the Buckel Foundation.* Stanford University: Stanford University Press, 1915.

i Review of "Osceola: An Educational Utopia," by Ellwood P. Cubberley, *Stanford Alumnus*, 1915, *16*, 180-182.

j (With H. E. Knollin) "Some Problems Relating to the Detection of Borderline Cases of Mental Deficiency," *J. Psycho-Asthen.*, 1915, *20*, 3-15.

k (With G. Lyman, G. Ordahl, L. Ordahl, N. Galbreath, and W. Talbert) "The Stanford Revision of the Binet-Simon Scale and Some Results from Its Application to 1000 Non-selected Children," *J. Educ. Psychol.*, 1915, *6*, 551-562.

1916—a "The American School Hygiene Association," *Soc. Serv. Rev.*, 1916, *4*, 23.

b "Assaying Intelligence," *Stanford Illus. Rev.*, 1916, *2*, 174-175; 184-187.

c "The Binet Scale and the Diagnosis of Feeblemindedness," *J. Crim. Law Criminol.*, 1916, *7*, 530-543.

d "The Binet Scale and the Diagnosis of Feeblemindedness," *Nat. Educ. Assn. J.*, 1916, *1*, 874-879.

e "The Building Situation and Medical Inspection." In *Denver School Survey*. Pt. V. Denver, 1916.

f "The Measurement of Intelligence." In *Young People's Encyclopedia*. Chicago: Hudson Bellows, 1916.

g *The Measurement of Intelligence.* Boston: Houghton Mifflin, 1916.

h (With others) "Mentality Tests: A Symposium," *J. Educ. Psychol.*, 1916, *7*, 348-360.

i Review of "Being Well Born," by M. F. Guyer. *Sierra Educ. News*, 1916, *12*, 170.

j Review of "The Criminal Imbecile," by Henry H. Goddard. *J. Delinqu.*, 1916, *1*, 56-57.

k Review of "Man: An Adaptive Mechanism," by Geo. W. Crile. *J. Delinqu.*, 1916, *1*, 158-160.

l Review of "Mendelism and the Problem of Mental Defect," by Karl Pearson. *J. Delinqu.*, 1916, *1*, 102-104.

m Review of "Self Reliance," by Dorothy Canfield Fisher. *Sierra Educ. News*, 1916, *12*, 554.

n Review of the Vineland Translation of Articles by Binet and Simon. *J. Delinqu.*, 1916, *1*, 256-272.

o "Some Comments on Dr. Haines' Comparison of the Binet-Simon and Yerkes-Bridges Intelligence Scales," *J. Delinqu.*, 1916, *1*, 115-117.

p *The Stanford Revision of the Binet-Simon Tests.* Boston: Houghton Mifflin, 1916.

1917—*a* "Feeble-minded Children in the Public Schools of California," *Sch. & Soc.*, 1917, *5*, 161-165.

b "The Intelligence Quotient of Francis Galton in Childhood," *Amer. J. Psychol.*, 1917, *28*, 209-215.

c "The Mental Powers of Children and the Stanford Revision and Extension of the Binet-Simon Intelligence Scale," *Child*, 1917, *7*, 287-290.

d (With G. Lyman, G. Ordahl, L. E. Ordahl, N. Galbreath, and W. Talbert) "The Stanford Revision and Extension of the Binet-Simon Scale for Measuring Intelligence." *Educ. Psychol. Monogr.*, 1917, No. 18.

e "A Trial of Mental and Pedagogical Tests in a Civil Service Examination of Policemen and Firemen," *J. Appl. Psychol.*, 1917, *1*, 17-29.

1918—*a* (With Virgil Dickson and Lowry Howard) "Backward and Feeble-minded Children in the Public Schools of "X" County; California." In *Surveys in Mental Deviation in Prisons, Public Schools, and Orphanages in California.* Sacramento: California State Board of Charities and Corrections, 1918. Pp. 19-45.

b "Errors in Scoring Binet Tests," *Psychol. Clin.*, 1918, *12*, 33-39.

c "An Experiment in Infant Education," *J. Appl. Psychol.*, 1918, *2*, 219-228.

d "Expert Testimony in the Case of Alberto Flores," *J. Delinqu.*, 1918, *3*, 145-164.

e (With D. Wagner) "Intelligence Quotients of 68 Children in a California Orphanage," *J. Delinqu.*, 1918, *3*, 115-121.

f (With H. E. Knollin) "A Partial Psychological Survey of the Prison Population of San Quentin, California, Based on Mental Tests of 155 Consecutive Entrants." In *Surveys in Mental Deviation in Prisons, Public Schools, and Orphanages in California.* Sacramento: California State Board of Charities and Corrections, 1918. Pp. 6-19.

g (With Irene Cuneo) "Stanford-Binet Tests of 112 Kindergarten Children and 77 Repeated Tests," *Pedag. Sem.*, 1918, *25*, 414-428.

h "Tests of General Intelligence," *Psychol. Bull.*, 1918, *15*, 160-167.

i (With M. B. Chamberlain) "Twenty-three Serial Tests of Intelligence and Their Intercorrelations," *J. Appl. Psychol.*, 1918, *2*, 341-354.

j "The Use of Intelligence Tests in the Army," *Psychol. Bull.*, 1918, *15*, 177-187.

k "The Vocabulary Test as a Measure of Intelligence," *J. Educ. Psychol.*, 1918, *9*, 452-466.

1919—a *The Intelligence of School Children.* Boston: Houghton Mifflin, 1919.

b "Dental Clinics." In *Bulletin No. 60.* Washington: Children's Bur., U. S. Dept. Labor, 1919. Pp. 234-237.

c "Some Data on the Binet Test of Naming Words," *J. Educ. Psychol.*, 1919, *10*, 29-35.

1920—a (With others.) *National Intelligence Tests, with Manual of Directions.* Yonkers: World Book, 1920.

b (With J. M. Chase) "The Psychology, Biology and Pedagogy of Genius," *Psychol. Bull.*, 1920, *17*, 397-409.

c "Scholarship and Success," *Stanford Cardinal*, 1920, *29*, 265-266.

d *Terman Group Test of Mental Ability.* Yonkers; World Book, 1920.

e "The Use of Intelligence Tests in the Grading of School Children," *J. Educ. Res.*, 1920, *1*, 20-32.

1921—a (With E. D. Whitmire) "Age and Grade Norms for the National Intelligence Tests, Scales A and B," *J. Educ. Res.*, 1921, *3*, 124-132.

b (With T. L. Kelley) "Dr. Ruml's Criticism of Mental Test Methods," *J. Phil.*, 1921, *18*, 459-465.

c (With others) "Intelligence and Its Measurement: A Symposium," *J. Educ. Psychol.*, 1921, *12*, 127-133.

d "Intelligence Tests in Colleges and Universities," *Sch. & Soc.*, 1921, *13*, 481-494.

e "Mental Growth and the I.Q.," *J. Educ. Psychol.*, 1921, *12*, 325-341; 401-407.

f (With J. C. Fenton) "Preliminary Report on a Gifted Juvenile Author," *J. Appl. Psychol.*, 1921, *5*, 163-178.

g "Methods of Examining: History, Development and Preliminary Results." In Robert M. Yerkes (Ed.), *Psychological Examining in the United States Army. Mem. Nat. Acad. Sci.*, Vol. 15, Part II. Washington: Government Printing Office, 1921. Pp. 299-546.

h "The Status of Applied Psychology in the United States," *J. Appl. Psychol.*, 1921, *5*, 1-4.

i (With Jessie C. Fenton and Giles M. Ruch) *Suggestions for Children's Reading.* Stanford University: Stanford University Press, 1921.

j *Suggestions for the Education and Training of Gifted Children.* Stanford University: Stanford University Press, 1921.

k "$20,000 Grant by Commonwealth Fund of New York for Work with Gifted Children," *Sch. & Soc.*, 1921, *13*, 694-695.

1922—a "Adventures in Stupidity: A Partial Analysis of the Intellectual Inferiority of a College Student," *Sci. Mon.*, 1922, *14*, 23-38.

b "The Great Conspiracy, or the Impulse Imperious of Intelligence Testers, Psychoanalyzed and Exposed by Mr. Lippmann," *New Repub.*, 1922, *33*, 116-120.

c (With Virgil Dickson and others) *Intelligence Tests and School Reorganization.* Subcommittee's Report to the Commission on the Revision of Elementary Education, National Education Association Yonkers: World Book, 1922.

d "Mental Measurement Work Told," *Stanford Illus. Rev.*, 1922, *23*, 44; 457; 464.

e "A New Approach to the Study of Genius," *Psychol. Rev.*, 1922, *29*, 310-318.

f "The Problem." In Terman, L. M., and others. *Intelligence Tests and School Reorganization.* Yonkers: World Book, 1922. Pp. 1-31.

g "The Psychological Determinist, or Democracy and the I.Q.," *J. Educ. Res.*, 1922, *6*, 57-62.

h Review of "Intelligence of High School Seniors," by William F. Book. *Indiana U. Alumni Quart.*, 1922, *9*, 443-444.

i "Were We Born That Way?" *World's Work*, 1922, *44*, 655-660.

1923—*a* Editor's Introduction to: Dickson, Virgil E. *Mental Tests and the Classroom Teacher.* Yonkers: World Book, 1923.

b Editor's Introduction to: Wood, Ben D. *Measurement in Higher Education.* Yonkers: World Book, 1923.

c Foreword to: Cady, Vernon M. *The Estimation of Juvenile Incorrigibility.* Whittier, California: Calif. Bur. Juv. Res., Whittier State Sch., 1923.

d (With O. L. Elliott, T. L. Kelley, and others) *Report of Subcommittee of Leland Stanford Junior University Committee on Scholarship and Student Ability.* Stanford University: Stanford University Press, 1923.

e (With E. P. Cubberley, J. B. Sears, J. H. Van Sickle, and J. Harold Williams). *School Organization and Administration.* Yonkers: World Book, 1923.

f (With T. L. Kelley and G. M. Ruch) *Stanford Achievement Test.* Manuals of Directions for Primary Examination and Advanced Examination. Yonkers: World Book, 1923.

1924—*a* "American Psychological Association," *Science*, 1924, *59*, 546-548.

b "Conservation of Talent," *Sch. & Soc.*, 1924, *19*, 359-364; *Nat. Educ. Assn. Proc.*, 1923, 152-158.

c Editor's Introduction to: Stedman, Louise. *Education of Gifted Children.* Yonkers: World Book, 1924.

d (With J. C. DeVoss) "The Educational Achievements of Gifted Children." In *Yearb. Nat. Soc. Stud. Educ.*, 1924, *23*, Pt. I. Pp. 169-184.

e Introduction to: Bigelow, Maurice A. *Adolescence.* New York: Funk & Wagnalls, 1924. (National Health Series.)

f "Mental Measurements," *Wash. Educ. J.*, 1924, *3*, 133-136; 151.

g "The Mental Test as a Psychological Method," *Psychol. Rev.*, 1924, *31*, 93-117.

h "The Physical and Mental Traits of Gifted Children." In *Yearb. Nat. Soc. Stud. Educ.*, 1924, *23*, Pt. I. Pp. 155-167.

i "The Possibilities and Limitations of Training," *J. Educ. Res.*, 1924, *10*, 335-343.

j "Tests and Measurements of Gifted Children," *Wash. Educ. J.*, 1924, *3*, 172-173; 189-190.

1925—*a* "Bright Children Upset Notions About Genius," *N. Y. Times*, July 19, 1925, Sec. 8, p. 14.

b "Die Pflege der Begabung," (The Conservation of Talent) *Z. pädag. Psychol.*, 1925, *26*, 137-144.

c Editor's Introduction to: Otis, Arthur S. *Statistical Method in Educational Measurement.* Yonkers: World Book, 1925.

d Editor's Introduction to: Peterson, Joseph. *Early Conceptions and Tests of Intelligence.* Yonkers: World Book, 1925.

e (With others) *Genetic Studies of Genius. I. Mental and Physical Traits of a Thousand Gifted Children.* Stanford University: Stanford University Press, 1925.

f "Research on the Diagnosis of Pre-delinquent Tendencies," *J. Delinqu.*, 1925, *9*, 124-130.

g Review of "The Mental Growth of the Child," by Arnold Gesell. *Science*, 1925, *61*, 445-446.

h (With K. M. Cowdery) "Stanford Program of University Personnel Research," *J. Person. Res.*, 1925, *4*, 263-267.

1926—a "Biographical Note on Henry Cowell," *Amer. J. Psychol.*, 1926, *37*, 233-234.

b (With Margaret Lima) "Children's Reading," *Nat. Educ. Assn. J.*, 1926, *15*, 169-170.

c (With M. Lima) *Children's Reading: A Guide for Parents and Teachers.* New York: Appleton, 1926. 2nd ed., 1931.

d Editor's Introduction to: Fenton, Norman. *Self-Direction and Adjustment.* Yonkers: World Book, 1926.

e Editor's Introduction to: Goodenough, Florence L. *Measurement of Intelligence by Drawings.* Yonkers: World Book, 1926.

f Cox, C. M., assisted by Terman, L. M., and others. *Genetic Studies of Genius. II. The Early Mental Traits of 300 Geniuses.* Stanford University: Stanford University Press, 1926.

g "Independent Study Plan at Stanford University," *Sch. & Soc.*, 1926, *24*, 96-98.

h "The 1927 Yearbook of the National Society for the Study of Education, on the Possibilities and Limitations of Training," *Sch. & Soc.*, 1926, *23*, 404-406.

i "The Possibilities and Limitations of Training," *J. Educ. Res.*, 1926, *13*, 371-373.

j Review of "Elementary Psychology," by Arthur I. Gates. *J. Educ. Psychol.*, 1926, *17*, 214-216.

1927—a Editorial, "Fred Nelles, Practical Idealist," *J. Delinqu.*, 1927, *11*, 212-214.

b Editor's Introduction to: Kelley, Truman L. *Interpretation of Educational Measurements.* Yonkers: World Book, 1927.

c   Editor's Introduction to: Ruch, Giles M., and Stoddard, George D. *Tests and Measurements in High School Instruction.* Yonkers: World Book, 1927.

d   Editor's Introduction to: Wells, Frederic L. *Mental Tests in Clinical Practice.* Yonkers: World Book, 1927.

e   Review of "Behaviorism," by John B. Watson. *Amer. J. Psychol.*, 1927, *38*, 135-138.

f   Review of "Gifted Children: Their Nature and Nurture," by Leta S. Hollingworth. *J. Educ. Res.*, 1927, *15*, 63-64.

1928—a   Editorial, *J. Delinqu.*, 1928, *12*, 193-195.

b   Editor's Introduction to: Hull, Clark L. *Aptitude Testing.* Yonkers: World Book, 1928.

c   "Growth Through Professional Reading," *Nat. Educ. Assn. J.*, 1928, *17*, 137-138.

d   "The Influence of Nature and Nurture upon Intelligence Scores: An Evaluation of the Evidence in Part I of the 1928 Yearbook of the National Society for the Study of Education," *J. Educ. Psychol.*, 1928, *19*, 362-373.

e   "Introduction to: Nature and Nurture. I. Their Influence Upon Intelligence." In *Yearb. Nat. Soc. Stud. Educ.*, 1928, 27 Pt. I. Pp. 1-7.

f   "Testing for the Crime Germ," *Sunset*, 1928, *60*, 24-25, 54-56.

g   "Ultimate Influence of Standard Tests," *J. Educ. Res.*, 1928, *17*, 57-59.

1929—a   "Ability and Personality Tests," *Indep. Educ.*, 1929, *3*, 5-6.

b   (With J. C. Almack) *The Hygiene of the School Child.* (Rev. and enlarged ed.) Boston: Houghton Mifflin, 1929.

c   (With T. L. Kelley, G. M. Ruch, and others) *New Stanford Achievement Test.* Yonkers: World Book, 1929, 1940, 1953.

d   (With C. C. Miles) "Sex Difference in the Association of Ideas," *Amer. J. Psychol.*, 1929, *41*, 165-206.

1930—a   Editor's Introduction to: Hildreth, Gertrude H. *Psychological Service for School Problems.* Yonkers: World Book, 1930.

b   Editor's Introduction to: Madsen, I. N. *Educational Measurement in the Elementary Grades.* Yonkers: World Book, 1930.

c   (With B. S. Burks and D. W. Jensen) *Genetic Studies of Genius. III. The Promise of Youth: Follow-up Studies of a Thousand Gifted Children.* Stanford University: Stanford Univeristy Press, 1930.

d   "Talent and Genius in Children." In V. F. Calverton and S. D. Schmalhausen (Eds.), *The New Generation.* New York: Macaulay, 1930. Pp. 405-424.

1931—a   Editorial, *Child Study*, 1931, *9*, 1.

b   Editor's Introduction to: Stutsman, Rachel. *Mental Measurement of Preschool Children.* Yonkers: World Book, 1931.

c   "Educational Psychology." In E. M. East (Ed.), *Biology in Human Affairs.* New York: McGraw-Hill, 1931. Pp. 94-122.

d   "The Gifted Child." In C. A. Murchison (Ed.), *Handbook of Child Psychology.* Worcester: Clark Univ. Press, 1931. Pp. 568-584.

e   Introduction to: Fryer, Douglas. *The Measurement of Interests in Relation to Human Adjustment.* New York: H. Holt, 1931.

f   "Psychology and the Law," *Los Angeles Bar Assn. Bull.*, 1931, *6*, 142-153; *Commercial Law J.*, 1935, *40*, 639-646.

1932—a   Editor's Introduction to: Dunlap, Jack W., and Kutz, Albert K. *Handbook of Statistical Monographs, Tables, and Formulas.* Yonkers: World Book, 1932.

b   Editor's Introduction to: Washburne, Carleton, W. *Adjusting the School to the Child.* Yonkers: World Book, 1932.

c   "Intelligence Tests." In *White House Conference on Child Health and Protection*, Growth and Development of the Child, Part IV, Appraisement of the Child. New York: Century Co., 1932. Pp. 26-60.

d   "Mentally Superior Children." In *White House Conference on Child Health and Protection*, Growth and Development of the Child, Part IV, Appraisement of the Child. New York: Century Co., 1932. Pp. 61-75.

e   (With M. A. Merrill) "Preliminary Notes on a Revision of the Stanford-Binet Scale," *Psychol. Bull.*, 1932, *28*, 589.

f   "Trails to Psychology." In C. A. Murchison (Ed.), *A History of Psychology in Autobiography*, vol. II. Worcester: Clark Univ. Press, 1932. Pp. 297-332.

1933—a   (With Barbara S. Burks) "The Gifted Child." In C. A. Murchison (Ed.), *Handbook of Child Psychology.* (Second Ed. Rev.) Worcester: Clark Univ. Press, 1933. Pp. 773-801.

b   Introduction to: Bennett, M. E. *College and Life.* New York: McGraw-Hill, 1933, 1941, 1946, 1952.

1934—a   "The Measurement of Personality," *Science*, 1934, *80*, 605-608.

b   "Objective of Social Control and Motivation in a Planned Society." Chairman's Report of a Discussion Group: Soc. Sci. Res. Conf. of Pacific Coast, San Francisco, June 13-15, 1934. In *Proc. 4th Annual Conf.* Pp. 48-51.

c   "The Present Status of Personality Measurement," *Psychol. Bull.*, 1934, *31*, 584.

1935—*a*   (With Maud A. Merrill) "Analysis of Intelligence Test Scores." In G. W. Baehne (Ed.), *Practical Applications of the Punched Card Method in Colleges and Universities.* New York: Columbia University Press, 1935. Pp. 230-234.

 b   Introduction to: Fenton, Norman. *The Delinquent Boy and the Correctional School.* Claremont, California: Claremont Colleges Guidance Center, 1935.

 c   (With P. Buttenweiser) "Personality Factors in Marital Compatibility," *J. Soc. Psychol.*, 1935, *6*, 143-171; 267-289.

 d   (With W. B. Johnson) "Personality Characteristics of Happily Married, Unhappily Married, and Divorced Persons," *Charact. & Pers.*, 1935, *3*, 290-311.

 e   "Psychology." In C. G. Wrenn (Ed.), *University Training and Vocational Outlets.* Stanford University: The University, 1935. Pp. 61-64.

 f   (With Roger G. Barker) Review of "A Dynamic Theory of Personality," by Kurt Lewin. *Charact. & Pers.*, 1935, *4*, 91-92.

1936—*a*   (With E. L. Kelly & C. C. Miles) "Ability to Influence One's Score on a Typical Paper-and-Pencil Test of Personality," *Charact. & Pers.*, 1936, *4*, 206-215.

 b   (With C. C. Miles) *Attitude-Interest Analysis Test.* New York: McGraw-Hill, 1936.

 c   (With C. C. Miles) *Sex and Personality: Studies in Masculinity and Femininity.* New York: McGraw-Hill, 1936.

 d   (With Quinn Mc Nemar) "Sex Differences in Variational Tendency." *Genet. Psychol. Monogr.*, 1936, *18*, No. 1.

1937—*a*   (With M. A. Merrill) *Measuring Intelligence.* Boston: Houghton Mifflin, 1937.

 b   (With M. A. Merrill) *Revised Stanford-Binet Scale.* Boston: Houghton Mifflin, 1937.

1938—*a*   (With C. C. Miles) *Manual of Information and Directions for Use of Attitude-Interest Analysis Test.* New York: McGraw-Hill, 1938.

 b   *Psychological Factors in Marital Happiness.* New York: McGraw-Hill, 1938.

1939—*a*   "Educational Suggestions from Follow-up Studies of Intellectually Gifted Children," *J. Educ. Sociol.*, 1939, *13*, 82-89.

 b   "The Effect of Happiness or Unhappiness on Self-report Regarding Attitudes, Reaction Patterns, and Facts of Personal History," *Psychol. Bull.*, 1939, *36*, 197-202.

c "The Gifted Student and His Academic Environment," *Sch. & Soc.*, 1939, *49*, 65-73.

d (With W. B. Johnson) "Methodology and Results of Recent Studies in Marital Adjustment," *Amer. Sociol. Rev.*, 1939, *4*, 307-324.

e Review of "Plan for Marriage," by J. K. Folsom (Ed.) *Amer. J. Sociol.*, 1939, *45*, 136-137.

f Review of "The Student and His Knowledge," by William S. Learned and Ben D. Wood. *J. Higher Educ.*, 1939, *10*, 111-113.

1940—a "Frank Angell: 1857-1939," *Amer. J. Psychol.*, 1940, *53*, 138-141.

b "Intelligence in a Changing Universe," *Sch. & Soc.*, 1940, *51*, 465-470.

c "Personal Reactions of the Yearbook Committee, Nat. Soc. Stud. Educ." In *Yearb. Nat. Soc. Stud. Educ.*, 1940, *39* Pt. I. Pp. 460-467.

d "Psychological Approaches to the Biography of Genius," *Science*, 1940, *92*, 293-301.

e (With Melita Oden) "The Significance of Deviates. II. Status of the California Gifted Group at the End of Sixteen Years. III. Correlates of Adult Achievement in the California Gifted Group." In *Yearb. Nat. Soc. Stud. Educ.*, 1940, *39* Pt. I. Pp. 67-89.

f (With W. B. Johnson) "Some Highlights in the Literature of Psychological Sex Differences Published Since 1920," *J. Psychol.*, 1940, *9*, 327-336.

1941—a Introduction to: Howard, Lowry S. *The Road Ahead*. Yonkers: World Book, 1941.

b Review of "Human Nature and the Social Order," by E. L. Thorndike. *Science*, 1941, *94*, 236-238.

c Review of "Sex in Development," by Carney Landis and others. *Amer. J. Psychol.*, 1941, *54*, 453-455.

d "Should the Historian Study Psychology?" *Pac. Hist. Rev.*, 1941, *10*, 2, 209-216.

e (With Quinn McNemar) *Terman-McNemar Test of Mental Ability*. Yonkers: World Book, 1941.

1942—a Editor's Introduction to: Hollingworth, Leta. *Children Above 180 I.Q.* Yonkers: World Book, 1942.

b "The Revision Procedures." In Quinn McNemar, *The Revision of the Stanford-Binet Scale*. Boston: Houghton Mifflin, 1942. Pp. 1-14.

c "The Vocational Successes of Intellectually Gifted Individuals," *Occup.*, 1942, *20*, 493-498.

1943—a "Education and the Democratic Ideal," *Educ. Forum*, 1943, 7: sup., 5-8.

b Foreword to: Fernald, Grace M. *Remedial Techniques in Basic School Subjects.* New York: McGraw-Hill, 1943.

1944—a "Barbara Stoddard Burks (1902-1943), *Psychol. Rev.*, 1944, *51*, 136-141.

b Review of "Leta S. Hollingworth: A Biography," by H. L. Hollingworth. *J. Apl. Psychl.*, 1944, *28*, 357-359.

1946—a Editor's Introduction to: Cattell, Raymond B. *The Description and Measurement of Personality.* Yonkers: World Book, 1946.

b (With Winifred B. Johnson, George Kuznets, and Olga W. McNemar) "Psychological Sex Differences." In Leonard Carmichael (Ed.), *Manual of Child Psychology.* New York: John Wiley & Sons, 1946. Pp. 954-1000.

c Review of "How a Baby Grows: A Story in Pictures," by Arnold Gesell. *Science*, 1946, *103*, 60.

d *The Stanford Study of Gifted Children. Condensed Summary 1921-1946.* Stanford University: Stanford University Press, 1946. Printed for private distribution only.

1947—a "Factors in the Adult Achievement of Gifted Men." In *Miscellanea Psychologica Albert Michotte.* Louvain (Belgium): Institut Superieur de Philosophie, 1947. Pp. 371-381.

b (With Melita H. Oden) *Genetic Studies of Genius. IV. The Gifted Child Grows Up; Twenty-five Years Follow-up of a Superior Group.* Stanford University: Stanford University Press, 1947.

c "Marital Adjustment and Its Prediction." In M. Fishbein and E. W. Burgess (Eds.), *Successful Marriage.* New York: Doubleday, 1947. Rev. Ed. 1955. Pp. 113-126.

d "Psychological Approaches to the Biography of Genius." *Occasional Papers on Eugenics.* London: The Eugenics Society and Hamish Hamilton Medical Books. 1947, No. 4.

Note: The above was published originally as an article in *Science* in 1940. The same article, with an addendum, was published as a separate monograph in 1947.

e Review of "The Psychology of Human Differences," by Leona Tyler. *J. Appl. Psychol.*, 1947, *32*, 216-217.

f Review of "22 Cells in Nuremberg," by Douglas M. Kelley. *Psychol. Bull.*, 1947, *44*, 483-484.

1948—"Kinsey's 'Sexual Behavior in the Human Male': Some Comments and Criticisms." *Psychol. Bull.*, 1948, *45*, 443-459.

1949—*a* "A Critique of the Evaluations of the Study of Bernadine G. Schmidt entitled: 'Changes in Personal, Social, and Intellectual Behavior of Children Originally Classified as Feeble-minded,' " *J. Except. Child.*, 1949, *15*, 228-230.

    b Review of "Psychologist Unretired; The Life Pattern of Lillian J. Martin," by Miriam Allen deFord. *Calif. Med.*, 1949, *70*, 141-142.

    c (With Paul Wallin) "The Validity of Marriage Prediction and Marital Adjustment Tests," *Amer. Sociol. Rev.*, 1949, 14, 497-504.

    Note: The above article appears also in R. E. Winch and R. McGinnis (Eds.), *Selected Studies in Marriage and the Family.* New York: Henry Holt, 1953. Pp. 507-518.

1950—*a* "Predicting Marriage Failure from Test Scores," *Marriage Fam. Liv.*, 1950, *12*, 51-54.

    b (With M. R. Sumption and Dorothy Norris) "Special Education for the Gifted Child." In *Yearb. Nat. Soc. Stud. Educ.*, 1950, *49*, 259-280.

1951—*a* (With Nancy Bayley, Helen Marshall, Olga McNemar, and Melita Oden) "Correlates of Orgasm Adequacy in a Group of 556 Wives," *J. Psychol.*, 1951, *32*, 115-172.

    b Review of "The New You and Heredity," by Amram Scheinfeld. *Psychol. Bull.*, 1951, *48*, 457-458.

    c (With Melita H. Oden) "The Stanford Studies of the Gifted." In Paul Witty (Ed.), *The Gifted Child.* Boston: D. C. Heath, 1951. Pp. 20-46.

    Note: The above chapter appears in abridged form as "The Development and Adult Status of Gifted Children," in R. S. Kuhlen and G. G. Thompson (Eds.), *Psychological Studies of Human Development.* New York: Appleton-Century-Crofts, 1952. Pp. 199-210.

1952—Review of "Predicting Adjustment in Marriage," by Harvey J. Locke. *Sociol. & Soc. Res.*, 1952, *36*, 339-342.

1953—*a* Foreword to: Lehman, H. C., *Age and Achievement.* Pub. for Amer. Phil. Soc. by Princeton Univ. Press, 1953.

    b (With Maud A. Merrill) "1937 Stanford-Binet Scales." In A. Weider (Ed.), *Contributions Toward Medical Psychology.* New York: Ronald Press, 1953. Pp. 510-521.

c Review of "A History of Psychology in Autobiography," Vol. IV, by E. G. Boring, H. S. Langfeld, H. Werner, R. M. Yerkes (Eds.). *Psychol. Bull.*, 1953, *50*, 477-481.

d Review of "Mental Prodigies," by F. Barlow. *J. Appl. Psychol.*, 1953, *37*, 325-326.

1954—a "The Discovery and Encouragement of Exceptional Talent," *Amer. Psychologist*, 1954, *9*, 221-230.

b (With Melita Oden) "Major Issues in the Education of Gifted Children," *J. Tchr. Educ.*, 1954, *5*, 230-232.

c (With Leona Tyler) "Psychological Sex Differences." In Leonard Carmichael (Ed.), *Manual of Child Psychology*. New York: John Wiley & Sons, 1954. Pp. 1064-1114.

d "Scientists and Nonscientists in a Group of 800 Gifted Men." *Psychol. Monogr.*, 1954, *68*, No. 7 (Whole No. 378).

1955—a "Are Scientists Different?" *Scientif. Amer.*, 1955, *192*, 25-29.

b Foreword to: Lantz, Beatrice. *Easel Age Scale*. Los Angeles: California Test Bureau, 1955.

c "Louis Leon Thurstone (1887-1955)," *Yearb. Amer. Phil. Soc.*, *1955*, 504-508.

1956—a *Concept Mastery Test*. New York: Psychological Corp., 1956.

b Review of "Selection and Guidance of Gifted Students for National Survival," by Arthur E. Traxler (Ed.). *J. Contemp. Psychol.*, 1956, *1*, 359.

1958—"What Education for the Gifted Should Accomplish." In *Yearb. Nat. Soc. Stud. Educ.*, 1958, *57*, Pt. 2, pp. 15-19.

1959—(With Melita H. Oden) *Genetic Studies of Genius*. Vol. V. *The Gifted Group at Mid-life: Thirty-five Years Follow-up of the Superior Child*. Stanford University; Stanford University Press, 1959.

Unpublished Manuscripts
of Lewis M. Terman

1928—*a* (With Katherine Ames Taylor) "Brains Won't Hurt You!" 15 pages.

    b "Editorial," 4 pages.

1929—*a* "The Education of Gifted Children in the United States," 5 pages.

    b "Worry," 1 page.

1930—"Comments on the Norwegian Program for Race Hygiene," 1 page.

1934—*a* "Discovery of the Gifted Child," 1 page.

    b "How Gifted Children Turn Out," 8 pages.

1935—"Edmund S. Conklin: Principles of Adolescent Psychology," 2 pages.

1938—"Samuel Kahn: Mentality and Homosexuality," 2 pages.

1940—*a* "Leadership in the Present Emergency," 3 pages.

    b "Maturational Factors in Child Development," 24 pages.

    c "Why Stanford Wants Gifted Students," 5 pages.

1941—*a* "Human Intelligence and Achievement," 26 pages.

    b "A Lesson in Window Dressing," 5 pages.

1942—*a* "Some of the Things I Think About," 10 pages.

    b "Ten Vows of the Stanford Emeriti Graduates of 1942," 1 page.

1946—(with W. B. Johnson) "Marriage," 14 pages.

1947—*a* "Educating and Training the Gifted Child," 7 pages.

    b "If Your Child is Gifted———," 7 pages.

1948—*a* "The Education and Training of Gifted Children," 2 pages.

    b "My Faith," 6 pages.

1949—"The Prediction of Marriage Failure from Scores on Tests of Marital Happiness, Marital Aptitude, and Sex Adjustment," 9 pages.

1950—*a* "How Far Shall We Go in Aping Totalitarian Methods of Educational Control?" 2 pages.

    b "The 1937 Stanford-Binet Scales," 16 pages.

1953—"I Was Lucky," 10 pages.

1955—"Paper Read by Lewis M. Terman at the APA Meeting in San Francisco, September 1, 1955," 7 pages.

Ph.D. and M.A. Research Sponsored by Terman

Year	Department	Degree	Student	Title
1914	Education	M.A.	Galbreath, Neva L.	A revision of the Binet-Simon scale for measuring the intelligence of school children
1914	Education	M.A.	Lyman, Grace	Intelligence tests in relation to the analysis of intelligence
1915	Education	M.A.	Otis, Arthur S.	Some logical and mathematical aspects of the measurement of intelligence by the Binet scale
1916	Education	Ph.D.	Williams, J. Harold	The intelligence of the delinquent boy
1917	Education	M.A.	Cuneo, Irene	Individual differences among kindergarten children as shown by Stanford-Binet intelligence tests
1917	Education	M.A.	Dickson, Virgil E.	The relation of mental testing to school administration with special reference to children entering school
1917	Education	M.A.	Hopwood, Margaret B.	A study of superior children
1917	Education	M.A.	Knollin, Herbert E.	The relation of intelligence to unemployment and crime
1918	Education	Ph.D.	Darsie, Marvin L.	The intelligence of American-Japanese children
1918	Education	M.A.	Barr, Frank E.	A scale for measuring mental ability in vocations and some of its applications

1918	Education	M.A.	Horn, John L.	A study of fifty-three juvenile court wards and a case of pathological day dreaming
1918	Education	M.A.	Sullivan, Elizabeth	A study of certain tests and their significance in the administration of the high school curriculum
1919	Education	Ph.D.	Dickson, Virgil E.	The relation of mental testing to school administration (with E. P. Cubberley)
1919	Education	Ph.D.	Kohs, Samuel C.	Intelligence measurement; a psychological and statistical study based upon the block-design tests
1919	Education	M.A.	Howard, Lowry S.	A mental and pedagogical survey of the Redwood City school system
1920	Education	Ph.D.	Otis, Arthur S.	An absolute point scale for the group measurement of intelligence
1920	Education	Ph.D.	Stockton, James L.	The definition of intelligence in relation to modern methods of mental measurement
1920	Education	M.A.	Borncamp, Frederick F.	The mental development of the Oriental
1920	Education	M.A.	Gillan, Lela	Group tests and school success in the case of 277 high school pupils
1920	Education	M.A.	Merrill, Maud A.	The relation of intelligence to ability in the "three R's" in the case of retarded children
1920	Education	M.A.	Thomson, Mildred	Validity of Stanford-Binet tests as a basis or prediction of school success
1920	Education	M.A.	Whitmire, Ethel D.	A preliminary study of sex differences from the results of the National Intelligence Tests as given to 1340 unselected school children
1921	Education	M.A.	Fenton, Jessie Chase	A study of character and social adjustments in relation to superior intelligence

1921	Education	M.A.	Henry, Mary Bess	The department of research in a small city
1921	Education	M.A.	Remer, Laura L.	A comparative study of a borderline defective and a normal child of the same mental age
1921	Education	M.A.	Rensch, Grace E.	A study of 365 pairs of siblings with reference to the influence of heredity on mental ability
1921	Education	M.A.	Strachan, Lexie	A study of the vocabulary test of the Stanford revision of the Binet-Simon intelligence tests
1922	Education	Ph.D.	Merriman, Curtis	The intellectual resemblance of twins
1922	Education	Ph.D.	Ruch, Giles M.	The influence of the factor of intelligence on the form of the learning curve
1922	Education	Ph.D.	Young, Kimball	Mental differences in certain immigrant groups (with E. P. Cubberley)
1922	Education	M.A.	Cowdery, Karl M.	General intelligence as a factor in trade learning
1922	Education	M.A.	Hambleton, Frances E.	A study of gifted children: their responses to tests of general information
1922	Education	M.A.	Lantz, C. M. Beatrice	Intelligence and fecundity: a study of the comparative fecundity of various intelligence levels in Palo Alto, California
1922	Education	M.A.	Lantzeff, George V.	Results of the use of mental tests in the study of delinquency
1922	Education	M.A.	Nolds, Ida G.	A study of a group of superior children
1923	Psychology	Ph.D.	Merrill (James), Maud	On the relation of intelligence to achievement in case of mentally retarded children

207

1923	Psychology	Ph.D.	Raubenheimer, A. S.	An experimental study of some behavior traits of the potentially delinquent boy
1923	Education	M.A.	Bell, Gertrude	The testing and teaching of a backward girl
1923	Education	M.A.	Hao, Yao-Tung	A study of supernormal mentality
1923	Education	M.A.	Willoughby, Raymond R.	Some characteristics of a group of gifted California high school children
1923	Psychology	M.A.	Eyre, Mary	Achievement test for graduate nurses for use by state examining boards in examination for licensure
1923	Psychology	M.A.	Laslett, Herbert R.	On the effects of sleeplessness on the ability to do mental work
1923	Psychology	M.A.	Lima, Ida M.	The reading interests of gifted children
1924	Psychology	Ph.D.	De Voss, J. C.	The unevenness of the abilities of gifted children in California
1924	Psychology	Ph.D.	Goodenough, Florence	The intellectual factor in children's drawings
1924	Psychology	Ph.D.	Sullivan, Ellen B.	Attitude in relation to learning
1925	Education	Ph.D.	Cady, Vernon M.	The estimation of juvenile incorrigibility
1925	Psychology	Ph.D.	Cox (Miles), Catherine	On the early mental development of a group of eminent men
1925	Psychology	Ph.D.	Fenton, Norman	A survey of war neurosis and its aftermath
1925	Psychology	M.A.	Davidson, Helen	Some effects of training on the Stanford-Binet scale
1925	Psychology	M.A.	Durkheimer, Rita	The effects of retesting on the IQ of the retarded child
1925	Psychology	M.A.	Harter, Doris I.	Some results of coaching some of the tests of the Stanford revision of the Binet-Simon scale

1926	Psychology	Ph.D.	Willoughby, R. R.	Some characteristics of a group of gifted California high school children
1926	Psychology	M.A.	Bell, Mary Ann	On sex differences in non-intellectual mental traits
1926	Psychology	M.A.	Casey, Mary Louise	Some results of training in material similar to the Stanford revision of the Binet-Simon scale
1928	Psychology	Ph.D.	Davidson, Helen P.	An experimental study of bright, average, and dull children at the four year mental level
1928	Psychology	M.A.	Hogan, Verda	An experimental study of the picture absurdity test
1928	Psychology	M.A.	Rulon, Phillip Justin	An experimental study of the verbal absurdities test
1929	Psychology	Ph.D.	Burks (Ramsperger), Barbara	The relative influence of nature and nurture upon mental development; a comparative study
1929	Psychology	Ph.D.	Jensen (Osborn), Dortha	The evaluation of literary juvenilia
1929	Education	M.A.	Brintle, Shirley L.	A study of a set of twelve-year-old quadruplets in the light of nature and nurture hypothesis
1931	Psychology	Ph.D.	Bernreuter, R. G.	The evaluation of a proposed new method for constructing personality trait tests of foster parent-child resemblance and true parent-true child resemblance
1931	Psychology	M.A.	Murray, Margaret Elizabeth	A study of test technique for the detection of emotional maladjustments in adolescent boys
1932	Psychology	Ph.D.	McNemar, Quinn	Twin resemblances in motor skills, and the effect of practice thereon

1932	Psychology	M.A.	Green, Helen J.	A qualitative method for scoring the vocabulary test of the new revision of the Stanford-Binet
1934	Education	Ph.D.	Seagoe, May V.	Perceptual units in learning: an evaluation of the whole-part problem
1935	Psychology	Ph.D.	Buttenweiser, Paul	The relation of age to skill of expert chess players
1935	Psychology	Ph.D.	Challman, R. C.	An experimental study of resistance to impulse in normal and subnormal children of the same mental age
1937	Psychology	Ph.D.	White, Ralph K. (in absentia with L. L. Thurstone)	A factor analysis of tests designed to measure fluency, atypicality, and intellectual curiosity

APPENDIX D

Related Publications

ALBEE, GEORGE W., and others. (1969) "Statement by SPSSI on Current I.Q. Controversy: Heredity and Environment." *Amer. Psychologist*, *24*, 1039-1040.

ALBERT, ROBERT S. (1969) "Genius: Present-Day Status of the Concept and its Implications for the Study of Creativity and Giftedness." *Amer. Psychologist, 24*, 743-753.

ANASTASI, ANNE. (1970) "On the Formation of Psychological Traits." *Amer. Psychologist, 28*, 899-910.

BAGLEY, WILLIAM C. (1922) "Educational Determinism: or Democracy and the I.Q." *School and Society, 15*, 373-384.

BAYLEY, N. (1955) "On the Growth of Intelligence." *Amer. Psychologist, 10*, 805-818.

BECK, R. H. (1956) "Lewis M. Terman: Educational Leadership, 1906-1956." *Phi Delta Kappan, 37*, 164.

BERLE, BEATRICE BISHOP. (1939) "In Quest of a Yardstick." *Survey, 75*, 59-60.

BINET, A. (1911) "Nouvelles Recherches sur la Mesure du Niveau Intellectuel chez les Enfants de L'Ecole." *L'Année Psychol., 17*, 145-210.

BINET, A., and SIMON, T. (1905) "Methodes Nouvelles pour le Diagnostic du Niveau Intellectuel des Anormaux." *L'Année Psychol., 11*, 191-244.

BINET, A, and SIMON, T. (1908) "Le Developpement de L'Intelligence chez les Enfants." *L'Année Psychol., 14*, 1-94.

BORING, EDWIN G. (1923) "Intelligence as the Tests Test It." *New Repub., 35*, 35-37.

BORING, EDWIN G. (1945) *Psychologist at Large: An Autobiography and Selected Essays.* New York: Basic Books.

BORING, EDWIN G. (1959) "Lewis Madison Terman: 1877-1956." *Biographical Memoirs of the National Academy of Sciences, 33*, 414-440.

BORING, MOLLIE D. (1948) "Masters and Pupils among the American Psychologists." *Amer. J. Psychol., 61*, 527-534.

BURT, CYRIL. (1972) "Inheritance of General Intelligence." *Amer. Psychologist, 27*, 175-190.

BUSWELL, G. T. (1925) "Two New Book Lists for Children's Reading." *Elem. School J., 26*, 548-551.

211

"Children's Reading: A Guide for Parents and Teachers." *Elem. School J.*, 1926, *26*, 387.

"Children's Reading: A Guide for Parents and Teachers." *N. Y. Times*, Feb. 14, 1926, *26*.

"Children's Reading: A Guide for Parents and Teachers." *Survey*, 1925, *55*, 378.

COLE, MICHAEL, and BRUNER, JEROME S. (1971) "Cultural Differences and Inferences about Psychological Processes." *Amer. Psychologist, 26*, 867-876.

COTTRELL, LEONARD S. (1939) "Psychological Factors in Marital Happiness." *Amer. J. Sociol., 44*, 570-574.

COWELL, HENRY. (1926) "The Process of Musical Creation." *Amer. J. Psychol., 37*, 233-236.

CRONBACH, L. J. (1949) *Essentials of Psychological Testing.* New York: Harper.

DuBois, PHILLIP H. (1970) "Varieties of Psychological Test Homogeneity." *Amer. Psychologist, 25*, 532-536.

Education for the Gifted: The Fifty-seventh Yearbook of the National Society for the Study of Education, Part II. Chicago: National Society for the Study of Education, 1958.

EELLS, K. (1951) *Intelligence and Cultural Differences.* Chicago: University of Chicago Press.

FARIS, ROBERT E. L. (1948) "The Gifted Child Grows Up." *Amer. J. Sociol., 54*, 169.

FARRAR, ELIZABETH. (1947) "The Gifted Child Grows Up." *Atlantic Bookshelf, 180*, 177.

FENTON, JESSIE C. (1932) "Lewis M. Terman." *Understanding the Child, 2*, 18-20.

FREEMAN, FRANK N. (1925) "Where Genius Begins." *Survey, 55*, 378.

FREEMAN, FRANK N. (1938) "The Revised Stanford-Binet Tests of Intelligence." *Elem. School J., 38*, 387-388.

FULTON, J. T. (1951) *Experiment in Dental Care: Results of New Zealand's Use of School Dental Nurses.* Geneva: World Health Organization.

"The Gifted Child Grows Up." *U. S. Quarterly Bkl.*, 1948, 4, 79-80.

GOODENOUGH, FLORENCE. (1949) *Mental Testing: Its History, Principles and Applications.* New York: Rinehart.

HALL, G. STANLEY. (1923) *Life and Confessions of a Psychologist.* New York: Appleton.

"Health Work in the Schools." *Educ. Res.*, 1915, *49*, 98.

HILGARD, ERNEST R. (1957) "Lewis Madison Terman: 1877-1956." *Amer. J. Psychol., 70*, 472-479.

HOLLINGWORTH, H. L. (1938) "Review of *Psychological Factors in Marital Happiness.*" *Psychol. Bull.*, *36*, 191-203.

HOLZINGER, KARL J. (1926) "Review of *Genetic Studies of Genius.*" *Elem. School J.*, *26*, 387-390.

HONZIK, M. P.; MACFARLANE, J. W.; and ALLEN, I. (1948) "The Stability of Mental Test Performance between Two and Eighteen Years." *J. Exp. Educ.*, *18*, 309-324.

"How We Happen to Read the Good." *Educ. Res.*, 1926, *72*, 249-250.

"The Intelligence of School Children." *Nation*, 1919, *109*, 306.

JENSEN, ARTHUR R. (1968) "Social Class, Race, and Genetics: Implications for Education." *American Educational Research Journal*, *5*, 1-42.

JENSEN, ARTHUR R. (1969a) "Criticism or Propaganda?" *Amer. Psychologist*, *24*, 1040-1041.

JENSEN, ARTHUR R. (1969b) "How Much Can We Boost I.Q. and Scholastic Achievement?" *Harv. Educ. Rev.*, *39*, 1-123.

JENSEN, ARTHUR R. (1969c) "Reducing the Heredity-Environment Uncertainty." *Harv. Educ. Rev.*, *39*, 449-483.

JENSEN, ARTHUR R. (1973) "Let's Understand Skodak and Skeels, Finally." *Educ. Psychologist*, *10*, 30-35.

KLAISS, DONALD. (1939) "Psychological Factors in Marital Happiness." *Social Forces*, *17*, 580-581.

KREUTER, GRETCHEN. (1962) "Vanishing Genius: Lewis Terman and the Stanford Study." *Hist. Ed. Q.*, *2*, 6-18.

LANE, WINTHROP D. (1913) "The Teacher's Health." *Survey*, *30*, 68.

LEWIS, WILLIAM B. (1951) "Professor Lewis M. Terman." *Brit. J. Statistic. Psychol. 10*, 65-68.

LIPPMANN, WALTER. "The Mental Age of Americans." *New Repub.*, 1922, *32*, 213-215. "The Mystery of the 'A' Men." *New Repub.*, 1922, *32*, 246-248. "The Reliability of Intelligence Tests." *New Repub.*, 1922, *32*, 275-277. "The Abuse of the Tests." *New Repub.*, 1922, *32*, 297-298. "Tests of Hereditary Intelligence." *New Repub.*, 1922, *32*, 328-330. "A Future for the Tests." *New Repub.*, 1922, *33*, 9-10. "A Postscript." *New Repub.*, 1922, *33*, 10-11. "The Great Confusion: A Reply to Mr. Terman." *New Repub.*, 1922, *33*, 145-146.

MCCULLERS, JOHN C. (1969) "G. Stanley Hall's Conception of Mental Development and Some Indications of Its Influence on Developmental Psychology." *Amer. Psychologist*, *24*, 1109-1114.

MCNEMAR, QUINN. (1940) "A Critical Examination of the University of Iowa Studies of Environmental Influences upon the I.Q." *Psychol. Bull.*, *37*, 63-92.

"The Measurement of Intelligence." *Elem. School J.*, 1916, *17*, 87.

MEYLAN, GEORGE L. (1914a) "Review of Hoag and Terman's Health Work in the School." *Survey, 33,* 270.

MEYLAN, GEORGE L. (1914b) "Review of Terman's Hygiene of the School Child." *Survey, 32,* 346.

ODEN, MELITA H. (1968) "The Fulfillment of Promise: Forty-Year Follow-Up of the Terman Gifted Group." *Genet. Psychol. Monogr., 77,* Pt. 1.

PASTORE, NICHOLAS. (1949) *The Nature-Nurture Controversy.* New York: King's Crown.

PINTNER, RUDOLF; DRAGOWITZ, ANNA; and KUSHNAER, ROSE. (1944) *Supplementary Guide for the Stanford-Binet Scale.* Stanford: Stanford University.

"Psychological Factors in Marital Happiness." *Amer. J. Psychol.,* 1939, *52,* 656.

REUTER, E. B. (1937) "Sex and Personality." *Amer. J. Socio., 42,* 753-754.

"Review of *Children's Reading.*" *Wis. Lib. Bull.,* 1926, *22,* 69.

"Review of *Hygiene of the School Child.*" *Educ. Res.,* 1914, *48,* 212.

"A Review of Terman's *Children's Reading* and Mary Graham Gonner's *A Parent's Guide to Children's Reading.*" *Outlook,* 1926, *142,* 575.

RIVERS, WILLIAM L. (1965) "Terman of Stanford." *Stanford Today,* Series 1, No. 14, 2-8.

ROE, ANNE. (1952) *The Making of a Scientist.* New York: Dodd Mead.

SCRIVEN, MICHAEL. (1970) "The Values of the Academy (Moral Issues for American Education and Educational Research Arising from the Jensen Case)." *Rev. Educ. Res., 40,* 541-549.

SEARS, ROBERT R. (1957) "L. M. Terman, Pioneer in Mental Measurement." *Science, 125,* 978-979.

"Sex and Personality: Studies in Masculinity and Femininity." *Amer. Sociol. Rev.,* 1937, *2,* 790.

SILVERMAN, MILTON, and SILVERMAN, MARGARET. (1952) "So That's What Happens to Child Prodigies." *Sat. Eve. Post, 224,* 22-23.

SKEELS, HAROLD M. (1940) "Some Iowa Studies of the Mental Growth of Children in Relation to Differentials in the Environment: A Summary." *Yearb. Nat. Soc. Stud. Educ.,* Pt. II, *39,* 281-308.

STERN, WILLIAM. (1912) "Die psychologischen Methoden der Intelligenz-prüfung." *Bericht über den V. Kongress für experimentelle Psychologie, 5,* 1-109.

STERN, WILLIAM. (1914) "The Psychological Methods of Testing Intelligence." *Educ. Psychol. Monographs,* No. 13, p. 160. Baltimore: Warwick and York.

STODDARD, GEORGE D. and WELLMAN, BETH L. (1940) "Environment and the I.Q." *Yearb. Nat. Soc. Stud. Educ.,* Pt. I, *39,* 405-442.

SWARD, KEITH. (1948) "The Gifted Child Grows Up." *Amer. J. Psychol.*, *61*, 443-446.

"The Teacher's Health: A Study in the Hygiene of an Occupation." *ALA Bkl.*, 1913, *9*, 391.

THORNDIKE, R. L. (1940) " 'Constancy' of the I.Q." *Psychol. Bull.*, *37*, 167-186.

TRAXLER, ARTHUR E. (1937) "A Guide to the New Revision of the Stanford-Binet Tests." *School Rev.*, *45*, 549-550.

TUDDENHAM, READ D. (1962) "The Nature and Measurement of Intelligence." In *Psychology in the Making*, Ed. Leo Postman, pp. 469-525. New York: Knopf.

WECHSLER, D. (1958) *The Measurement and Appraisal of Adult Intelligence.* Baltimore: Williams and Wilkins.

WECHSLER, DAVID. (1937) "Sex and Personality." *Amer. J. Psychol,* *49*, 328-329.

WELLMAN, BETH L. (1940) "Iowa Studies on the Effects of Schooling." *Yearb. Nat. Soc. Stud. Educ.*, Pt. II, *39*, 377-399.

WELLMAN, B. L., SKEELS, H. M. and SKODAK, M. (1940) "Review of McNemar's Critical Examination of Iowa Studies." *Psychol. Bull.*, *37*, 93-111.

WILLIAMS, J. HAROLD. (1924) *Graphic Methods in Education.* Boston: Houghton Mifflin.

WOLF, THETA H. (1961) "An Individual Who Made a Difference." *Amer. Psychologist, 16*, 245-248.

WOLF, THETA H. (1964) "Alfred Binet: a Time of Crisis." *Amer. Psychologist, 19*, 762-771.

WOLF, THETA H. (1966) "Intuition and Experiment: Alfred Binet's First Efforts in Child Psychology." *J. Hist. Behavioral Sciences, 2*, 233-239.

WOODWORTH, ROBERT S. (1942) "Introduction" in *Studies in Personality*, Eds. Robert G. Bernreuter and others, i-vi. New York: McGraw-Hill.

Selected Unpublished Manuscripts

HUMAN INTELLIGENCE AND ACHIEVEMENT*

One who undertakes to discuss the relationship between intelligence and achievement labors under a double handicap in that he has no accurate measure of either of these variables. To the physical scientist this lack may well seem fatal. However, accuracy is a relative term. In the strict sense, no measurement that man can make of anything is completely accurate. Even those of the physicist have their margin of error, be it only 1 part in ten thousand or 1 in ten million. The psychologist, working both with cruder tools and with less stable phenomena, is usually happy if he can reduce the probable error of his determinations to 1 or 2 percent, or in some cases to 5 percent. No one who is a born perfectionist should ever launch himself on a psychological career.

The thing to note is that even the crude techniques of psychometrics are better than guesses or subjective estimates, and that used with appropriate caution they are capable of leading to important generalizations. In nearly a half a century of experimental work on the adaptive behavior of animals and human subjects genuine progress has been made. At present, the psychologist will undertake to measure for you the intelligence of any animal from earthworm to ape, or of any human subject from idiot to Einstein. Moreover, in comparison with the wide range of intelligent behavior between the simplest and the most complex, the errors in his measurements are by no means entirely discouraging.

What it boils down to is that intelligence is the ability to acquire and manipulate concepts—the shorthand symbols without which abstract thinking is impossible. It took Dr. Field's rats practically all their lives and thousands of learning periods to form one crude concept—in this case indicated by the ability to react uniformly to triangularity in a visual stimulus whatever the shape or size or background of the particular trial presented. At the opposite extreme are the complex types of abstraction found in higher mathematics, the theory of atomic structure, the bio-chemistry of the genes, or analysis of the constitution and mass of a distant

---

*Sigma Xi address at Stanford, Spring 1941

universe. The higher the level of thinking, the greater the degree of abstraction; whether in the physical, the biological, or the social sciences, whether in one or another of the arts. Aptitude for concept formation is a *sine qua non* of creative thinking in any field, though, as we shall see, it is possible for one to have the aptitude without using it for effective achievement.

For many years my own interests have been largely concerned with the relation between intelligence and achievement at the upper intellectual levels, and particularly with the relationship between early superiority in intelligence and the achievements of adult life. Two methods of approach are here possible: (1) We may start with the historical genius who has achieved greatly and attempt to trace his development in reverse order and discover the characteristics of his childhood; or (2) We may begin with the living gifted child, measure his abilities, and decades later evaluate his life achievements. Thanks to generous research grants from the Commonwealth Fund, the Carnegie Corporation, the National Research Council, and other sources—grants which, to date, total more than $100,000—we have been able at Stanford to experiment with both of these approaches. On the one hand, a study has been made of the early mental development of 300 geniuses; on the other hand, we have identified by means of intelligence tests some 1300 gifted children, have investigated their mental and physical characteristics, and have since followed their development for almost twenty years.

The study of historical geniuses was carried out by Catherine Cox. Her first problem was to obtain by means as objective as possible an unbiased sampling of subjects (avoid handpicking to prove a theory). Following the example of Galton, she selected her group by the criterion of eminence as measured by space in biographical dictionaries. Although possessing the merit of objectivity, this criterion, admittedly, is far from ideal in that eminence is influenced by circumstances other than intellectual achievement. The population it affords is the result of innumerable selective factors which vary from age to age, and from culture to culture. The genius who survives as such has successfully run the gauntlet of premature death, the stupidities of formal education, the social and ethical pressures of his immediate environment, and the more general cultural influences that have given direction and content to the civilization in which he was born. Moreover, a man's eminence is not a static thing; it rises and falls with the value transformations that cultural changes inevitably bring (Farnsworth). Genius in the sense of eminence is not a biological concept, though it does have biological prerequisites in ancestral genes, nutrition, and escape from mortal disease. The study of historic personages tells us nothing about potential geniuses who failed to achieve eminence. Even so, I feel warranted in asserting that the study by Cox has made a substantial contribution to our knowledge of the early mental traits that underlie prodigious achievement of adult life. It has exposed certain tendencies to error in biographical interpretation, especially in regard to the alleged one-sidedness of genius and the still more frequently alleged dangers of intellectual precocity.

It was, in fact, a striking example of such erroneous interpretation that led me to apply for a grant to finance the Cox research. Karl Pearson, in his *Life, Letters, and Labors of Galton*, presented an extraordinary array of documentary evidence regarding his subject's early accomplishments. Francis learned to read at the age of two and a half years and wrote a letter before he was four that has been preserved. By the age of five he could read "most any English book" and some French, could cast up any sum in addition, had mastered all the multiplication table except 9s and 11s, knew the table of English money, and could tell time by the clock. Now it happens that all these and other dated performances of Galton have been standardized by psychologists on unselected children of different ages, and that the mental age necessary for each performance is known. By the use of such norms it is possible, in the case of Galton, to estimate with considerable assurance the lowest IQ that would account for the facts. This was unquestionably in the neighborhood of 200, a figure not equalled by more than one child in 50,000 of the generality [Terman, 1917b]. Yet, Pearson was so unaware of the significance of the performances he had described as to assert that there was nothing unusual about them: "I do not think we can say more than that Francis Galton was a normal child with rather more than average ability."

In selecting her subjects, Cox began with Cattell's list of the 1,000 most eminent individuals of history as determined by amount of space devoted to them in biographical dictionaries. Taking the 500 most eminent of Cattell's list, she eliminated from this group those born before 1450, those who belonged to the hereditary aristocracy or nobility, and a few others, arbitrarily, whose eminence had little or no basis in intellectual achievement. This left her with 300 subjects.

Cox and her assistants combed the biographies of her 300 subjects for data on early mental development as indicated by interests, education, school standing and school progress, friends and associates, reading, and production and achievement. Special attention was given to evidence of a documentary kind, such as dated letters, compositions, poems, mothers' diaries, etc. The material thus assembled ran to 6,000 typed pages. The evidence for each subject was then examined independently by three psychologists who were intimately acquainted with age norms of mental performance. Their task involved two things: (1) estimation of the minimum IQ that would account for a subject's known childhood performances, and (2) a rating of the reliability of the evidence on which the IQ estimate was based. The average of the three estimates for an individual subject was the primary data for this part of the study. It must be emphasized that the IQ thus reckoned is an estimate of the lowest IQ that could reasonably account for the recorded facts; the actual childhood IQs of historical geniuses are, of course, indeterminate.

218

For the entire group, the estimated minimum IQs ranged from 100 to 200, with an average of 155. The latter figure is more than three standard deviations above the mean of the generality. Low estimates in the range of 100 to 120 IQ occurred only when there was little biographical information about the early years. The mean was highest for philosophers (170), and next highest for poets, novelists, dramatists, and revolutionary statesmen (160). The lowest was for soldiers (125), the next lowest for artists (140), and musicians (145). The mean for scientists (155) was identical with that for the total group.

It will be understood, I trust, that IQ estimates of this kind are not to be taken too literally. For a majority of the subjects, the information on which the estimates were based was far short of what could be desired. Cox was careful to provide the reader with probable errors of the IQ estimates, with reliability ratings of the data on which the estimates were based and with other cautions against literal-mindedness. Despite the admitted inadequacies of her study, I believe that the author's main conclusion is warranted: namely, that the genius who achieves highest eminence is one whom intelligence tests would have identified as gifted in childhood. The author warns us that the converse of this does not follow; we may not conclude that every child who tests high will become eminent. Her data suggest that those who do achieve greatly are characterized not only by superior intellectual ability, but also "by persistence of motive and effort, confidence in their abilities, and great strength or force of character."

That personality traits are influential in determining both the level and the direction of achievement is a matter of common observation. One must also take account of the part played by chance. For a given type of achievement to be possible, one must be born not too far from a given time and place. It is an interesting game to try to imagine how differently any list of eminent persons might read if every one now in it had been born a generation or two earlier or later. The soldiers would nearly all bear strange names, perhaps a majority of the statesmen, especially revolutionary statesmen, and doubtless many of the writers and scientists. Apart from time and place of birth, there are other chance factors in vast number that are capable of shaping the life of a gifted youth. Newton, at 15, had left school and was tending his mother's farm; but for the timely visit of an uncle, who had attended Cambridge, it is unlikely that he would ever have received the education that made possible his great discoveries. Victor Cousin was bred in the gutter and was illiterate at the age of ten when he happened to befriend a bully's victim in a street fight, with the result that the latter's mother sought him out and gave him an education. Faraday left school at 13 and at 14 was apprenticed to a bookbinder. It was the reading of an article on electricity in an encyclopedia given him to bind that first stimulated his interest in science. Even this would probably have got him nowhere had not Humphrey Davy been near to lend a helping hand.

In a study like that of Cox, special interest attaches to certain eminent persons who have been cited as examples of childhood backwardness. In every one of these cases, the facts clearly belie the legend. Goldsmith was characterized by Samuel Johnson as "a plant that flowered late," and a childhood teacher said of him in her old age, "never was so dull a boy." Actually Goldsmith was writing verse at the age of 7 and at 8 was reading Ovid and Horace. His IQ was probably 140 or higher. Sir Walter Scott is said to have been a dunce when he attended the Musselburgh School. The facts are that he never attended this school; that when only 7 years old he read widely in poetry and his prose used correctly such words as 'melancholy' and 'exotic'; that by age 10 he had collected a small library of ballads, and that at 13 he lay awake nights reading Shakespeare when he was supposed to be asleep. His IQ was at least 150. Other alleged dullards represent a type often encountered in the old-fashioned Latin school, i.e., the youth who hated Latin and Greek, but had a natural talent for science. Liebig, the founder of physiological chemistry, was the despair of his language teachers. At 15, he left school and was apprenticed to an apothecary because he wanted to be a chemist. At 17, he managed to enter a university, and at 20 was awarded the Ph.D. degree. John Hunter, British surgeon and anatomist, left Latin school at 13 and spent four apparently idle years roaming the woods and fields, watching the ants, the bees, the birds, the tadpoles, and caddis-worms, pestering people "with questions about which nobody knew or cared anything." Alexander von Humboldt and his brother Wilhelm, two years older, were privately tutored along the usual classical lines. Wilhelm liked languages and was recognized as gifted; Alexander, caring only for nature, was considered mentally slow. Both became eminent, but Alexander outstripped his brother.

In the cases just cited one notes a tendency for the direction of later achievement to be foreshadowed by the interests and preoccupations of childhood. I have tried to determine how frequently this was true of the 100 subjects in Cox's group whose childhood is best documented. Very marked foreshadowing was noted in the case of more than half of the group, none at all in less than a fourth. Macaulay, for example, began his career as historian at the age of 6 with what he called a "Compendium of Universal History," filling a quire of paper before he lost interest in the project. Goethe's literary juvenilia are perhaps the most remarkable that ever have been preserved. Ben Franklin, before the age of 17, had displayed nearly all the traits that characterized him in middle life: manual skill, scientific curiosity, religious heterodoxy, wit and buffoonery, political and business shrewdness, and ability to write. At the age of 70, when on a diplomatic mission to England, he dug up an article which he had written in his teens, published it practically without change, and created a political sensation. At 11, Pascal wrote a paper on sound and was so interested in mathematics that his father thought best to deprive him of books on this subject until the boy had first mastered Latin and Greek.

Pascal secretly proceeded to construct a geometry of his own and covered the ground as far as the 32nd proposition of Euclid. At 14, Leibnitz was writing on logic and philosophy and composing what he called "An Alphabet of Human Thought." He relates that, at this age, he took a walk one afternoon to consider whether he should hold the "doctrine of substantial forms."

The data collected by Cox also throw interesting light on the versatility of genius. While the versatility of a few geniuses has long been stressed by biographers (da Vinci), the less spectacular cases are usually overlooked. People prefer to believe that the genius, as a rule, is no better than the rest of us except in one particular. The facts are very different. Except in music and the arts, which draw heavily on specialized abilities, there are few persons who have achieved great eminence in one field without displaying more than average ability in one or more other fields. Using the biographical information assembled by Cox, White and another psychologist rated each subject on the ability shown in 23 different fields. The results indicated that a majority of the subjects displayed more than average ability in 5 to 10 different areas of accomplishment. The mean versatility index was highest for Non-fiction Writers, Statesmen, and Philosophers (around 7.5); somewhat lower for Scholars, Religious Leaders, Scientists, Poets, Mathematicians, Novelists, and Dramatists (around 6.7); much lower for Soldiers and Artists (4.3 and 4.0); and lowest of all for Musicians (only 2.7).

Cox selected 100 of the most eminent subjects representing the various fields of achievement and obtained for each ratings on home influences, formal education, amount of early reading and travel, seven aspects of interests, and numerous character traits. It is chiefly on these data that she based her conclusions regarding the high importance of zeal, persistence, self-confidence and other character traits as determiners of life achievement.

So much for this particular approach to our problem. Anyone who has tried to get the real facts from the always incomplete and often distorted information in biographical works is keenly aware of the limitations of his material. One's interpretations are, at best, only tentative and suggestive, lacking the finality of positive proof. It is a relief to turn to living gifted subjects who can be studied first-hand at successive age levels, for in this way, and no other, is it possible to establish the true relationship between early promise and life achievement.

Most of my 1300 subjects were located by sifting a school population of a quarter million in the larger cities of California. The method of search was thorough enough to identify about 90 per cent of all cases capable of earning an IQ of 140 or higher. Whatever is true of this group may be regarded as substantially true of gifted children in general of this level of ability.

It should be noted that the gifted child is here quite arbitrarily defined as one whose score in tested intelligence is equalled by about one child in two hundred of the school population. The population studied by Galton was twenty times as highly selected, since it included only the most eminent in 4000 of the generality. The American *Who's Who* population is ten or twelve times as highly selected as my gifted group, and Cattell's galaxy of starred scientists about 500 times as aristocratic. It is necessary to hold these comparative figures in mind in order to appraise justly the life achievements of the subjects I have studied.

The data secured for this group in 1922 include, for a majority of the subjects, two or more intelligence scores; scores from a four-hour test of school achievement; scores from three tests of character, personality, and interests; 34 anthropometric measurements; the results of a one-hour medical examination; ratings by parents and teachers on 25 traits; and a large amount of case-history information supplied by parents, teachers, and field assistants. What is the gifted child like when we find him?

For one thing, he carries no earmarks that make his identification easy. My search for subjects proved that if you want to know who is the brightest child in a classroom, your chance of catching the right one is slightly better if you arbitrarily take the youngest than if you take the one the teacher selects for you.

Gifted children are found in every racial group represented in California, but are least numerous among the Mexicans and Negroes and most numerous among the Jews. Nearly two-thirds of the occupations of the fathers were classified as professional, semi-professional, or higher business; less than 1 percent as unskilled.

The medical examination and anthropometric measurements showed the typical gifted child physically superior to the average. The tests of personality and character yielded scores far superior to those of average children of corresponding age.

In school achievement the gifted subjects score almost as high as in intelligence. A majority of them had, in fact, acquired a good mastery of the curriculum as far as two, three, or even four school grades beyond that in which they were enrolled.

One-sidedness in achievement was no more prevalent in the gifted group than in a control group of unselected subjects. More or less irregularity was found with both groups, but on a high level with the gifted and on a low level with the controls. Whereas the mean intelligence quotient of the group was about 150, the mean achievement quotient in reading, arithmetic, language usage, spelling, science information, literary information, historical information, and art information, were all in the narrow range between 137 and 152. The relative uniformity of these scores establishes beyond question that a high degree of versatility is the rule in a group of this kind.

So much for the central tendencies that characterized this group of subjects. I hasten to add that the individual members of the group, far from following a single pattern, showed considerable diversity with respect to all the traits studied. The variation was least in intelligence, but even here the range was from 140 IQ to 200 IQ.

This is where our biographical study of gifted children began in 1922. It has now been under way long enough to give some indication of the probable life achievement of such a group. The thousand who were below high school age in 1922 now range from 23 to 35 years of age, with a median of about 28. The 1922 high school subjects range from 30 to 38 with a median of 34. I am still in contact with more than 95 percent of the original group.

For several years, after 1922, the subjects were followed by information blanks that were filled out and mailed to me annually by the parents and teachers. In 1928, a second grant from the Commonwealth Fund made it possible to have field assistants retest most of the subjects and obtain a large amount of additional information from parents, teachers, and the subjects themselves. The next follow-up was conducted chiefly by mail in 1936-1937, but a liberal grant from Carnegie Corporation two years ago made it possible to keep three research associates in the field last year. As not all of the latest data have yet been statisticized, [Spring, 1941], most of the figures I shall report will be in round numbers, subject to later corrections that will not materially affect the picture.

First, a few vital statistics. The mortality rate of the group, to date, is below that of the generality of corresponding age. The same is true of the insanity rate. The incidence of suicide approaches more closely that of the generality, but the incidence of arrests and imprisonment is extremely low.

At the present time, two-thirds of the members of the group are, or have been, married—the proportion being about the same for men and women. The divorce rate is below that of the generality in California of corresponding age. Among those who have married, 40 percent of the men and 50 percent of the women married college graduates. The mean intelligence score of the subjects is well above that of their spouses, but the latter also test high. Girls do better!

The group has, thus far, produced about 500 offspring. Tests recently given to 300 above the age of two years have yielded a mean IQ of approximately 127, which represents about the expected regression toward the mean of the generality.

Has the intellectual superiority shown by this group in 1922 been maintained? In terms of intelligence test scores the answer is emphatically yes. The retests given both in 1928 and during the past two years showed a majority of the subjects close to the 99th percentile of the generality. This is true even of those whose careers have not been particularly successful. Although there are exceptions to the rule, the intellectually gifted individual can be identified almost as accurately in the third elementary grade as at age 30.

With regard to educational achievement, the average member of the group enters high school at 13 and college at 17. In high school more than two-thirds of the grades are As, and failure in any school subject is almost unknown. Nearly 90 percent enter college and of those entering about 93 percent graduate. Although averaging nearly two years younger than their classmates, they engage more extensively in extracurricular activities, receive more student-body honors, and are several times as likely to graduate with distinction.

Approximately two-thirds of the men who graduate, and half of the women, go on for graduate work. Of some 350 men who have completed their graduate studies, about 60 received a Ph.D. degree, about the same number a medical degree, about 90 a law degree, and about 40 a degree in engineering or architecture. Less than one-tenth as many women as men have obtained a graduate degree beyond the M.A. For the sexes combined, the incidence of higher professional degrees is perhaps twenty or thirty times as great as for the general population.

In appraising the life achievements of these subjects it is necessary to take account of the severe economic depression that has spanned most or all of their adult years. This circumstance has made harder the way of many and has diverted some permanently from their original goals.

The average earned income of the men at age 30 is around $3,000 a year. About a dozen of the men are earning between $10,000 and $15,000 a year. In general, the women who are gainfully employed earn only about half as much as the men, and the maximum reached by women is only about one-fifth the maximum for men. Income, however, is a poor measure of achievement, particularly in the case of a young man just starting on his professional career. Some of the most promising members of the group are, at present, earning less than $2,500 a year.

Turning to other indications of achievement, we find that about 60 of the men and about 15 of the women are teaching in colleges or universities throughout the country. At least 8 of the men are already executive heads of departments.

Publications by the total group number many hundreds of articles in professional or technical journals, at least 20 books, and a vast number of short stories, popular articles, and poems. The books include textbooks, scholarly treatises, a semi-popular book on invention, several volumes of fiction, and two books of poems. Two writers of fiction and one poet have a national reputation. Eighty or more patents have been issued to men of the group, none to any of the women.

In the case of historical geniuses we have noted that the direction of adult accomplishment is often foreshadowed during the early years. In order to find whether this is true of my gifted group the records of men in the various fields are being compared with respect to childhood hobbies, school marks, achievement test scores, amount and kinds of early reading, trait ratings by parents and teachers, early social adjustment, and other variables. Although the analysis has not been completed, the data are showing more than chance agreement between some of these variables and the field of adult achievement. This is particularly true of those who have accomplished the most. Achievement in music, literature, and art is always foreshadowed in some degree. However, in all fields except music there are individuals whose early records give no hint of later performance. Because of the large common factor in the abilities necessary for success in the various professions, the direction of adult achievement is greatly influenced by chance factors and specialization of interests.

The range of success in my group is very wide for both sexes and, at the present time, extends downward to occupations as humble as those of policeman, carpenter, gardener, gas station operator, department store floorwalker, store clerk, house-to-house canvasser, small rancher, seaman, telephone operator, typist, and filing clerk. In a depression-ridden world some of the men have not scorned the work of common laborer (carpenter, policeman, cannery worker). Usually the humbler jobs have been followed by better, though not in every case. The question arises what factors other than intelligence are important determiners of achievement in such a group.

One, obviously, is sex. Although the women equal or exceed the men in school achievement from the first grade through college, after school days are over the great majority cease to compete with men in the world's work. If they do not marry at once they accept whatever kind of respectable employment is at hand. After marriage they fall into the domestic role and only in exceptional cases seek other outlet for their talents. The woman who is a potential poet, novelist, lawyer, physician, or scientist usually gives up any professional ambition she may have had and devotes herself to home, husband, and children. The exclusive devotion to domestic pursuits robs the arts and sciences of a large fraction of the genius that might otherwise be dedicated to them. My data strongly suggest that this loss must be debited to motivational causes and limited opportunity rather than to lack of ability.

Since the achievement of women is so largely determined by extraneous circumstances and is, in any case, so difficult to estimate, our investigation of the causes of success and failure has been confined to the male group. The data I shall report here were obtained fifteen to eighteen years after the subjects had been given their first tests. Three psychologists, working independently, examined the records of 600 men and rated each subject on life success. The criterion of "success" was the extent to which a subject had made use of his superior intellectual ability. The judges were instructed to give little weight to earned income except insofar as this was clearly related to achievement as just defined.

On the basis of these ratings the men were tentatively classified into three groups, composing roughly the highest fourth, the middle 50 percent, and the lowest fourth. The highest and lowest fourths in terms of life success, or the A and C groups as we have called them, were then compared with respect to test scores of 1922 and 1928, family records, home environment, case histories, health data, trait ratings, and many other items of information, in the hope that by reading the records backwards, so to speak, some light might be thrown on the factors that influence achievement. The compared groups were arbitrarily matched with respect to age, the range being 23 to 35, and the mean 27.

The educational and occupational records of these two groups present a vivid contrast. Of the As, 98 percent entered college and 90 percent graduated; of the Cs, 70 percent entered but only 50 percent graduated. Three-fourths of the As but only a fifth of the Cs completed one or more years of graduate work. Among those graduating, nearly half the As but only 4 percent of the Cs were elected to Phi Beta Kappa or Sigma Xi. Half of the As but only 10 percent of the Cs had received appointment to scholarships, fellowships, or assistantships. In professional or semi-professional pursuits were 96 percent of the As as compared with 28 percent of the Cs. Although salary had been given little weight in the success ratings, the average earned income of the As was two and a third times that of the Cs. Earnings of the As increased steadily with age, reaching about $4,000 by age 28 and $6,000 by age 35. Earnings of the Cs increased little and did not average above $2,000 at any age.

Let us turn now to the childhood records and test scores of the two groups to see what facts or circumstances are associated with differences in adult accomplishment. We note first that, during the elementary school years, As and Cs were about equally successful. Their average grades were almost identical and the average scores on a four-hour objective achievement test were only a trifle higher for the A group. In high school, the groups began to draw apart as a result of lower grades in group C, but it was not until the college period that the slump of this group assumed alarming proportions. The slump cannot be blamed upon extra-curricular activities, for these were almost twice as common among the As as among the Cs. Nor can it have been caused by intellectual deterioration, for on every mental test—from childhood to adult years—the average score of the Cs has been only a few points lower than that of the As. In a population so highly selected for intelligence that each person in it rates within the top one percent of the generality, the differences in achievement must necessarily be due chiefly to non-intellectual factors.

For one thing, the family backgrounds of the two groups differ markedly. Nearly twice as many A parents as C parents had graduated from college, and a similar difference was found between the siblings of the As and Cs. Fathers of the As were far more often in the professional classes. The important point here is that the educational tradition was stronger in families of the A group. In line with this is the fact that the Jewish element is three times as large among the As as among the Cs. The Jewish child is under heavy pressure to succeed, with the result that he seems to accomplish more per unit of intelligence than do children of any other racial stock.

Significant differences between the groups were found in the childhood data on emotional stability, social adjustment, and various traits of personality. The case histories and trait ratings obtained from parents and teachers in 1922 reflect these differences clearly. All the 1922 trait ratings, except those relating to physique, averaged lower for the C group. That is, fifteen or more years prior to the classification of these subjects on the basis of adult achievement, teachers and parents had been able to discern personality differences that would later characterize the two groups.

The A-C differences are further evidenced in the marital records. The incidence of marriage is higher in the A group and the age of marriage is lower. Moreover, the A's marry better than the C's; the A spouses score higher in intelligence tests and include nearly twice as large a proportion of college graduates. Especially significant is the contrast in marital adjustments, for the incidence of separation or divorce is only a third as high in the A group as in the C group. This difference extends even to the parents of the two groups, the incidence of separation or divorce being only half as great for A parents as for C parents. (Nature and nurture both involved.)

The A-C differences in marital adjustments appear to be symptomatic of more basic differences in emotional stability and integration of personality. With the aid of funds from the National Research Council, a special study is being made of marital success or failure in the entire gifted population. This has shown that the A group scores higher than the C group in present marital happiness, also higher in a test designed to measure happiness of temperament as it relates to social adjustment. The superiority of the As in what might be called aptitude for happiness is evident in the case history data obtained during the childhood of the subjects.

The facts just reported appear to be in direct opposition to the Lange-Eichbaum theory that great achievement is associated with emotional tensions which border on the abnormal. (Hitler.) In my gifted group, success is associated with emotional stability rather than instability, with absence rather than presence of disturbing conflicts, with happiness of temperament, and with freedom from excessive frustration. This does not necessarily mean that the Lange-Eichbaum theory has nothing in it. It is conceivable that the personality factors that make for ordinary achievement under ordinary conditions are different from those that make for eminence of a superlative order. The two approaches agree in the conclusion that beyond a certain high level of intellectual ability, success is largely determined by non-intellectual factors and that the number of persons who are endowed with abilities equal to great achievement is immensely greater than the number who will attain eminence.

Looking forward to the future, I regard it as unlikely that more than 50 or 100 of my 1300 subjects will become eminent in Galton's sense of the term. It would be surprising if a hundred years hence even one should be found among the thousand most eminent persons of recorded history. In sheer intellectual ability, however, I am sure that my group overlaps Cattell's thousand most eminent of history. Although the group probably contains no intellect at all comparable with that of Newton or Shakespeare, I believe it contains many who are intellectual equals of Washington, the nineteenth most eminent in Cattell's list, and some who are intellectual equals of Napoleon, the most eminent man of history. (Soon to give place to Hitler?) I believe that several of my group are probably as well endowed with literary gifts as were Longfellow, Hawthorne, or George Sand. These specific estimates are, of course, not amenable to objective proof. They are offered merely as illustrations of a larger truth that no one can doubt who has studied either a group of historical persons or a group of living gifted subjects: namely, that intellectuality and achievement are far from perfectly correlated. Why they are so poorly correlated, what circumstances affect the fruition of human talent, are questions of transcendent importance that should be investigated by every method that promises the slightest reduction of our present ignorance. So little do we know about our available supply of potential genius, the environmental factors that favor or hinder its expression, the emotional compulsions that give it dynamic quality, or the personality distortions that make it dangerous! And viewing the present crisis in world affairs, one cannot doubt that these things are potent factors in deciding the fate of civilizations.

TEN VOWS OF THE STANFORD EMERITI GRADUATES OF 1942
(Their Ten Commandments as formulated by L.M.T.)

1. Whatever sufferings, disappointments, and griefs beset us we will not feel sorry for ourselves.

2. While doing all in our power to combat the ills that may beset our bodies and our bodies-politic, we will strive to maintain a reasonable degree of philosophical detachment.

3. We will endeavor to keep an open mind toward the newer trends that appear in our respective fields of scholarship and research.

4. We will never commit the ancient folly of condemning wholesale the younger generation.

5. We will not allow our minds to dwell upon, nor our tongues to enlarge upon, our life accomplishments.

6. We will not cultivate the illusion that our most important achievements are probably ahead of us.

7. We will try to keep alive such sense of humor as God in His mercy may have endowed us with—but not by overmuch practice on our stored up reserves of jokes and stories.

8. We will emulate especially those members of our emeritus group who have shown that age is no bar to zest for life and for service.

9. We will not refuse the little services we *can* render, because we are no longer equal to the bigger things we could once have done.

10. We will never allow ourselves to be beguiled by the flattery of friends who tell us that we look as young as we did twenty or thirty years ago.

EDUCATING AND TRAINING THE GIFTED CHILD*

If you have a child who shows unusual promise, either by the intelligent questions he asks, his general alertness, his interest in learning to read without being taught, his leaning towards atlases, dictionaries, scientific toys, etc., or if his intelligence and achievement tests score two or three grades above that in which he is located, you have, no doubt, a gifted child. You have, too, a definite responsibility for yours is the first chance to fashion him into what he will be tomorrow. Following are a few suggestions which we have gathered through long experience on the education and training of exceptional children.

1. *His social development.* Since gifted children are inclined to become absorbed in reading and less interested in outdoor play, it is imperative that they spend from 10 to 20 hours a week in normal play and other activities with children their own age. Otherwise they will grow up unhappy and introverted. While the companionship of parents is fine it will never take the place of such organizations as the Boy Scouts, Campfire Girls, church clubs, etc., for normal social development.

2. *Don't overpraise.* Probably the gifted child is not by nature more inclined to egotism than the average child but, many have been ruined by conceit because parents, teachers, relatives, and friends constantly call the child's attention to his superiority or overpraise him for his accomplishments. No child is more universally disliked than one who has become obsessed with a sense of his own importance. It is not necessary to belittle the child's ability or accomplishments. You can hardly prevent a child, who is mentally several years ahead of his age, from knowing that he is brighter than the average child, but anything which savors of boasting or showing off should be definitely frowned upon. Newspaper publicity particularly should be avoided. Acquaintances and relatives should never discuss the child's intelligence in his presence. He should not be placed in a position which practically compels him to play the role of the child prodigy. He should be taught to judge himself in terms of a high standard, and not be content merely because he has done well what most children can do. He should rate himself in comparison with somebody smarter than he—the great men and women of history, and the more brilliant of his fellow students.

3. *Industrious habits should be inculcated early.* This is quite a problem if the child is held back two or three grades below the level to which he has mastered his school subjects. A school simply doesn't expect enough of such children and often fails to cultivate pride in achievement, holding the gifted to a standard of the best *they* can do, not merely the

---

*Prepared summer, 1947

average of the class. On the other hand, a child shouldn't be hustled through school in the shortest possible time. The important consideration is not to save time, but to keep the youngster profitably employed and, at the same time, give opportunity for normal social development with children of his own age and size. One solution to the problem would be special classes for gifted children in the public schools. There are many cities which provide for a considerable proportion of their gifted children in this way. They provide a highly enriched curriculum, and make no effort to accelerate the child's school progress by more than a year or two. In such classes, gifted children of eleven or twelve are often found doing better research on their special projects than many a college freshman is able to do. Those opposed to such classes call them undemocratic. It seems a curious way to think about democracy. If it isn't democratic to make the most of every child's talents then I don't know what democracy is. But lacking the enriched curriculum, half day attendance at school may be resorted to with supplementary reading or study or devotion to hobbies at home.

4. *Beware of undertaking intensive training of children in babyhood.* It doesn't do any good and it often does harm to undertake intensive training of children while still too young. "Prodigy making" by such methods is at best a sorry business and at worst almost criminal. There is an erroneous belief that any child can be made a genius by intensive mental culture during the first four or five years of its life. This is not true. There is no psychological or pedagogical alchemy by which intellectual commonplaceness can be transmuted into the gold of genius. Such intensive cultivation is not even necessary for the fullest development of the natural born genius. Many of the most promising youngsters, among the gifted in our records, have had no formal instruction of any kind until the age of six, seven, or even eight years of age. One boy, who did not know his letters at the age of eight and a half years, graduated from Stanford University at barely twenty years with a higher average grade than any of his 300 classmates. So follow the lead of the child's interest. Forced culture breeds an unnatural priggishness and in other ways leads to disappointment. The mind should be allowed to develop at its natural rate without artificial stimulation.

5. *Give information when it is called for and help the child to help himself.* Knowledge acquired when it is wanted is like food eaten when one is hungry. It is quickly assimilated and becomes a part of the mental structure. Parents who take the innumerable questions of the child seriously and answer them as fully and truthfully as their intelligence will justify, or their own information will permit, are satisfying the most important of the child's educational needs in the preschool period. The gifted child not only asks more questions than the average, but he asks more intelligent ones and asks them more insistently. This, in fact, is one of the best indications of mental superiority. It's a good plan to look up the answers with the child or, better still, have the child look it up for

himself with a little direction from the parents. There are few delights more satisfying, after all, than to find things out for one's self. To make a pretense of knowing what one does not know, or to give an answer which is incorrect or inexact, is worse than to ignore the child's question altogether. The parent who accompanies the child on these voyages of discovery not only renders one of the richest of all services but helps to renew his youth in the process.

6. *Encourage hobbies.* Even though it may be inconvenient and annoying to other members of the household to stumble over wireless apparatus, photography equipment, butterfly collections, or a doll's dressmaking establishment, encourage your youngster to any activity which helps him to think, and to do, and to learn for himself. Many a boy learns more in physics in working with his motor or radio outfit than the high school can teach him in a year. Many another lays a solid foundation of biological knowledge in his bird studies, butterfly collecting, animal raising, etc. Geography, mineralogy, chemistry, botany, zoology, and history are all subjects in which the bright child can make rapid progress by means of collections or amateur experimentation. Children who have no hobbies may develop them by being exposed to those of other children. Though they lose a large part of their educational value, if one succeeds another too rapidly, never try to prolong a hobby after a child's spontaneous interest in it has vanished and never, never try to force your own hobbies on your children or to boss theirs.

7. *Provide the best books and in large variety.* If there is anything in which quality is more important than quantity it is in children's reading. This does not mean that a child's reading should be mainly of the "improving" or "moralizing" kind but the word quality refers to first class literature of all kinds, from stories and jingles suitable for babies to the best of the world's fiction, poetry, biography, and drama. Libraries can supply you with special reading lists as a rule. The child of superior intelligence is likely to show a preference for books generally read by older children. This is entirely natural and should not be discouraged. If a gifted ten-year-old can read a play of Shakespeare's or a novel by H. G. Wells and enjoy it, there is no reason why he should not do so. On the other hand, no pressure should be exerted to force the child's reading interest to precocious maturity. But books aren't all. Care should be taken that the gifted child doesn't spend so much of his time reading that he loses contact with the world of reality. Interest in every aspect of his material environment should be encouraged, including: trees, flowers, animals, local industries, state legislatures and points of scenic or historical interest. The child should be made alive to the things going on around him. In this connection a certain amount of work is valuable. Every child should have certain regular home duties to perform. No greater mistake can be made than to encourage in a child an attitude of superiority towards the everyday affairs of the household. No matter how gifted a

child may be, he should be trained early in habits of helpfulness and in a sense of responsibility. Avoid, at all costs, giving him so much service that he takes it as his natural due. The mother of a certain gifted boy of eight years continued to dress and undress him, to give him his bath, and to do for him all sorts of things which any sensible mother would have taught her child to do for himself at an early age. Her excuse was, that for her boy to do such commonplace things would rob him of the time needed for creative thinking! Absurd, but it happened.

8. *The choice of a vocation.* Parents of the gifted child are often too much and too early concerned about the choice of a vocation. It is not generally understood that until a child's abilities and interests have had time to mature, the right choice cannot be made except by chance. During the period of rapid mental growth one interest after another develops, only to disappear and be succeeded by something else. This is usual and proper. Each wave of interest, if made the most of while it lasts, adds its own special contribution to the making of the many-sided man or woman. The common mistake is to interpret the onrush of interest in drawing, writing, or rock collecting as an indication that the child should forthwith begin preparation for a life career in art, authorship, science, etc. Some parents are much disturbed by the apparently fleeting nature of the child's interests, and do their utmost to keep them from abandoning old intellectual pastures for new. A little girl of ten years, of somewhat more than average ability but far from being a genius, wrote some poems which were published in a local newspaper. Many thousands of little girls do the same thing, but, in this case, the father thought it meant she must become a poet, and when the interest in authorship left her a little later he tried scolding, shaming, and prizes in a vain attempt to bring it back. "She is going backward," he kept saying, "she is going backward." He was mistaken. She was merely going forward to new interests. The world is full of interesting experiences and the child is right in sampling as many of them as possible.

The occupational preferences which the child spontaneously expressed from time to time may be extremely fickle or relatively lasting. The wise parent will neither attempt to discourage such preferences, nor take them too seriously. It is wiser to nourish the interest at hand and wait for developments. With a majority of gifted children nothing is to be gained and much is to be lost by "casting the die" too early. Such children, as a rule, have fairly all-round ability. Many of them, for example, would probably succeed equally well in law, medicine, teaching, authorship, engineering, or business. The final choice will often hinge upon interests rather than upon special innate genius for this or that vocation. Of course, specialized talent plays a larger role in determining fitness for a career of music, painting, poetry, and the arts generally. The child who shows extraordinary genius in one of those fields may well begin his vocational training at an early age. But in the large majority of cases the wisest course to pursue with the gifted child is to give the broadest possible school training, to encourage the greatest possible number of intellectual contacts, and then to wait for the settling and shaping effects of maturity. Until then the main problem is to feed to the limit a large variety of interests and, to this end, travel, libraries, and the pursuit of hobbies are fully as important as any formal training the school can offer.

MY FAITH*

In the thinking of some the crucial test of one's religious faith is belief in the existence of God. The trouble with this criterion is that there are so many meanings of the word "God." If the term is used as a mere synonym for the universe of being, it would of course be a semantic contradiction to deny God's existence. But if God is conceived in the anthropomorphic sense as a personal, spiritual entity who planned, created, and governs the cosmic world, it seems to me unreasonable to make acceptance of this concept a *sine qua non* of one's faith. Logical proofs of God's reality do not impress me, and theological or philosophical discussions of the exact nature of God seem to me presumptuous if not sacrilegious.

Another criterion of faith that has been stressed is belief in the continuation of life after death. Here again I am an agnostic. It is simply not given us to know. Like almost all psychologists, I place no credence in the spirit communications reported in certain investigations of psychical researchers. This is not to deny that the world might be better if everyone tried to live in such a way that the possibility of a future life could be faced without fear. For one who is unsure of immortality in this sense, there is the alternative faith that the important thing is so to live that the good we do will continue to influence the minds and hearts of those who come after us.

A third criterion of faith—really a corollary of the first one—is belief in the efficacy of prayer. But there are various kinds of prayer. The kind which merely asks God for favors, as a child begs favors of his parents, does not appeal to me. Prayer as communion with one's better self—the taking stock of one's acts and motives, the search for strength to resist evil, and the purposeful cultivation of good will—is the kind in which I have greatest faith.

I especially reject the idea that any particular belief about the origin of the universe can be a just criterion of the religious attitude. Both the origin and the ultimate nature of the cosmos are beyond the grasp of man's mentality. The wonders revealed by astronomy, physics, and chemistry stagger the imagination and almost inevitably inspire a degree of reverence. Those revealed by biological researches in the fields of evolution, heredity, adaptation, and animal behavior are equally awe inspiring. Yet, all of the physical and all of the biological sciences combined are unable to give us a final explanation of matter or of life. The 200-inch telescope at Palomar will doubtless raise as many questions as it will answer, just as each advance in nuclear science and each discovery about the behavior of genes poses new problems *ad infinitum*.

---

*Presumably written during the summer of 1948.

The fact that science cannot reveal final causes does not mean that it is futile or that it is incompatible with religious attitudes. Indeed, science itself is almost a form of religion, one that commands the highest type of sacrifice and devotion. In his never ending quest of knowledge the scientist is responding to one of the finest impulses of the human mind. His discoveries have made possible vast increase in human populations, lengthened the average span of life, reduced the amount of human suffering, and given us comforts without number. More important, they have helped to free man from material bondage and have given more room to the life of the spirit. It could be argued that science brings us closer to God, if there is a God, than does blind faith, for faith that knows nothing of nature's laws is at the bottom of every superstition.

If one believes in an ultimate Good, perhaps it does not matter whether one believes in a personal God. Either belief, of course, is an act of faith, for our notion of the Good is as much determined by emotional attitudes as by intellect. Science alone cannot define it. The guidance and inspiration afforded by religion have been, and still are, among the most powerful influences for good, even though terrible evils are sometimes perpetrated in its name. It is, of course, the spirit rather than the form of religion that is important. All will agree that one can be religious without subscribing to any particular dogma, and that there are professed Christians who are strangers to the ethical ideals of Jesus.

If man has any divinity, it rests upon two things: his ability to think and his capacity for love. Both are necessary ingredients. A man may be an intellectual giant, but without love he can be a monster of evil. Despite man's intelligence and his capacity for altruism, it is not easy to be optimistic about his future in the atomic age. That future will depend on the use he makes of his intelligence and the extent to which understanding and good will can replace selfishness, fear, and distrust.

Lecomte du Noüy dwells repeatedly on the "immeasurable gap" that separates spiritual man from his animal forebears, and the author of an earlier article in this series refers to attributes of human nature "which we share not at all with other creatures." This alleged uniqueness of man is held to be proof of his divine origin. It is true that man does differ in many ways from the animals below him, but it is easy to exaggerate the differences. As a psychologist, I do not know of any attribute of human behavior that is not shared in some degree by other creatures. Apes, for example, solve intellectual problems that are beyond the capacity of the average two-year-old child. They can be taught the value of differently colored food tokens and thus to acquire the rudiments of a money-sense. They learn to cooperate in a common effort; quite literally, they learn to "pull together" when that is necessary to draw a weighted box of food within reach. Like man, alas, some of them also learn to cheat in this cooperative task by pulling less than their share. The emotional behavior of the apes parallels remarkably that of man. These primates show not only fear and anger, but also affection and the clear beginnings of sympathy and altruism. Their social behavior affords highly interesting examples of leadership, dominance, submission, trading of sex for food or other favors (prostitution), and collusion of several to dethrone a tyrant (the beginning of political strategy). On occasion they exhibit something resembling shame or remorse, which could well be the forerunner of our human conscience.

Mind has indeed evolved by the most minute steps, and its evolution is as fascinating as that of the world of matter. Consider the capacity to profit from experience. We find its beginning in the amoeba and can trace its development on up through the earthworms, the reptiles, and the mammals to its flowering in *genus homo*. In man we can trace its development from the new-born to the adult, and from the level of idiocy to the intellect of an Einstein. No other differences among people are so important as their differences in intelligence, unless it be their differences in moral outlook. But whereas the limits of one's intelligence are largely determined by the genes of his ancestors, moral attributes are to a great extent the product of cultural patterns and training.

Significant in this connection is the ever increasing tempo of cultural change, in striking contrast to the glacial slowness of organic evolution. We do not know how long it took for the making of fire, the flaking of flint, or the use of bow and arrow to spread to all the world, but it was probably many thousands of years. It took a hundred years for the use of gunpowder in firearms to supercede more primitive weapons in the countries of Western Europe alone. Now, within a few decades after their invention or discovery, we find telephones, automobiles, airplanes, moving pictures, radios, hybrid corn, and synthetic vitamins in remote areas of the earth. The first atomic bomb was exploded in 1945, and there is every prospect that others like it or more destructive will be manufactured in all "civilized" countries before 1955.

The increasing tempo of cultural change is, of course, due to improved methods of transportation and communication. Each new invention has an effect like the atom-smashing cyclotron, which, by the application of successive bursts of energy, gives to the bombarding missile an ever-increasing acceleration. At present, the impact of culture upon culture, of ideology upon ideology, is having a hurricane effect upon the established order. Whatever the final outcome may prove to be, the immediate result is devastating and unsettling to our social institutions. The one thing we can be sure of is, that the new world will be different; we can only hope that it will be better. This hope cannot be fulfilled by clinging stubbornly to the old, but only by making greater effort to assimilate the new. If we are to be saved from chaos it can only be by increasing the tempo of man's social and moral evolution.

At present, our knowledge of human nature and of ways to improve it is not keeping pace with progress in the physical sciences. It is for religion, psychology, education, and all the social sciences to set themselves diligently and cooperatively to the task of civilizing man's impulses and emotions, so that nations and peoples everywhere will learn, before it is too late, that it is possible to live together in peace, justice, and good will. The end is one that calls for concerted and heroic effort. We dare not rest our hopes on a pollyannaish faith that man's social and moral evolution is predestined to lead forever upward. The stresses of this atomic age threaten to send it into a tailspin. From my point of view, the whole-hearted dedication of one's life to the promotion of social justice, mutual understanding, racial tolerance and equalization of opportunity, is as good evidence of a truly religious spirit as any beliefs one might hold about miracles, immortality, or a personal God.

I WAS LUCKY*

My story will be unusual, for although I have had numerous bouts with tuberculosis I have lost an estimated total of not more than eight months from work, have been bedridden with the disease less than half of that time, and recovered quickly from every attack. Nevertheless, I have had my full share of anxieties; the possibility of a premature death was a nightmarish specter that haunted me for years.

I was born on a farm in Indiana, the twelfth of fourteen children, the eldest of whom died of tuberculosis when I was a small child. As our home was overcrowded I was, of course, exposed to contagion. There seems to have been some hereditary susceptibility in my paternal ancestry. My grandfather was said to have strangled to death at age 72 during a hemorrhage of the lungs, and most of my father's nine siblings died of "consumption" before the age of 50. My father himself had "spat blood" a time or two when he was a young man but he lived to the age of 76.

Throughout my childhood I was exceptionally healthy. I began making a full hand on the farm before I was 12 years old, working close to ten hours a day, six days a week, from April to September. I was 19 when I had my first serious illness, which proved to be typhoid fever. It was a severe case and for a time I was not expected to live. I have always suspected that this illness may have made me less resistant to tuberculosis; at any rate, it was just three years later when I had my first hemorrhage of the lungs.

Or was it from the lungs? After all, there were only two or three mouthfuls of blood, followed by a faint trickle that was over in a few minutes. If I had not known about the consumptive taint in my father's family I should probably not have given the matter a second thought, but the memory of that taint led me to consult a doctor. When the examination disclosed nothing wrong the doctor was inclined to think that the blood had not come from my lungs, but probably from injury to a tiny blood vessel in my throat. He told me to take my temperature twice a day, to eat heartily, get lots of sleep, and avoid strenuous physical activity; then if no symptoms had shown up by the end of the month I could forget that anything had happened. None appeared, and a few weeks later I was married. We settled in an old farmhouse near the country high school where I had taught the previous year. In June of the following year our son was born. In August I came down with a disabling attack of pleurisy that was diagnosed as tubercular. The country doctor I had then was ill-trained, but in the light of events that followed I have little doubt that his diagnosis was correct. He kept me in bed for two or three weeks

---

*Written in 1953

until my temperature was normal and the pains of pleurisy had subsided. When I was able to be up and around a little he told me bluntly that if I did not want to die from tuberculosis in a year or two I had better resign my job and move to a better climate. Badly scared as I was, I could not take his advice because I had nothing on which to support myself and family while getting well. I decided to stay where I was but to ask for a month's leave of absence in the hope that I could then return to work. The leave was granted; I improved steadily and went back to my job at the end of October, though I was still worried about the final outcome.

My regimen that year may be of interest. I usually rose early and took a brief walk in the near-by fields or woods before breakfast. As soon as school was dismissed at four in the afternoon, I strolled off again unless it was raining or snowing. On Saturdays and Sundays the walks were somewhat longer though still carefully rationed. I took my temperature every day and counted my pulse at the end of my walks. As a measure of safety to my family I slept in a separate room, which was larger and had cross ventilation. All through the winter I slept with doors and windows wide open, often waking to find snow drifted half way across the room. I came to enjoy "outdoor" sleeping and during most of my life since then I have usually slept in open or half-open rooms.

By the following spring my health appeared so completely normal that I decided to enter Indiana University as a first step toward becoming a psychologist. My normal school training would allow me to enter as a junior undergraduate and I hoped to get both my A.B. and M.A. degrees in two years by crowding three years of work into two. This was accomplished without any symptoms of ill health. My wife managed, by taking in roomers, to get us through the two years on only $1,000, all of which was borrowed. Before the end of the second year our family was increased to four by the birth of a daughter and it seemed absolutely necessary for me to find a job that would enable me to pay my debts. My professors insisted, however, that I should continue to the doctorate without further delay and they obtained for me the offer of a fellowship at Clark University. Relatives agreed to finance me for another two years.

My first ten months at Clark were uneventful so far as my health was concerned. The new environment was stimulating and I worked harder than ever before, averaging about 80 hours a week. At the end of the school year I began preparations for a doctoral research that would have to be completed the following year. But around the middle of the vacation period, just after I had finished a game of tennis, a hemorrhage broke loose in such quantity as to leave no doubt as to its origin. Four years had passed since the attack of pleurisy and I had pretty well recovered from the fright it had given me. The shock I experienced from the new threat was profound, particularly after the nature of it was confirmed by a TB specialist. When I informed the doctor of my desperate situation—a wife and two children, debts of more than $1,500, and the necessity of getting my degree the following year—I fully expected to be told to forget my plans and spend a year regaining my health. Instead, he suggested that I go to bed for two or three weeks to see how things developed. If there were no further symptoms he thought it might then be safe to work a few hours daily provided I rested in bed the remainder of the day. I have always believed that if I had been sentenced to a year in a sanatorium I should probably have died of worry about the future of my family and my career. As it turned out, I was feeling so well within a month or two that I was working six or seven hours a day.

Although no symptoms reappeared during the following school year, I developed something like an anxiety neurosis which remained fairly quiescent during the day but often woke me in the middle of the night and left me sleepless for hours, worrying about my health, my debts, and my chances of getting the degree. Before that year I had never experienced insomnia, but for the next five years I was rarely free from it. However, as the months passed and my health improved, the anxiety abated somewhat and my working efficiency increased. I completed my dissertation, passed the examinations, and in June received my degree.

The immediate goal had been won but my worries would not be over until I obtained a position in a favorable climate and at a salary that would enable me to start paying the debts that now amounted to nearly $2,500 (the equivalent of three times that amount today). I wanted, of course, a university position, but the only offer I received of that kind carried a salary much too low to support my family, to say nothing of paying off any debts. Later I was offered the high school principalship at San Bernardino, California. This was far from being the kind of job I wanted, but I accepted it because the semi-arid region of Southern California had the kind of climate that I thought would be safest for me.

It was September of 1905 when we arrived at San Bernardino after an unforgettable ride through the Mohave Desert. As our train coasted down through the Cajon pass, and the San Bernardino valley opened before us almost encircled by mountains of 4,000 to 11,000 feet, the valley seemed to be truly the paradise that the chamber-of-commerce literature had depicted it. Here, if anywhere, I should be able to rid myself of the threat that had been hanging over me. The people we met were so proud of their climate that I was constantly being told of this or that person who had come to San Bernardino twenty or thirty years ago as a "one-lunger" and was soon restored to health. My new friends who told me these stories could not know what an eager listener I was!

The high school work proved to be interesting; the teachers were competent and cooperative and the townspeople were as friendly and kind as the climate itself. Life was so pleasant and so filled with hope that I was ill-prepared for the shock that came eight weeks later when I awoke about five o'clock on a Thursday morning with my mouth full of blood. The hemorrhage lasted several minutes and was more copious than any other I was ever to experience.

Imagine my predicament. No one in San Bernardino knew that I had ever had TB, and to admit the fact now might have serious consequences. Instead of calling a doctor, I reported to the school that I was not feeling well and would remain at home the rest of the week. During the following week I was on duty half of each day to attend to administrative matters, while other faculty members taught my classes. Just eleven days after the hemorrhage I went back to work on a full-time basis! The desperate gamble I had taken paid off, for there was no serious trouble the rest of the school year. I carried my duties as lightly as possible, avoided over-exertion, and went to bed early. As soon as school ended in June we packed off to the mountains where we camped out in tents for nearly three months. By the time we had to leave I felt so well that I could look forward to next year's work with confidence.

And I needed both health and confidence, for my work next year would be different; I had accepted a position in the Los Angeles State Normal School as teacher of child study and pedagogy. The offer had come quite unexpectedly. I had not applied for that position or any other; I was happy in San Bernardino, had been reappointed at an increase in salary, and expected to stay at least another year. But the normal school position was so much nearer to my ultimate goal that it could not be refused. Perhaps after a few years there I could get a university position.

The first year after our move we lived in Hollywood, then a quiet suburb of 4000 population. The following summer was again spent in the mountains where we had camped the previous summer. In the meantime we had bought an acre-lot in an orange grove at the foot of the Verdugo mountains in San Fernando Valley, and had drafted plans for a house. It was ready for us in November and we lived there nearly three years. The location was ideal, for in those pre-smog years the climate of San Fernando Valley rivaled that of Redlands or San Bernardino. I commuted to Los Angeles by interurban trolley and was usually able to get home in the afternoon in time to work an hour or more in the garden before dinner, where I also spent much of my time on Saturdays and Sundays.

My teaching schedule during those four years in the normal school was reasonably light and required only a moderate amount of preparation. The only outside work I took on was an occasional lecture before teachers' institutes in various counties of Southern California. I prepared these lectures with considerable care, and it was fortunate I did, because one of them was largely responsible for an invitation from Professor E. P. Cubberley (who had heard that lecture) to join his faculty at Stanford University as Assistant Professor of Education.

At last I found the opportunity I had so long wanted, in a perfect climate and with the university I would have chosen in preference to any other. But for the TB, which had brought me to California, it is unlikely that this opportunity would ever have come. When I think of this I feel repaid for all the anxiety the disease has caused me. We moved to

Stanford in 1910, and were fortunate to find a charming cottage in the country a mile and a half from the University by bicycle. It had (besides living room, bath, and a large kitchen) a study, two bedrooms, and a screened sleeping porch more than forty feet long where the entire family could sleep.

My light teaching load of eight lectures a week left more than half of my time for research and writing. In research I began where I had left off when I finished my doctoral experiment, namely with mental tests. The first writing I undertook (apart from a few research articles) was motivated by my health history and resulted in two books, "The Hygiene of the School Child" and (coauthored with a physician) "Health Work in the Schools." These had a combined sale of about 200,000 copies and seem to have had considerable influence. This crusade in a field that was outside my area of major competence points up the truth there is in the old saying that "if you scratch a health reformer you are pretty sure to find an invalid."

My health at Stanford was excellent for many years. Although I worked an average of sixty hours a week, I continued my long-established practice of resting in bed an hour or two daily. In 1913, I was able to get $10,000 of life insurance at the normal rate, after having previously been turned down by two insurance companies, and in 1918 I got $10,000 in government insurance when I was accepted for a commission in the Army. These policies added greatly to my peace of mind.

Apart from three attacks of pneumonia, there have been only two additional threats to my health from lung trouble. In the summer of 1928 I had a light hemorrhage, but no positive sputum was found and my temperature remained at or near normal. I spent a week or two in bed then gradually returned to my writing and research. In the summer of 1936 X-rays taken after a severe cold were interpreted as indicating renewed tubercular activity. As I had been tired for some time and felt in need of a considerable rest, I entered a TB sanatorium and remained there six weeks. The physician in charge confirmed the diagnosis of my Palo Alto doctor, but still my sputum remained negative and my temperature close to normal. The sanatorium experience was on the whole pleasant. The 2500 feet elevation and the dry air had a bracing effect, the food was superb, and most of the patients I came to know were interesting and not too despondent.

That I was able to win so many bouts with tuberculosis despite my reckless return to work after only a few weeks (or days) of rest from each, and with so little medical help during the earlier years, must mean that I was just plain lucky; either I had more than the ordinary amount of resistance to tubercle bacilli or the strain that I harbored was exceptionally weak. I hope that the reading of this chapter will not influence anyone to take the kinds of chances that happened to "work" for me. I express this hope all the more earnestly because of the fact that it took all the science and skill of modern medicine to pull my son through his two-year battle-for-life against this disease. Without such prolonged and expert treatment, Frederick Emmons Terman would never have lived to become the world figure he is in electronic science.

Since coming to Stanford I have undergone many thorough medical check-ups, usually once a year, or oftener. The late Dr. Philip Pierson, of the Stanford Medical School, collected all my X-rays and used them for years as prize exhibits in his medical school classes. He called them the most valuable series he had seen, as they revealed so clearly the scar tissues which had sealed off the many lesions that had occurred during the long course of my disease. The numerous calcareous deposits showing white in the lung structure always reminded me of multiple concrete reinforcements.

Approaching 77 now, I have lived more years than I dared hope for a half century ago and have accomplished more than I ever dreamed possible, probably as much as I would have accomplished if I had never had TB. From this distance, it is possible to look back upon the threats of those earlier years without reviving the raw anxiety they caused me. Though I long ago lost my fear of death from tuberculosis (or anything else), I still find myself occasionally counting my pulse or reaching for the clinical thermometer that lies on a table by my bed—perhaps out of habit, perhaps because I want to finish another book and to watch for a while longer developments on the world scene. Besides there are my 1400 gifted "children," now at mid-life, who were selected by mental tests in 1922; I have already followed their careers for thirty years and should like so much to follow them for another thirty!

PAPER READ BY LEWIS M. TERMAN AT THE A.P.A. MEETING
IN SAN FRANCISCO, SEPTEMBER 1, 1955

It has been suggested that in leading off this symposium I summarize briefly the characteristic traits of gifted children and then present some of the results of recent follow-up studies.

It is now 34 years since the Stanford study was launched as an empirical attempt to find the answer to two questions: What are gifted children like, and what kind of adults do they tend to become? For our purpose the gifted child was defined arbitrarily as one who rates in the top 1 percent for his age on the 1916 Stanford-Binet test or, in the case of high school children, makes a correspondingly high rating on the Terman Group Test of Mental Ability. The number of subjects tested who met this criterion was 1528, counting a few who had been tested prior to the main search for subjects in 1921-22 and a few who were admitted to the group during the first field follow-up six years later. Careful checks on the methods of search employed indicate that close to 90 percent of children who could have met our standard in the schools canvassed were identified, thus affording a sample sufficiently unbiased to permit of generalization. The age range of the subjects when tested was from 3 to 18 years, with only a small number who were below 5 or above 17. The mean age was approximately 11 years.

Those familiar with the methods we have used in assessing the traits of these subjects will recall that we tried to make them objective enough to permit others to repeat the experiment at will and thus verify or refute the conclusions we have drawn. It appears that to date few of our *major* conclusions have been seriously questioned.

To what extent do our findings support the beliefs current a half century ago that intellectually precocious children are especially likely to be queer, one-sided, sickly, neurotic, or otherwise poor bets for the future? The answer is almost no support at all.

The physical measurements, health histories, and medical examinations show conclusively that the typical child in our group was a better physical specimen that the average child in the generality. The interests of the children were not as a rule one-sided, but instead covered a wide range, were avidly pursued, and revealed a maturity two or three years above the age norm. On a battery of seven character tests the children scored above unselected children on every one, and on total score of the battery the gifted at age 9 scored as high as unselected children at age 12. Ratings of the children by teachers and parents on 25 personality and character traits confirmed the evidence from tests and case histories. Moreover, a 3-hour battery of achievement tests showed that in mastery of school subject matter the average gifted child was accelerated 44 percent of his age, whereas in grade placement he was accelerated only 14 percent of his age. The result was that the average member of our group was being kept at school tasks about two full grades below the level of achievement he had already attained.

Such are the outstanding traits of gifted children expressed in terms of composite portraiture, a method which is useful as a basis for generalization and as a guide for educational practice. Actually, of course, there was a wide range of variability within the group on every trait we tried to measure. Among these children one could find individual examples of almost every type of personality defect, social maladjustment, behavior problem, and physical frailty; but the fact remains that the incidence of unfavorable deviations was, in varying degrees, well below that in the general child population.

But doubtless you are more interested in knowing what these subjects are like as adults. In our many years of follow-up we have obtained an immense amount of information bearing on this, but it would be far too much to claim that we have found all the answers. The follow-up has included field studies involving interviews and retests in 1927-28, 1939-40, and 1951-52, supplemented by more frequent follow-up by mail. Despite the high mobility of the subjects we have completely lost track of fewer than 30 of the original group. At a given time there may be a good many more whom we cannot locate immediately, but diligent enquiry from their relatives or friends nearly always brings them to light. Our statistics on the adult gifted are not appreciably biased by loss of subjects.

Mortality in the group, as computed from the tables of Dublin and Lotka showing expected mortality to given ages for persons who were alive at age 11, was below that for the generality both in 1940 and 1952. In 1952, the subjects rated their health on a 5-point scale as very good, good, fair, poor, or very poor. Ratings of very good were given by 92 percent of men and 87 percent of women. Ratings of poor or very poor were given by 1.7 percent of men and 2.7 percent of women. Before this mixed audience I hesitate to venture an explanation of the greater frequency of poor health reported by the women.

As for mental health, the proportion of those who have ever been hospitalized for mental difficulty is certainly not above and is probably below that in the general population of corresponding age. There is a margin of uncertainty in this comparison because our figures are cumulative and complete, whereas those for the generality usually are not. Our figure is close to 3 percent, of whom not more than three or four remain hospitalized. However, the proportion of gifted who have consulted a psychiatrist is certainly much greater than it is in the general population, a fact readily explained by the superior intelligence and high economic status of our group. The incidence of alcoholism and of suicide is in each case below that for the generality, and the delinquency rate is but a tiny fraction of that in the general population.

But if our gifted are not especially prone to die young or become mentally addled, the question remains whether many of them do not later regress to average intelligence. Thus far we have found no such case. The scores they make on our difficult Concept Mastery Test indicate that the great majority of them rate nearly as high in comparison with adults as they rated in childhood in comparison with other children. What is more, when those who were given Form A of this test in 1940 were given equated Form B in 1952, the group was found to have made a highly reliable gain in the 12-year interval. The increases in score occurred in all educational and occupational levels, in all grades of ability, and at all ages. (For details see the extremely important article by Nancy Bayley and Melita Oden in the *Journal of Gerontology* for January 1955).

Additional evidence on the maintenance of ability is afforded by the educational and occupational histories of the group. Approximately 86 percent entered college and 70 percent graduated. Of those graduating, two-thirds of the men and nearly three-fifths of the women completed one or more years of graduate work. A Ph.D. or equivalent degree was obtained by 96 of the group, the M.D. degree by 55, and a graduate law degree by 90. Not counting any of the above persons, 213 have taken the M.A. Lastly, there were 161 who had a year or more of graduate work without taking any graduate degree.

On the Minnesota (7-point) Occupational Scale, 85 percent of the men were by 1951 in class I or II; that is, either in the professional group or the semi-professional and managerial group. Only 3 percent were below class III. Some 125 of the men and a dozen women have a substantial record of research in the physical, biological, or social sciences. The number in the group who are known to have been listed in *American Men of Science* is 64, and in *Who's Who in America* 20. These numbers, especially the *Who's Who* listings, can be expected to increase greatly, since the average age of the group was only 43 years when the last *Who's Who* went to press. It is reasonable to expect that ultimately at least 100 members of the total group (about 90 of them men) will have been listed in one or the other or in both of these publications. In the case of men this would mean more than 10 percent, or perhaps 8 or 10 times the proportion for the generality of college graduates in the United States, and perhaps 50 times the proportion in the general population. The group includes nationally known leaders in almost every professional field (not excepting psychology), and several who are internationally eminent. There is not time to tell you about the nearly 100 books that members of the group have authored, about their 2000 or more articles covering many fields of science, scholarship, and literature, or about the 200 patents they have been granted.

The median earned income of the men for 1954, when their average age was 43 years, was almost $10,000. Nearly 30 percent earned $15,000 or more, and 10 percent $25,000 or more. Some 15 reported 1954 incomes of $50,000 to more than $100,000. Only one man in four earned less than $7,000. Following are the median and top earned incomes of 1954 for men in a few professional and business occupations:

1. Practising physicians and surgeons, median $20,000 plus, top $40,000. The most eminent physicians, however, were research men on salaries who earned much less than the practitioners.
2. Executives in business and industry, median $16,000 plus, top more than $100,000.
3. Producers, writers, and directors in radio, TV, and motion pictures, median $15,000 plus, top more than $100,000.
4. Lawyers, median $15,000 plus, top around $50,000.
5. Physical scientists, engineers, and university teachers and researchers, median about $9,000 with one in ten earning above $15,000. Science attracts some of the best brains but its dollar rewards are far below those for practising physicians, business executives, entertainers, and lawyers.

But it may seem to you that I have been accentuating the positive too much. What about the other side of the picture? Why, for example, did only 70 percent graduate from college, and why did only 27 percent of the men get a Ph.D. or other degree requiring three or four years of graduate work? There are many reasons, but inadequate mental ability was rarely if ever the decisive factor. Those who never entered college score higher on our Concept Mastery Test than our highly selected Stanford seniors, who themselves average 130 I.Q. The failure of so many gifted youths to graduate from college is an old story. Wolfle, in his book, *America's Resources of Specialized Talent*, estimates that even now in the United States only 59 percent of youths who are in the top 1 percent for mental ability graduate from college. This is 11 percent below the record for our gifted subjects, many of whom had the bad luck to reach college age at or near the beginning of the great depression.

One of the important causes of such deplorable waste of intellectual resources is the lack of adequate counseling in high schools. Hardly any was available in the high schools our group attended, and I am told that good counseling service is still the exception rather than the rule. As for occupational success, if a test like the 1938 edition of Strong's vocational interest test had been available for our gifted boys at high school graduation a good many of them might have chosen an occupation that would have led to greater vocational achievement.

Although failure to achieve was in certain cases the result of social maladjustment or other defect of personality, it was more often due to lack of ambition or drive to achieve. We know of several in the group who deliberately chose not to enter the usual American rat-race for material success. Nor can I find it in my heart to criticize those who made this choice; it may well be that their fewer honors and lower incomes have been fully compensated by greater contentment and a lower incidence of anxiety and ulcers.

Index

achievement tests, 24, 45, 69, 90, 222
  See also *Stanford Achievement Test*
Adjusting the School to the Child (Washburn), 78.
adolescent psychology, 39, 139.
adopted children: study of, 120
age scale: for mental tests, 42, 44f
Alexandria Bay statement, 151, 161
Almack, J. C., 60
America First Committee, 156, 159-60
American Association of Marriage Counselors, 148
American Men of Science, 24, 97, 98, 178, 247
American Psychological Association, 111-12, 120, 138;
  and Terman, 64, 65, 67, 79, 107, 113, 177, 178, 183;
  Terman's paper at, 245-49
American Psychological Foundation, 178
American Vocational Guidance Association, 178
American Weekly, 179
America's Resources of Specialized Talent (Wolfle), 248
Angell, Frank, 108, 110
animal psychology, 141
anti-Semitism, 56, 136, 149
applied psychology, 113
  See also mental tests
Applied Psychology Monographs, 75
Aptitude Testing (Hull), 77
Army mental testing, 65-68, 79, 113, 115;
  Lippmann on, 114-15
Army Alpha Test, 65-66, 68
Army Beta Test, 66
Army General Classification Test, 67
Association for Child Health, 112
Atlantic Union Committee, 164

Bagley, William C., 107, 113-14, 116
Ban the Books movement, 164

Banta, Arthur, 6, 144
Barnard College, 100
Bayley, Nancy, 183, 247
Bennett, Margaret, 133-34
Bergstrom, 17, 19, 23, 34, 35
Berle, Adolph, 85
Berlin Diary (Shirer), 151
Bernreuter, Robert, 70, 134, 169
Bernreuter Personality Inventory, 142
Binet, Alfred:
  Terman and, 17, 18, 24, 43-54, 63, 186;
  mental tests of, 41-43;
  and age scale, 42
Binet-Simon Scale, 42;
  Terman's revision of, 40, 44-54;
  criticism of, 42-43
  other tests derived from, 45, 47, 51, 70
Bingham, Walter Van Dyke, 65, 177
biography:
  and Terman's studies, 86, 140-141;
  for gifted children, 92
black population, 91, 119-23, 168, 222
Block Design Test, 51, 56
Bohr, Neils, 85
Boisen, Anton, 17, 179
Book, W. F., 24, 25
Book of Knowledge, 93
Bonbright, Betsy, 176
Boring, E. G.:
  Terman and, 63, 110, 112, 139-40, 162, 176;
  and Army testing, 65;
  biography of Terman by, 67, 183;
  on nature-nurture issue, 116
Boy Scouts, 21, 74, 230
British Journal of Educational Psychology, 75
British Journal of Psychology, 44
British Journal of Statistical Psychology, 183
British Psychological Society, 178
Bryan, William Lowe, 17, 19

Buckel Fellowship, 55, 62
Burks, Barbara, 51, 95
Burlingame, L. L., 88
Burnham, W. H., 17, 23-24, 55
Burt, Cyril, 43, 74, 120
Bush, Vannevar, 126

Cady, Vernon, 51
California, University of, 164, 178
Carnegie Corporation, 94, 217, 223
Carter, Harold, 132
Cattell, James McKeen, 17, 21, 41, 61, 80;
    on historical eminence, 86, 97, 218, 222
Central Normal College, 8-9
Challman, R. C., 51
Charcot, Jean Martin, 17
child psychology, 21, 24, 39, 41;
    Terman and, 12, 25-26, 168
    See also gifted child
Children Above 180 IQ (Hollingworth),
    78
Children's Reading (Terman), 92
Childs, H. G., 40, 46, 49
Christian Science Monitor, 162
Church of Jesus Christ, Scientist, 60, 149
Civil War, 3
Clark School for the Deaf, 63
Clark University, 19-27, 178
Cleveland, A. A., 24, 25
College and Life (Bennett), 78
Committee for Research on Problems of
    Sex, 144
Committee on Classification of Personnel,
    64
Commonwealth Fund, 94, 217
Concept Mastery Test, 70, 96, 98, 247, 248
Conference on the Gifted Child, 182
Conklin, E. S., 139
Connecticut State College, 137
Conradi, Edward, 25, 30
Consumer's Union, 150, 164
Coover, J. E., 109-10
Council on Intolerance in America, 150
Cousin, Victor, 87, 219
Cowell, Henry, 82-84
Cox, Catherine, see Miles, Catherine Cox
creativity, 101
Crile, George, 58
criminality:
    Terman on, 17, 51, 61-63
Cronbach, Lee, 99, 183

Cubberley, Elwood, 35, 40, 55, 60, 135
Cuneo, Irene, 47

Darsie, Marvin L., 56
Darwin, Charles, 9, 10
Davidson, Helen, 51
Davis, Allison, 119
delinquency, juvenile:
    studies of, 51, 61-63;
    tests identifying, 62, 141
Delinquent Boy and the Correctional
    School (Fenton), 78
dental health: Terman on, 57-58
Description and Measurement of Person-
    ality (Cattell), 78
Dewey, John, 21
Dickson, Virgil, 49-50, 56
Dies committee, 150, 165
Draw-a-Man Test, 51, 74

Early Conception and Tests of Intelligence
    (Peterson), 77
Easel Age Scale (Lantz), 78
Ebbinghaus, Hermann, 17, 44
Edison, Thomas, 85
"Educating and Training the Gifted Child"
    (Terman), 230-34
Education Film Magazine, 75
Education of Gifted Children (Stedman),
    76
Educational Institute of Scotland, 178
Educational Measurement in the Elementary
    Grades (Madsen), 78
Einstein, Albert, 85
Electrical Engineering Department, Stan-
    ford University, 127-28
Engineering, Stanford School of, 173
environment: and intelligence, 46, 97,
    113-23, 228
Estimation of Juvenile Incorrigibility
    (Cady), 78
Eugenics Research Association, 112, 178
European Recovery Plan, 165
evolution: Hall on, 21
Experimentelle Pädagogik (Meumann), 44

Faraday, Michael, 87, 219
Farnsworth, Paul, 83, 110, 122, 124, 182,
    217
feeblemindedness, see mental deficiency
Fenton, Jesse Chase, 88
Fenton, Norman, 51, 63

Fernald, Grace, 62
Fernald, Mabel, 65
Fight for Freedom Committee, 150
Fisher, Dorothy Canfield, 62
Flesch, Rudolf, 134
Foch, Ferdinand, 85
Ford, Henry, 85
foreign languages: Terman's use of, 17, 38
foreign policy: Stanford faculty on, 151-63
Fourth International Congress on School Hygiene, 45
Franklin, Benjamin, 85, 87, 220
Freud, Sigmund, 24;
    psychology of, 141, 142, 143
Fuller, Florence, 88

Galbreath, Neva, 49
Galton, Francis:
    Terman and, 17, 81, 86, 142;
    study of intelligence by, 80, 97, 113, 122, 222
Genetic Psychology Monographs, 75
Genetic Studies of Genius (Terman, ed.):
    volume I, 75, 87, 91f; volume II, 86;
    volume III, 95; volume IV, 95, 97;
    volume V, 98, 170, 183
genius, 17-18, 221;
    historical study of, 86-87, 217-21, 224
    See also gifted child
Genius and Stupidity: A Study of Some of the Intellectual Processes of Seven "Bright" and Seven "Stupid" Boys (Terman), 28
George Peabody College, 167
Gesell, Arnold, 21, 25, 32-34, 59, 176
Gestalt psychology, 141
gifted child:
    Terman on, 26, 101-6, 185;
    Binet's studies of, 41;
    identification of, 71, 101, 103;
    education of, 71-72, 80, 100-5;
    case studies of, 81-85;
    definition of, 85-86, 87, 101, 221-22;
    historical study of, 86-87;
    longitudinal study of, 87-100, 170, 217, 221-28;
    characteristics of, 92-93, 95-97, 222-28, 245-49;
    and M-F test, 142-43;
    religion and, 179
Goddard, H. H., 21, 33, 43, 45, 65, 122
Goethe, von, Johann, 87, 220
Goldsmith, Oliver, 87, 220
Goodenough, Florence, 51, 74, 88, 90, 169

Goodwin Watson Test of Fair-Mindedness, 141-42, 149
grants: for research, 85, 94, 101, 144-46, 217, 223
Guershayst, Hugo, 85

Haines, Thomas Harvey, 45
Hall, G. Stanley, 17f, 112, 133, 139;
    at Clark University, 21-29;
    and mental tests, 43, 75
Hamsum, Knute, 85
Handbook of Statistical Monographs, Tables and Formulas (Dunlap and Kurtz), 78
Harlow, H. F., 111, 136, 149, 176
Harvard University, 21, 173
Hawthorne, Nathaniel, 97, 228
Hayes-Binet test, 51
health studies, *see* hygiene
Health Work in the Schools (Terman and Hoag), 59, 60
Huxley, Thomas Henry, 9, 10
Herbert Hoover Medal for Distinguished Service to Stanford, 174
heredity, 21, 88;
    vs. environment, 113-23
Herring-Binet test, 51
Hilgard, E. R., 112, 139, 183
History of Experimental Psychology, 67
History of Psychology in Autobiography, 140
Hitler, Adolf, 149-63 *passim*
Hoag, E. B., 59
hobbies: for gifted children, 232
Hoover, Herbert, 85, 151, 153-63
Hoover-Stimson Doctrine, 152-54
Huey, E. B., 25, 33, 34, 43, 44
Hughes, Charles, 85
"Human Intelligence and Achievement" (Terman), 216-228
Humboldt, von, Alexander, 87, 220
Hunter, John, 87, 220
Hunter College Elementary School, 100
hygiene:
    in schools, 33-34, 38, 39, 45, 55-63, 81, 85;
    in prisons, 61
Hygiene of the School Child, The (Terman), 55, 59-60

IQ, *see* intelligence quotient
"I Was Lucky" (Terman), 239-44
income: of gifted group, 224, 247-48

Independent Study Plan, 100-101, 111
Indiana, 1-19 passim
Indiana, University of, 16-19, 178
individual differences:
  Terman's work in, 39, 56, 61-62, 70, 120-22, 165, 168;
  Binet on, 41;
  teaching adapted to, 71;
  and the gifted, 80, 93
intelligence:
  Terman on, 27, 46, 80-81, 102;
  Binet's approach to, 42-44;
  studies on origins of, 51;
  and adjustment, 98;
  and nature-nurture controversy, 113-23;
  and achievement, 216-28.
  See also gifted child; mental tests
intelligence quotient (IQ),
  Terman's use of, 46-48, 50, 53;
  for school use, 73;
  estimated for historical study, 81, 86-87, 218-19, 223;
  of Henry Cowell, 84;
  of gifted group, 90, 95, 221-23;
  of Stanford seniors, 248.
  See also nature-nurture controversy
Intelligence of School Children, The (Terman), 70
intelligence tests, see mental tests
Intelligence Tests and School Reorganization (Terman), 72
interest tests, 142, 143, 222, 248
International Council for the Education of Exceptional Children, 112
Interpretation of Educational Measurement (Kelly), 77
Iowa, University of, 117-19

James, Maude Merrill, 50, 51, 52, 86, 108, 110, 169
James, William, 21, 34
Janet, Pierre, 25, 44
Jastrow, Joseph, 21
Jefferson, Thomas, 85
Jensen, Arthur, 119-20
Jensen, W. D., 95
Jewell, J. R., 25
Jewish population, 91, 222, 226-27.
  See also anti-Semitism
Johnson, Hiram, 61
Joint University Libraries, 167-68
Jordan, David Starr, 35, 109
Journal of Applied Psychology, 75
Journal of Delinquency, 62, 75
Journal of Educational Psychology, 75
Journal of Educational Research, 75

Journal of Genetic Psychology, 75
Journal of Gerontology, 247
Journal of Juvenile Research, 75
Journal of Personality, 75
Journal of Personnel Research, 75
Journal of Social Hygiene, 75
Junior Home, The, 75
juvenile delinquency, see delinquency, juvenile

Kant, Immanuel, 17
Kelley, Truman, 47, 65, 69, 108, 110
Kelly, E. L., 111, 133-38 passim, 145-46
Kennedy, John F., 83
Kinsey, Alfred Charles, 147-48
Knollin, Herbert, 51
Kohs, Samuel, 51, 56, 136, 149
Kraepelin, Emil, 17, 24, 44
Krafft-Ebing, Richard, 44
Kuhlman, F., 25, 27, 43, 50
Kulpe, Oswald, 17

Landis, Carney, 147
L'Annee Psychologique, 44
Lantz, Beatrice, 51
Lashley, Karl, 110
leadership: Terman's study of, 17-18, 26, 43
League for Medical Freedom, 60, 149
Leahy, Alice, 95
Leibig, physiological chemist, 87, 220
Leibnitz, Gottfried Wilhelm, 87, 221
Lewin, Kurt, 139, 150
Lewis, William B., 183
Libby, W., 25
Life, Letters and Labors of Galton (Pearson), 218
Lindley, 17, 19, 23, 55
Lippmann, Walter, 107, 114-16
Lima, Margaret, 93
Longfellow, Henry Wadsworth, 97, 228
Los Angeles Normal School, 32-34
loyalty oath, California, 164
Lyman, Grace, 49

Macaulay, Thomas B., 87, 220
magazine articles: by Terman, 60
Man, an Adaptive Mechanism (Crile), 58

Manual of Child Psychology (Carmichael), 144
marital happiness: study of, 144-48
Marquis, Don, 110, 112, 138
Marshall, Helen, 88-90, 95
Martineau, Harriet, 85
McCarthy Committee, 163
McGeoch, John, 139
McNemar, Quinn, 47, 69, 111, 165, 169
Measurement and Adjustment Series, 76-79, 92
Measurement in Higher Education (Wood), 76
Measurement of Intelligence, The (Terman and Childs), 40, 47-48
Measurement of Intelligence by Drawings (Goodenough), 77
Measurement of Interest in Relation to Human Adjustment (Fryer), 78
Mein Kampf (Hitler), 151
mental deficiency, 27, 50;
    Terman on, 17, 48, 51, 55, 57, 62, 92;
    Binet's tests of, 41-42, 45;
    vs. delinquency, 61
mental illness, 51
Mental Measurement of Pre-School Children (Stutsman), 78
mental tests:
    Terman on, 27-29, 38-39, 140-41, 165;
    Binet's work on, 41-43;
    scholarly reaction to, 42-43, 45, 70, 74;
    Terman's revision of Binet's, 45-54;
    verbal, 49;
    specializations of, 51, 56;
    non-verbal, 52, 68;
    for deaf persons, 63;
    and Army group tests, 64, 68;
    for schools, 68-73;
    textbook series on, 76-79;
    used in gifted study, 87-90, 222;
    and admission to Stanford, 100;
    and nature-nurture controversy, 113-23
Mental Tests and the Classroom Teacher (Dickson), 76
Mental Tests in Clinical Practice (Wells), 77
Mentality and Homosexuality (Kahn), 144
Merrill, Maud, *see* James, Maud Merrill
Merrill-Palmer Scale, 51
Merriman, Curtis, 51, 135
Meumann, Ernst, 44
Mexican population, 91, 222
M-F test (masculinity-femininity), 142-43, 148
Miles, Catherine Cox, 86-87, 143, 169, 217-21

Miles, Walter R., 110, 112
Mill, John Stuart, 85
Miller, Neal, 112
Milton, John, 85
Minnesota, University of, 107
Minnesota Occupational Scale, 247
minority groups, 51, 168;
    and gifted children, 91, 119-23, 222, 226-27
Minton, Reuben B., 11-12
monographs: Terman's use of, 44
Morse, Josiah, 25, 30, 149
Mussolini, Benito, 85, 165
"My Faith" (Terman), 235-38
My New Order (Hitler), 151
Myers, G. E., 25
Myth of the Total State (Reimann), 151

National Academy of Sciences, 67, 79, 174f, 183
National Association for the Study of Education, 107
National Intelligence Tests, 68, 89
National Research Council, 144
National Society for the Study of Education, 116-19
Nation's Schools, The, 75
nature-nurture controversy, 43, 107, 113-23, 164-65
Negroes, *see* black population
Nelles, Fred, 62
New Republic, 114, 116
New York Times, 162
New York University, 108
Newcomb, Theodore, 178
Newsweek, 156
Newton, Isaac, 87, 97, 219, 228
No Other Road to Freedom (Stowe), 151

Oakland Tribune, 162
Oden, Melita, 94, 95, 98, 99, 165, 183, 247
Oedipus complex, 143
Office of Naval Research, 98
Otis, Arthur, 47, 49, 65, 76
Otis Test of Mental Ability, 68
Our Nation's Foreign Policy, 152-53

Paderewski, Ignacy Jan, 85
Palo Alto Times, 153, 162
Pascal, Blaise, 87, 220
Pastore, Nicholas, 164, 165

Pattern of Conquest (Harch), 151
Pearson, Karl, 51, 81, 218
Pennsylvania, University of, 172, 178
People's World, The, 156
personality:
    Terman's interest in, 41, 61-62;
    tests of, 70, 74, 91, 140-41, 222;
    of gifted children, 227
personality tests, 70, 74, 91, 140-41;
    used in gifted study, 222
Plato the Teacher (Bryan), 10
Porter, J. P., 25
Preston School of Industry: and delin-
    quency study, 61
Price, Bronson, 57
prisons: Terman's hygiene studies in, 61
Psychological Factors in Marital Happiness
    (Terman), 146-47
Psychological Services for School Problems
    (Hildreth), 77-78
Psychologische Arbeiten (Kraepelin), 44
psychology:
    Terman and, 17, 45, 68, 79, 129, 140-141;
    at Clark University, 20-29;
    in Europe, 24-25, 41-43;
    mental testing defended as, 112-13;
    of animals, 141.
    See also child psychology; mental tests
psychometric methods, *see* mental tests

questionnaire method: Terman on, 26

Raubenheimer, Albert S., 51, 69
reading, 92, 232
religion: Terman on, 10, 141, 179, 235-38
Religion in Crisis and Customs (Boisen), 17
retardation, mental, *see* mental deficiency
Revolution of Nihilism (Rauschning), 151
Ribot, Theodule Armand, 17
Road Ahead, The (Howard), 78
Rockefeller, J. D., 85
Rockefeller Foundation, 101
Roe, Anne, 15, 135
Rollins College, 100
Roosevelt, Franklin D., 149, 151, 152
Ruch, Giles M., 51, 69
Rulon, Phillip, 51
Russia: twins study in, 142

San Bernardino, 30-32
San Francisco Chronicle, 156, 158, 162
San Francisco Examiner, 162

San Francisco News, 156, 162
San Quentin Prison: and delinquency
    study, 61
Sand, George, 97, 228
Sanford, E. C., 17, 21, 23, 27, 112
Scarritt College for Christian Workers, 167
Scott, Walter, 64, 65, 87, 220
schools: hygiene in, 33-34, 38, 39, 45,
    55-63, 81, 85;
    mental tests for, 68-73;
    special classes in, 71-72, 80, 103-5;
    gifted study and, 95;
    counseling in, 248
Sears, Jesse, 35, 157
Sears, Robert, 46, 94, 99, 112, 140, 183
Self-Direction and Adjustment (Fenton), 77
Self Reliance (Fisher), 62
Sex and Personality (Terman and Miles),
    143
sex differences: psychology of, 44, 47, 51,
    142-44, 225
Sexual Behavior in the Human Male
    (Kinsey), 147
Shakespeare, William, 97, 228
Shaw, G. B., 85
Simon, T., 41, 43
Skeels, H. M., 117, 120
Slaughter, J. W., 25
Smith College, 100
Southern California, University of, 178
Spearman, psychologist, 24, 27, 43, 44
speech correction, 62
Spoil of Europe (Reveille), 151
Sproul, Robert Gordon, 157
Stanford, Thomas Welton, 109
Stanford Achievement Test, 69, 75, 90,
    99, 183
Stanford Binet test, 40, 44-54, 79;
    revision of, 45-46, 50, 52, 94, 145, 177;
    validity of, 48, 52;
    Otis and, 65;
    gifted study and, 87-89, 245;
    and Army testing, 115
Stanford Convalescent Home, 125
Stanford Daily, The: on foreign policy
    questionnaire, 154;
    on America First, 160;
Stanford Dames, 125
Stanford Faculty Women's Club, 125
Stanford Mothers' Club, 125
Stanford Revision of the Binet, *see* Stanford
    Binet test

Stanford University:
Department of Education of, 34-106;
Psychology Department of, 65, 94,
107-48;
and foreign policy statement, 151-63;
Frederick Terman, Provost of, 173;
and Herbert Hoover Medal, 174
Statistical Method in Educational Measurement (Otis), 77
statistics: Terman and, 47;
and Otis, 49;
and gifted study, 90-91, 94
Stern, Louis William, 44, 46-47
Stedman, Louise, 92
Stoddard, George D., 117
Stone, Calvin P., 110, 112
Strategy of Terror (Taylor), 151
Strong, Edward K., 110
Strong Test of Vocational Interest, 142,
143, 248
Stuart, Graham, 157, 158
Studies in Personality, 168-69
success: of gifted men, 96-97
suicide rates, 62
Sward, Keith, 132
Swarthmore College, 100

Talbert, Wilfred E., 35
talent, 101
Talks to Teachers (James), 10
teachers: health of, 58;
and mental tests, 71, 73;
gifted children and, 105
Teacher's Reading Circle, 10, 58
"Ten Vows of the Stanford Emeriti Graduates of 1942," 170, 229
Terman, Anna Minton, 11-12, 27, 37,
124-25, 127, 131-32, 172-73, 180
Terman, Frederick Emmons, 12, 33, 36-37,
130, 175;
at Stanford, 126-28, 173-74, 182
Terman, Helen, 18-19, 36-37, 126, 130,
173, 175
Terman, James, 2-3
Terman, Lewis:
childhood of, 1-15;
illnesses of, 11-13, 26, 31, 129f, 170-71,
182, 239-44;
at Clark University, 19-29;
study of mental testing by, 27-29, 40-54
at Stanford, School of Education, 34-107;
and school hygiene, 38, 39, 55-63;
and Army testing, 64-68;
and group tests for schools, 68-79;

study of gifted by, 80-106, 217, 221-28;
at Stanford, Department of Psychology,
108-48;
and nature-nurture controversy, 132-39;
study of marital happiness by, 145-48;
statement of foreign policy by, 151-63;
retirement of, 167-83;
personal characteristics, 184-86;
selected manuscripts of, 216-49
Terman, Martha Cutsinger, 2-3
Terman, Sibyl Walcutt, 127
Terman Group Test of Mental Ability,
69, 73, 75, 89, 245
Terman-McNemar Test of Mental Ability,
74
They Wanted War (Tolischus), 151
Thompson, Sir Godfrey, 74
Thompson, J. J., 85
Thorndike, E. L., 24, 27, 44, 65, 139
Thurstone, Louis L., 74
Time Magazine, 156
Tinker, Miles, 135, 169
twins: studies of, 132, 142

Un-American Activities Committee, 99
Ungraded Magazine, 75
United States Children's Bureau, 57
University in Exile, 149, 150
Utah State College, 179

Vanderbilt University, 167
Vineland Training School, 43, 56, 57, 65
vocational education, 56-57
vocational guidance tests, 51, 71
Vocational Guidance Magazine, 75
Voice of Destruction (Rauschning), 151

Waddell, Charles, 25
Walter V. Bingham Lecture, 177
Washington, George, 97
Watsonian psychology, 141
Wechsler, D., 65
Wellman, B. L., 117
White House Conference on Child Health
and Protection, 92
Whittier State School for Boys: survey of,
61, 62
Who's Who in America, 97, 98, 136, 222,
247
Wilbur, Ray Lyman, 108, 109, 110, 151-63
Williams, J. Harold, 55, 82, 88
Wolfle, Dael, 183, 248

Woodworth, Robert S., 65, 169, 178
World Book Company, 65, 68, 75-76
World War I: testing in, 65-68
World War II, 97, 101, 150, 163.
  See also foreign policy
Wundt, Wilhelm Max, 17, 80

Yale University, 34
Yates, Dorothy, 88
Yerkes, Robert M.,
  and Army testing, 64-65, 67;

Terman and, 112, 130, 139-40, 144, 175, 176

You Can't Do Business With Hitler (Miller), 151
Young, Kimball, 51, 122

Zeitschrift für angewandte Psychologie, 44
Zeitschrift für pädagogische Psychologie, 44